Microsoft® SQL Server® 2017

ON LINUX

About the Author

Benjamin Nevarez is a database professional based in Los Angeles, California, who specializes in SQL Server query tuning and optimization. He is the author of three books, *High Performance SQL Server* (Apress, 2016), *Microsoft SQL Server 2014 Query Tuning & Optimization* (McGraw-Hill Education, 2014), and *Inside the SQL Server Query Optimizer* (Simple Talk Publishing, 2010) and has coauthored other books, including *SQL Server 2012 Internals* (Microsoft Press, 2013). Benjamin has also been a speaker at many SQL Server conferences and events around the world, including the PASS Summit, SQL Server Connections, and SQLBits. He writes a blog about SQL Server at www.benjaminnevarez.com and can be reached on Twitter at @BenjaminNevarez.

About the Technical Editor

Mark Broadbent is a Microsoft Certified Master in SQL Server and Microsoft Data Platform MVP with more than 30 years of IT experience and more than 20 years' experience working with Microsoft SQL Server. He is an expert in concurrency control, migration and upgrade, and high availability (and disaster recovery) and a lover of Linux, Golang, Serverless, and Docker. In between herding cats and rustling dogs, he can be found blogging at http://tenbulls.co.uk and tweeting as @retracement.

Microsoft® SQL Server® 2017

ON LINUX

Benjamin Nevarez

New York   Chicago   San Francisco
Athens   London   Madrid
Mexico City   Milan   New Delhi
Singapore   Sydney   Toronto

Cataloging-in-Publication Data is on file with the Library of Congress

McGraw-Hill Education books are available at special quantity discounts to use as premiums and sales promotions, or for use in corporate training programs. To contact a representative, please visit the Contact Us pages at www.mhprofessional.com.

Microsoft® SQL Server® 2017 on Linux

123456789   QFR   21201918

ISBN   978-1-260-12113-1
MHID   1-260-12113-5

Sponsoring Editor	**Technical Editor**	**Production Supervisor**
Lisa McClain	Mark Broadbent	Lynn M. Messina
Editorial Supervisor	**Copy Editor**	**Composition**
Patty Mon	Lisa Theobald	Cenveo Publisher Services
Project Manager	**Proofreader**	**Illustration**
Radhika Jolly,	Lisa McCoy	Cenveo Publisher Services
Cenveo® Publisher Services	**Indexer**	**Art Director, Cover**
Acquisitions Coordinator	Ted Laux	Jeff Weeks
Claire Yee		

This book is dedicated to the memory of my father, Humberto Nevarez.

Contents at a Glance

Contents

Foreword

I started working with SQL Server more than 30 years ago, when it was a Sybase product that ran on Unix (as well as on more than half a dozen other operating systems), and we did all our work on Unix machines. SQL Server didn't run on Windows at that time, because there was no Windows operating system. But several years later, when Sybase partnered with Microsoft to port its database product onto PC-based operating systems, few people could foresee just how powerful and ubiquitous these PCs would become. PC is hardly about only personal computers these days.

I've seen a lot of changes with SQL Server over these three decades, and some of the most interesting ones for me are when the product seems to circle back and add features or internal behaviors that were originally part of the product but had once been discarded. Some of the original ideas were not that far off base after all. Having SQL Server return to its roots and become available on Linux (a Unix-based OS) in SQL Server 2017 almost seems like coming home.

Benjamin Nevarez has been working with Unix-based operating systems almost as long as I've been working with SQL Server. He was also excited to see SQL Server make an appearance on Linux. It didn't take him long to decide to get his hands dirty and figure out how SQL Server professionals could get the maximum value out of the new OS. He wrote this book to make available to others all that he had learned.

I have known Ben for more than a dozen years, since he first started finding typos and other errors in my SQL Server 2005 books. We started a dialog, and I then asked him if he was interested in being a technical editor for some of my work. Through this technical collaboration, I have learned that when Ben sets out to learn something, he does it thoroughly. His attention to detail and passion for complete answers never cease to amaze me.

In this book, Ben tells you how to get started using SQL Server on Linux and how the database system actually works on the new platform. Chapters 1, 2, and 3 are particularly useful if you're new to Linux but experienced with SQL Server. Although most SQL Server books wouldn't go into operating system administration details, Chapter 3 does just that, to make the transition easier for people who have many years, if not decades, of experience with Windows. Of course, if you're already proficient with Linux, but new to SQL Server, you can focus on the following chapters when Ben's expertise with SQL Server shines through.

In Chapter 4, he tells you how SQL Server can be configured and blends SQL Server details with the Linux tools you need to access and control your SQL Server. Chapters 5 and 6 are very SQL Server focused. Chapter 5 provides some very detailed information about working with SQL Server queries, including how queries are optimized and processed, and how you can tune slow-running queries. Chapter 6 tells you all about some of the latest and greatest in SQL Server's optimization techniques in the most recent versions of SQL Server. Finally, in Chapters 7 and 8, he provides coverage of two critical focus areas for a database administrator: managing availability and recoverability, and setting up security. These are critical topics for any DBA, and because they involve the relationship between the database engine and the operating system, it's best to learn about them from someone who is an expert in both areas.

Although both Linux and SQL Server are huge topics and there is no way one book can provide everything you need to know about both technologies, Ben has done an awesome job of giving you exactly what you need to know, not only to get SQL Server running on the Linux operating system, but to have it performing well, while keeping your data safe and secure.

—Kalen Delaney
www.SQLServerInternals.com
Poulsbo, Washington, March 2018

Acknowledgments

A number of people contributed to making this book a reality. First of all, I would like to thank everyone on the McGraw-Hill Education team with whom I worked directly on this book: Lisa McClain, Claire Yee, and Radhika Jolly. Thanks to all for coordinating the entire project while trying to keep me on schedule. I also would like to thank my technical editor, Mark Broadbents, as his amazing feedback was critical to improving the quality of the chapters of the book. A very special thank you has to go out to Kalen Delaney for writing the Foreword for this book. Kalen has been my biggest inspiration in the SQL Server world, and it is because of people like her that I ended up writing books and presenting at technology conferences.

Finally, on the personal side, I would like to thank my family: my wife, Rocio, and three sons, Diego, Benjamin, and David. Thank you for your unconditional support and patience every time I need to work on another SQL Server book.

Introduction

I started my IT career working with Unix applications and databases back in the early '90s, and my first job ever was as a data processing manager for a small IT shop. Back then, I was running Unix System V Release 4 on an NCR system. With such big and expensive minicomputer systems, I was always wondering if I could have a Unix system on less expensive hardware, such as a PC, to learn and test without disrupting our shared test systems.

Then I read an article in a personal computing magazine about something called Linux. Nobody knew what Linux was back in those days. Very few people—mostly at universities—had access to the Internet back in those days. So I downloaded Linux on four or five floppy disks, installed it on a PC, and started playing with it. It was a distribution called Slackware. It was amazing that I could finally experiment and test everything I wanted on my own personal Unix system.

I continued to work with Linux and all the popular Unix commercial implementations, including IBM AIX, HP-UX, Sun Solaris, and others, throughout the '90s. For several years, people still didn't know what Linux was. It was not an immediate success. But by the end of the '90s I decided to specialize in SQL Server, and by doing that I left the Unix world behind.

So it looked like I was not going to touch a Unix system ever again. But one day in March 2016, Microsoft surprised the technology community by announcing that SQL Server would be available on Linux. When I first heard the news, I thought it would be cool to write a book about it. Because I was just finishing a book about SQL Server 2016, I decided to wait to see how the technology evolved and to take a break from writing. One day, as I was running while training for a marathon, I started thinking about the project again and decided it could be a great idea to write a book about SQL Server on Linux. Just after finishing my run, I went to my laptop and sent an e-mail to my contact at McGraw-Hill Education, who eventually connected me with Lisa McClain. Within a few days, I was now working on this new book project.

Let me tell you how I structured this book.

Chapter 1 shows you how to get SQL Server running on Linux as quickly as possible, so you can start using the technology, even though I haven't covered all the details yet. The chapter covers how to install SQL Server on Red Hat Enterprise Linux, SUSE Linux Enterprise Server, and Ubuntu and how to configure an image of SQL Server on a Docker container. More details of the setup and configuration are included in Chapter 4.

Chapter 2 covers some SQL Server history with different operating systems and explains some of the details about how SQL Server on Linux works. This includes describing the interaction between SQL Server and the operating system, decisions regarding its architecture, and information about its software implementation, among other related topics. It also covers details about the SQL Operating System (SQLOS), the Drawbridge technology, and the SQL Platform Abstraction Layer (SQLPAL).

I include an entire chapter dedicated to Linux for the SQL Server professional. Chapter 3 covers all the basic Linux commands you need to get started, including managing files and directories and their permissions, along with a few more advanced topics, including system monitoring.

Chapter 4 covers SQL Server setup and configuration in a Linux environment, and it is divided into three main topics: using the mssql-conf utility to configure SQL Server, which is required in Linux environments; using Linux-specific kernel settings and operating system configurations; and using some traditional SQL Server configurations for both Windows and Linux installations.

After spending time learning how to set up and configure SQL Server, you'll move to Chapter 5, which discusses how to use SQL Server to perform database operations. This chapter, in particular, covers query tuning and optimization topics, which are applicable both to Windows and Linux installations—and, in fact, to all the currently supported versions of the product.

Chapter 6 continues with query processing and covers the new features available in SQL Server 2017, such as adaptive query processing and automatic tuning.

Chapter 7 is about high-availability and disaster-recovery solutions for SQL Server on Linux and focuses on Always On availability groups. Availability groups on both Windows and Linux can be used in high-availability and disaster-recovery configurations and for migrations and upgrades, or even to scale out readable copies of one or more databases. The chapter also covers Pacemaker, a clustering solution available on Linux distributions.

Finally, I close the book with Chapter 8, which is about security. This chapter reviews security from a general point of view and includes details about some of the new security features in SQL Server, including Transparent Data Encryption, Always Encrypted, Row-Level Security, and Dynamic Data Masking.

Chapter 1

SQL Server on Linux: Getting Started

In This Chapter

▶ Creating a Virtual Machine

▶ Installing SQL Server

▶ Configuring SQL Server

▶ Connecting to SQL Server

▶ Installing Additional Components

▶ Installing on Ubuntu

▶ Installing on SUSE Linux Enterprise Server

▶ Running SQL Server on Docker

▶ Uninstalling SQL Server

▶ Summary

Although SQL Server has been a Windows-only software product for more than two decades, it originally started as a database engine for the then-new OS/2 operating system. The year was 1989 and the product was actually called Ashton-Tate/Microsoft SQL Server, originally written by Sybase using the C language. By the summer of 1990, after ending a marketing and distribution agreement with Ashton-Tate, it was renamed Microsoft SQL Server.

After the failure of OS/2 to gain market acceptance and the huge success of Windows, Microsoft SQL Server was eventually moved to the then-new Windows NT platform. SQL Server 4.21a, released in 1993, was the first version to run on Windows. The last version of SQL Server for OS/2, SQL Server 4.2B, was released that same year.

From then on, Microsoft focused on its software product as a Windows NT–only strategy. But that was about to change more than 20 years later when Microsoft announced in March 2016 that SQL Server would be available on the Linux platform. In 2017, Microsoft indicated that this version would be named SQL Server 2017 and would be available on Red Hat Enterprise Linux, Ubuntu, and SUSE Linux Enterprise Server, in addition to Docker containers. The product was released in October 2017.

I started my career in information technology with Unix applications and databases in the early 1990s and was, at the time, mostly unaware of these SQL Server developments. I worked with all the popular implementations of Unix, including Linux, for about a decade. These Unix platforms included System V Release 4, IBM AIX, and Hewlett-Packard HP-UX. I was one of the early Linux users, which I later deployed in production, but mostly to run web servers. I remember that Linux was not an immediate success, and nobody knew about Linux in those early days. I eventually decided to specialize in SQL Server and left the Unix/Linux world behind.

When I heard that SQL Server would be available on Linux, I was really excited about the possibilities. It was like going back to the old times. It was ironic and interesting that SQL Server would bring me back to Linux.

Although Chapter 2 continues the discussion of SQL Server history with different operating systems, this chapter will show you how to install SQL Server on Linux so you can start playing with the technology as quickly as possible. Chapter 2 also describes decisions about SQL Server on Linux architecture, software implementations, and how SQL Server interacts with the operating system, among other related topics. The remaining chapters focus on all the details and more advanced topics.

Creating a Virtual Machine

This chapter will show you how to install SQL Server on a virtual machine image with Linux preinstalled. You can obtain the Linux virtual machine in several ways—for example, by using a cloud provider such as Microsoft Azure or Amazon Web Services (AWS), or by using an image of a virtual machine created in the virtualization environment in your data center. You can also install Linux first on your own virtual machine or hardware and then follow the rest of the chapter.

Later chapters focus on more advanced details, such as configuring SQL Server or implementing high availability or disaster recovery solutions. The following Linux distributions are currently supported to run SQL Server:

- ▶ Red Hat Enterprise Linux 7.3 or 7.4
- ▶ SUSE Linux Enterprise Server v12 SP2
- ▶ Ubuntu 16.04
- ▶ Docker Engine 1.8+

If you want to install Linux directly on a virtual machine or hardware, these versions of the Linux operating system software are available:

- ▶ **Red Hat Enterprise Linux** https://access.redhat.com/products/red-hat-enterprise-linux/evaluation
- ▶ **SUSE Linux Enterprise Server** https://www.suse.com/products/server/
- ▶ **Ubuntu** https://www.ubuntu.com/download/server

NOTE

You can sign up for the Red Hat Developer Program, which provides no-cost subscriptions where you can download the software for development use only. For more details, see https://developers.redhat.com/ products/rhel/download.

In this section, I'll show you how to create a virtual machine in Microsoft Azure. If you need to use Amazon AWS, you can create an account and a virtual machine at https://aws.amazon.com/.

Start by visiting the Azure web site at https://azure.microsoft.com, where you can use an existing Microsoft Azure subscription or sign up for a free account with a US$200 free credit. After logging on with your credentials, proceed to the Microsoft Azure portal (https://portal.azure.com) by following the links. You may need to spend a few moments getting familiar with the Microsoft Azure portal.

To create a new virtual machine on the Microsoft Azure portal, choose Virtual Machines | Add. Hundreds of images may be available, so you need to enter a filter to help with the search. As of this writing, you can use two kinds of virtual machines:

- ▶ Virtual machines with only Linux installed
- ▶ Virtual machines with both Linux and SQL Server installed

If you select a virtual machine with both Linux and SQL Server installed, you will need to set the system administrator (sa) password and start the SQL Server service, which is a simple process that is covered in the section "Configuring SQL Server." If you select a virtual machine with only Linux installed, you'll also learn how to install SQL Server in that section.

If you are interested in finding a virtual machine with SQL Server already installed, enter **SQL Server Red Hat Enterprise Linux** or **SQL Server SUSE Enterprise Linux Server** or **SQL Server Ubuntu** in the Search bar. As of this writing, you can find images available for the Express, Developer, Web, Standard, and Enterprise editions for all the supported Linux distributions mentioned earlier. As suggested, the available choices may change at a later time. An example using SQL Server Red Hat Enterprise Linux is shown in Figure 1-1.

Clicking any of the results will show you the image details on the right side of the screen. For example, selecting Free SQL Server License: SQL Server 2017 Developer on Red Hat Enterprise Linux 7.4 (RHEL) will show you the following information (note that the message refers to the free SQL Server Developer edition; you still have to pay for the cost of running the Linux virtual machine):

> This image contains the Developer edition of SQL Server 2017 on Red Hat Enterprise Linux 7.4. This free edition (no SQL Server licensing cost) includes all the functionality of Enterprise edition, but it is licensed for development and testing only, not production. It provides comprehensive capabilities for mission-critical transactional processing, data warehousing, and real-time business intelligence.
>
> After provisioning, please run $sudo /opt/mssql/bin/mssql-conf set-sa-password to configure SQL Server.
>
> See documentation for additional details. https://docs.microsoft.com/azure/virtual-machines/linux/sql/provision-sql-server-linux-virtual-machine.

NAME	PUBLISHER	CATEGORY
SQL Server 2017 Web on Red Hat Enterprise Linux 7.4 (RHEL)	Microsoft	Compute
Free SQL Server License: SQL Server 2017 Developer on Red Hat Enterprise Linux 7.4 (RHEL)	Microsoft	Compute
Free SQL Server License: SQL Server 2017 Express on Red Hat Enterprise Linux 7.4 (RHEL)	Microsoft	Compute
SQL Server 2017 Standard on Red Hat Enterprise Linux 7.4 (RHEL)	Microsoft	Compute
SQL Server 2017 Enterprise on Red Hat Enterprise Linux 7.4 (RHEL)	Microsoft	Compute

Figure 1-1   *Microsoft Azure virtual machines search*

If you need to find a virtual machine without SQL Server installed, enter **Red Hat Enterprise Linux** or **SUSE Enterprise Linux Server** or **Ubuntu** in the Search bar. Be sure to select a supported version, as indicated earlier—for example, 7.3 or 7.4 for Red Hat Enterprise Linux 7.3 or 7.4.

Because I am going to show the entire installation process, for this exercise, select Red Hat Enterprise Linux 7.4. You may also choose a virtual machine with SQL Server installed, such as Free SQL Server License: SQL Server 2017 Developer On Red Hat Enterprise Linux 7.4 (RHEL) and still follow the rest of the chapter content. My selection shows the following description:

> Red Hat Enterprise Linux is the world's leading enterprise Linux platform built to meet the needs of today's modern enterprise. Red Hat Enterprise Linux is the preferred choice for enterprise Linux virtual machine (VM) workloads on Microsoft Azure. Red Hat Enterprise Linux is an open, reliable, and secure platform designed for customers who want deployment flexibility for their business-critical workloads—from the data center to the Azure cloud—backed by tightly integrated, enterprise-grade support from Red Hat and Microsoft.

Click Create To Continue. Leave the default deployment model set to Resource Manager. Although there is a second choice, Classic, the Azure Portal recommends that you use Resource Manager for new workloads.

The portal, which consists of four sections, will then ask you to provide information to create your virtual machine.

Step 1. Basics: Configure Basic Settings

The first section, shown in Figure 1-2, asks you to configure the virtual machine basic settings, such as server name, disk type, and authentication information.

Figures 1-2 through 1-5 do not show all the entire portal screens. You may need to scroll down on the web portal to see some parts of a screen, but all the choices are explained here. Some items offer a description. For example, you may wonder about the VM Disk Type or Resource Group choices shown in Figure 1-2. VM disk type is described as follows:

> Premium disks (SSD) are backed by solid state drives and offer consistent, low-latency performance. They provide the best balance between price and performance, and are ideal for I/O-intensive applications and production workloads. Standard disks (HDD) are backed by magnetic drives and are preferable for applications where data is accessed infrequently.

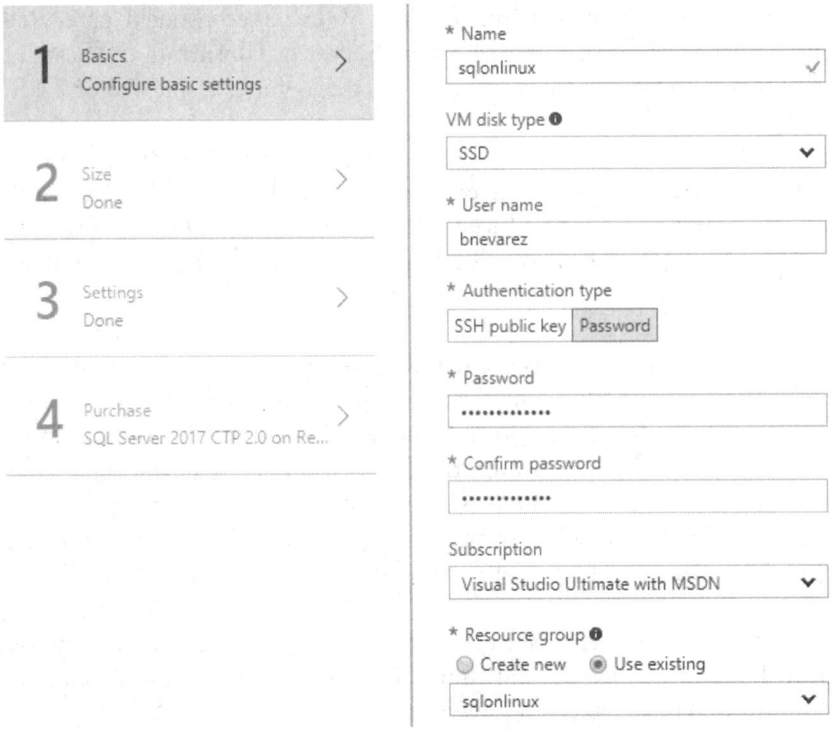

Figure 1-2   *Configure basic settings*

A resource group is defined as "a collection of resources that share the same lifecycle, permissions, and policies." To learn more about resource group, see https://docs .microsoft.com/en-us/azure/azure-resource-manager/resource-group-portal.

For Authentication Type, choose either Password or SSH Public Key. Finally, select a location near you if one is not already selected. Currently a large number of locations are provided; in my case, West US is selected by default. When you're done, click OK.

NOTE

For more details on how to generate a SSH key, see "How to Create and Use an SSH Public and Private Key Pair for Linux VMs in Azure" at https://docs.microsoft.com/en-us/azure/virtual-machines/linux/mac-create-ssh-keys. You can also find "How to Use SSH keys with Windows on Azure" at https://docs.microsoft.com/en-us/azure/virtual-machines/linux/ssh-from-windows.

Step 2. Size: Choose Virtual Machine Size

In this step, you'll choose a virtual machine size that basically defines the required number of processor cores, amount of memory, size of disk, number of data disks, and maximum input/output operations per second (IOPS). You made the choice between

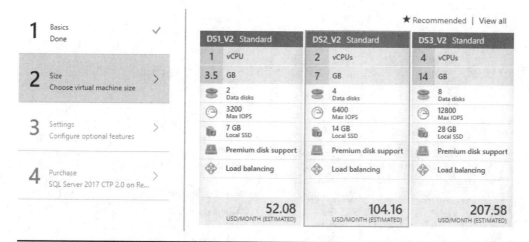

Figure 1-3   *Configure virtual machine size screen*

SSD and HDD (solid state drives and standard disks) in step 1. Be careful with your choices here, because they will impact your subscription cost. The estimated monthly cost is shown under each choice.

The portal recommends a few choices, but you can click the View All link to see all of them.

If you are new to Microsoft Azure or are not sure about what to choose, select the least expensive option and regularly monitor the resources used and cost. The recommendations are based on the hardware and software requirements for the virtual machine image you selected. A recommendation may also be indicated on the image description. For example, a selected choice may show something like this: "We recommend that you use a virtual machine size of DS2 or higher for development and functional testing. DS13 or higher for performance testing." Choose your virtual machine size and then click Select to continue.

Step 3. Settings: Configure Optional Features

Fortunately in our case, defaults are provided for all these features. For now, go with the defaults, and we will review some of them in later chapters. For completeness, I've included the descriptions of the items on the Azure portal (see Figure 1-4).

▶ **Use Managed Disks**   Enable this feature to have Azure automatically manage the availability of disks to provide data redundancy and fault tolerance, without creating and managing storage accounts on your own. (For more details, see https://docs.microsoft.com/en-us/azure/storage/storage-managed-disks-overview.)

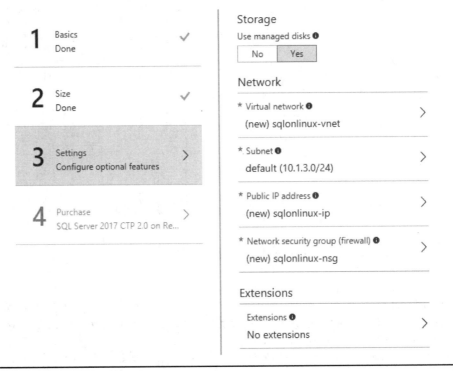

Figure 1-4   *Configure optional features screen*

▶ **Virtual Network**   Virtual networks are logically isolated from one another in Azure. You can configure their IP address ranges, subnets, route tables, gateways, and security settings, much like a traditional network in your data center. Virtual machines in the same virtual network can access each other by default.

▶ **Subnet**   A subnet is a range of IP addresses in your virtual network, which can be used to isolate virtual machines from one another or from the Internet.

▶ **Public IP Address**   Use a public IP address if you want to communicate with the virtual machine from outside the virtual network.

▶ **Network Security Group (Firewall)**   A network security group is a set of firewall rules that control traffic to and from your virtual machine.

▶ **Extensions**   Add new features, such as configuration management or antivirus protection, to your virtual machine using extensions. (For more details, see https:// docs.microsoft.com/en-us/azure/virtual-machines/windows/extensions-features.)

▶ **High Availability**   To provide redundancy to your application, I recommend that you group two or more virtual machines in an availability set. This configuration ensures that during a planned or unplanned maintenance event, at least one virtual machine will be available and will 99.95 percent meet the Azure service-level agreement (SLA). The availability set of a virtual machine can't be changed after it is created.

▶ **Monitoring**   Capture serial console output and screenshots of the virtual machine running on a host to help diagnose startup issues.

▶ **Guest OS Diagnostics**   Get metrics every minute for your virtual machine. You can use them to create alerts and stay informed about your applications.

▶ **Diagnostics Storage Account**   Metrics are written to a storage account so you can analyze them with your own tools.

To continue, click OK.

Step 4. Summary and Purchase

In this Summary section, you can review all the selected choices, as shown in Figure 1-5. Click Purchase to continue and create the virtual machine, which could take a few minutes.

After the virtual machine is created, the virtual machines page on the Azure portal should show something similar to Figure 1-6.

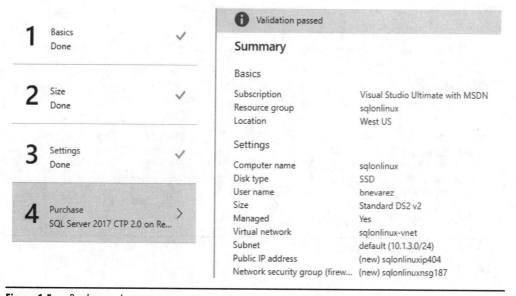

Figure 1-5   *Purchase and summary screen*

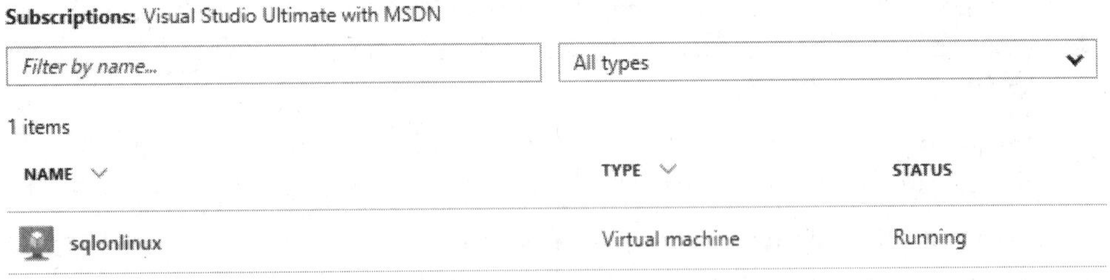

Subscriptions: Visual Studio Ultimate with MSDN

| Filter by name... | | All types | ⌄ |

1 items

NAME ⌄	TYPE ⌄	STATUS
🖥 sqlonlinux	Virtual machine	Running

Figure 1-6   *Virtual machines page*

As shown in Figure 1-6, after the virtual machine is created, it will be automatically started and you can connect to it. For more details about how to connect, click the virtual machine name, in this case, sqlonlinux. Microsoft Azure will show something similar to Figure 1-7.

You can see the public IP address you can use to connect to. Clicking Connect on the Azure portal will also show you how to connect. In my case, I see "To connect to your Linux virtual machine using SSH, use the following command: ssh bnevarez@104.210.38.105."

We will connect to this virtual machine via Secure Shell (SSH) in the following section. You can also find the public IP address on the Networking section on the Azure portal.

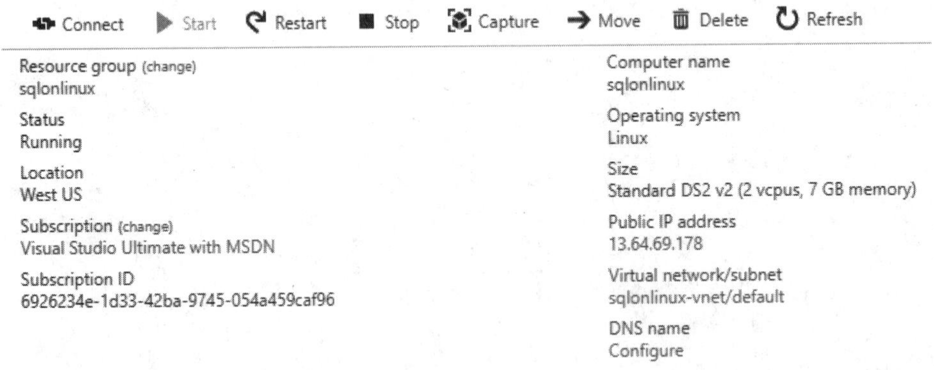

◄► Connect   ▶ Start   ⟲ Restart   ■ Stop   📷 Capture   → Move   🗑 Delete   ⟳ Refresh

Resource group (change) sqlonlinux	Computer name sqlonlinux
Status Running	Operating system Linux
Location West US	Size Standard DS2 v2 (2 vcpus, 7 GB memory)
Subscription (change) Visual Studio Ultimate with MSDN	Public IP address 13.64.69.178
Subscription ID 6926234e-1d33-42ba-9745-054a459caf96	Virtual network/subnet sqlonlinux-vnet/default
	DNS name Configure

Figure 1-7   *Virtual machine details*

Installing SQL Server

Now we'll download and install SQL Server. First we need to connect to the created Linux virtual machine—but to do that, we need a terminal emulator that can support an SSH session. A popular and free terminal emulator is PuTTY, which you can download from www.putty.org.

To connect, you need the public IP address provided earlier on the virtual machine details (Figure 1-5) and the user name and password provided during the configuration (Figure 1-2). Figure 1-8 shows an example of opening an SSH session using PuTTY.

SSH is a cryptographic network protocol and a suite of utilities that implement the protocol. It is used to connect to remote computer systems and designed as a replacement for other unsecured protocols such as telnet, rlogin, and rsh. (I remember using telnet heavily before SSH was available.) SSH uses the standard TCP port 22, which is selected by default in Figure 1-8.

Once you're connected to the Linux server, you will see the Linux prompt ($), or, more exactly, the Bash shell prompt. It may also contain the username and hostname:

```
[bnevarez@sqlonlinux ~]$
```

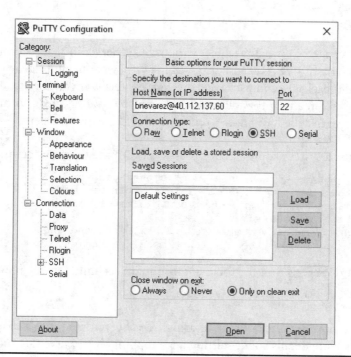

Figure 1-8   *Creating a PuTTY session*

I will first show you how to install and configure SQL Server for Red Hat Enterprise Linux. Instructions to perform the same operations on Ubuntu and SUSE Linux Enterprise Server are covered later in the chapter. How to run SQL Server 2017 on Docker is covered at the end of the chapter.

To continue with our Red Hat Enterprise Linux virtual machine, you need to download and install SQL Server using the curl and yum utilities. The `curl` command is designed to transfer data between servers without user interaction, and yum is a package manager utility that we will use to install the latest version of a package.

First, switch to superuser mode:

```
sudo su
```

`sudo` is a Linux command that enables you to execute a command as another user or as the superuser or root. A user needs to have prior privileges to perform such activity. The first time you run `sudo`, you will see a message such as the following:

```
We trust you have received the usual lecture from the local System
Administrator. It usually boils down to these three things:
    #1) Respect the privacy of others.
    #2) Think before you type.
    #3) With great power comes great responsibility.
```

If you have created a virtual machine without SQL Server installed, continue reading. If you already have SQL Server installed, you may still want to continue reading here to learn a bit about packages and package managers, especially if you are new to Linux, but you don't have to run any of the following commands. If you selected a virtual machine with SQL Server installed, you have to run only the following two steps:

1. Configure a system administrator password. Run the following script:

    ```
    $ sudo /opt/mssql/bin/mssql-conf set-sa-password
    Enter the SQL Server system administrator password:
    Confirm the SQL Server system administrator password:
    Configuring SQL Server...
    The system administrator password has been changed.
    Please run 'sudo systemctl start mssql-server' to start SQL Server.
    ```

2. Start SQL Server. Run the following command as hinted by the previous output:

    ```
    $ sudo systemctl start mssql-server
    ```

I will cover more details about configuring SQL Server later in this chapter and also in Chapter 4. More details about starting and stopping SQL Server are provided later in this chapter and also in Chapter 3. The remainder of the section assumes you do not have SQL Server installed.

Run the following commands to download the SQL Server Red Hat repository configuration file:

```
curl https://packages.microsoft.com/config/rhel/7/mssql-server-2017.repo >
/etc/yum.repos.d/mssql-server.repo
```

This should finish almost immediately, because this downloads a small file. If you look at its contents, at /etc/yum.repos.d/mssql-server.repo, you will see the following:

```
packages-microsoft-com-mssql-server-2017]
name=packages-microsoft-com-mssql-server-2017
baseurl=https://packages.microsoft.com/rhel/7/mssql-server-2017/
enabled=1
gpgcheck=1
gpgkey=https://packages.microsoft.com/keys/microsoft.asc
```

TIP

You can use several commands to view the contents of a file. For example, you can try `more/etc/yum.repos.d/mssql-server.repo`*. For information on these commands, see Chapter 3.*

Next, run the following commands to install the SQL Server package mssql-server:

```
yum install -y mssql-server
```

NOTE

Another difference from Windows is that in Unix and Linux commands are case-sensitive. An incorrect command name will return an error message and, in some cases, perhaps a recommendation as in the following examples:

```
$ Ls
Ls: command not found
$ Grep
No command 'Grep' found, did you mean:
 Command 'rrep' from package 'rrep' (universe)
 Command 'rep' from package 'rep' (universe)
 Command 'grep' from package 'grep' (main)
 Command 'prep' from package 'loki' (universe)
Grep: command not found
```

In this example, yum installs the package named mssql-server and the −y parameter is used to answer "yes" to any question during the installation. Here's the output, formatted for better readability:

```
Loaded plugins: langpacks, product-id, search-disabled-repos
Resolving Dependencies
--> Running transaction check
---> Package mssql-server.x86_64 0:14.0.3008.27-1 will be installed
--> Finished Dependency Resolution

Dependencies Resolved
Installing:
Package mssql-server
Arch x86_64
Version 14.0.3008.27-1
Repository packages-microsoft-com-mssql-server
Size 166 M

Transaction Summary
Install  1 Package

Total download size: 166 M
Installed size: 166 M
Downloading packages:
mssql-server-14.0.3008.27-1.x86_64.rpm  | 166 MB  00:00:02
Running transaction check
Running transaction test
Transaction test succeeded
Running transaction
Please run 'sudo /opt/mssql/bin/mssql-conf setup'
to complete the setup of Microsoft SQL Server
+-------------------------------------------------------------+
   Installing : mssql-server-14.0.3008.27-1.x86_64    1/1
   Verifying  : mssql-server-14.0.3008.27-1.x86_64    1/1

Installed:
  mssql-server.x86_64 0:14.0.3008.27-1

Complete!
```

At the moment the package was installed, SQL Server was not yet properly configured. We will do that in the next step. Also, close your root session as soon as it is no longer needed by running the exit command or pressing CTRL-D.

But before we continue, here's a quick introduction to package managers, which may be a new concept for most SQL Server developers and administrators. The process of installing, upgrading, configuring, and removing software is quite different on Windows platforms. Software in Linux distributions uses packages, and there are several *package management systems*, which are collections of utilities used to install, upgrade, configure, and remove packages or distributions of software. In this chapter, we will cover some package management utilities such as yum, apt, and zypper, which we will use with Red Hat, Ubuntu, and SUSE, respectively.

The yum (which stands for Yellowdog Updater Modified) package manager was written in Python. We use it to install the SQL Server package mssql-server by running the following:

```
yum install -y mssql-server
```

If you want to update the package, which is useful when there is a new CTP, RC, or cumulative update, you can use this:

```
yum update mssql-server
```

If you want to remove the package, use this:

```
yum remove mssql-server
```

NOTE

CTPs (Community Technology Previews) or RCs (Release Candidates) are versions of SQL Server used during their beta program before a final release. A final release is called RTM (release to manufacturing).

Finally, one of the major changes in SQL Server 2017 compared to previous versions is the new servicing model. Although service packs will still be used for SQL Server 2016 and previous supported versions, no more service packs will be released for SQL Server 2017 and later. The new servicing model will be based only on cumulative updates (and GDRs [General Distribution Releases] when required).

Cumulative updates will be released more often at first and then less frequently in the new servicing model. A cumulative update will be available every month for the first 12 months and every quarter for the remaining four years of the full five-year mainstream life cycle.

As of this writing, three repositories are defined for SQL Server on Linux:

▶ **Cumulative updates** This is the base SQL Server release and any bug fixes or improvements since that release. This is the choice we selected earlier using https://packages.microsoft.com/config/rhel/7/mssql-server-2017.repo.

▶ **GDR** The GDR repository contains packages for the base SQL Server release and only critical fixes and security updates since that release. The repository URL for GDR is https://packages.microsoft.com/config/rhel/7/mssql-server-2017-gdr.repo.

▶ **Preview repository** This is the repository used during the SQL Server beta period, consisting of CTPs and RCs. The preview repository URL is https://packages.microsoft.com/config/rhel/7/mssql-server.repo.

NOTE

Be aware that there may be a lot of code, articles, or documents published out there using the preview repository. So make sure that you refer to the correct repository.

Configuring SQL Server

The next step is to configure SQL Server. I'll show you how to install and run SQL Server on three supported Linux distributions, so I'll mention different options, depending on the choices.

Run the following command to configure and start SQL Server:

```
$sudo /opt/mssql/bin/mssql-conf setup
```

Answer the requested questions, including providing a strong password for the sa account. You may be asked if you want to start SQL Server and if you want to enable SQL Server to run at boot time. Answer yes in both cases. Also answer 2 to select the Developer edition.

```
$ sudo /opt/mssql/bin/mssql-conf setup
The license terms for this product can be downloaded from
http://go.microsoft.com/fwlink/?LinkId=746388
and found in /usr/share/doc/mssql-server/LICENSE.TXT.
Do you accept the license terms? [Yes/No]:Yes
Choose an edition of SQL Server:
  1) Evaluation (free, no production use rights, 180-day limit)
  2) Developer (free, no production use rights)
  3) Express (free)
  4) Web (PAID)
  5) Standard (PAID)
  6) Enterprise (PAID)
  7) I bought a license through a retail sales channel and have a product key to
enter.
```

```
ails about editions can be found at
ps://www.microsoft.com/en-us/sql-server/sql-server-2016-editions
 of PAID editions of this software requires separate licensing through a
rosoft Volume Licensing program.
 choosing a PAID edition, you are verifying that you have the appropriate
ber of licenses in place to install and run this software.
er your edition(1-7): 2
ting up Microsoft SQL Server
er the new SQL Server system administrator password:
firm the new SQL Server system administrator password:
rting Microsoft SQL Server...
bling Microsoft SQL Server to run at boot...
ated symlink from /etc/systemd/system/multi-user.target.wants/mssql-
ver.service to /usr/lib/systemd/system/mssql-server.service.
up completed successfully.
```

The mssql-conf utility can accept different parameters and can be used to initialize and set up SQL Server and to perform some other activities such as enable or disable a trace flag, set the collation of the system databases, or change the sa password. To see the list of possible options, run mssql-conf without any parameter or specify the –h or --help parameter.

Note that you need to specify a strong sa password or you may get one of the following errors:

```
 specified password does not meet SQL Server password policy requirements
ause it is too short. The password must be at least 8 characters.
 specified password does not meet SQL Server password policy requirements
ause it is not complex enough. The password must be at least 8 characters long
 contain characters from three of the following four sets: uppercase letters,
ercase letters, numbers, and symbols.
```

If you inspect the mssql-conf file, you will notice it is a basic bash script that calls a /opt/mssql/lib/mssql-conf/mssql-conf.py python script. /opt is a standard directory in the Unix file system that is used to install local software. There are many other standard directories, such as /bin, /dev, /etc, /home, /lib, /tmp, and /var—to list a few. More details about the Unix file system are covered in Chapter 3.

You can verify that SQL Server is running using the ps command old-school method:

```
$ ps -ef | grep sql
```

This returns something similar to the following:

```
mssql      2559      1   0 02:05 ?        00:00:00 /opt/mssql/bin/sqlservr
mssql      2580   2559   4 02:05 ?        00:00:06 /opt/mssql/bin/sqlservr
bnevarez   2775   2313   0 02:07 pts/0    00:00:00 grep --color=auto sql
[bnevarez@sqllinux ~]$
```

Or, more appropriately, use the `systemctl` command as in the following example:

```
systemctl status mssql-server
```

This will show you some interesting information, as shown next (plus the last ten lines of the SQL Server error log file, not included here, called the "journal" in systemctl terminology):

```
mssql-server.service - Microsoft SQL Server Database Engine
   Loaded: loaded (/usr/lib/systemd/system/mssql-server.service; enabled; vendor
preset: disabled)
   Active: active (running) since Fri 2017-07-14 06:45:02 UTC; 4min 6s ago
     Docs: https://docs.microsoft.com/en-us/sql/linux
 Main PID: 21560 (sqlservr)
   CGroup: /system.slice/mssql-server.service
           ├─21560 /opt/mssql/bin/sqlservr
           └─21581 /opt/mssql/bin/sqlservr
```

This will show you how long the SQL Server service has been running; the Linux processes IDs, which are the same as those shown earlier with the `ps` command; and even the location of the SQL Server documentation.

Intro to Unix Commands

A short introduction to some Unix commands is worth including here. The `ps` command is used to display information about the processes running in the system, and in this case we are using the pipe symbol or | to send the output of the `ps` command as the input to the `grep` command. The `grep` command searches the provided input for lines containing a match to the given pattern.

Many Linux commands have multiple options, all of which you can find in the command documentation. You can also get more help about these commands by reading the documentation, which you can access using the `man` command followed by the name of the command. Here are three examples:

```
man ps
```

Or

```
man grep
```

Or the following, to learn more about the `man` command itself:

```
man man
```

In addition, `systemd` is an init or initialization system used in Linux distributions to manage system processes that will run as daemons until the system is shut down. `systemd` has several utilities, such as `systemctl`, which you can use to start, restart, or stop a service or, as shown previously, to show runtime status information. The `systemctl` command is covered in detail in Chapter 3.

Connecting to SQL Server

Now let's connect to the instance we just installed. Although SQL Server is installed and running, the previous installation did not install SQL Server tools. Let's install them now. This time, we need to download them by switching to superuser mode again and running the following `curl` and `yum` commands:

```
sudo su
curl https://packages.microsoft.com/config/rhel/7/prod.repo >
/etc/yum.repos.d/msprod.repo
```

Similarly, the content of /etc/yum.repos.d/msprod.repo is

```
[packages-microsoft-com-prod]
name=packages-microsoft-com-prod
baseurl=https://packages.microsoft.com/rhel/7/prod/
enabled=1
gpgcheck=1
gpgkey=https://packages.microsoft.com/keys/microsoft.asc
```

Run the installation process:

```
sudo yum install mssql-tools unixODBC-devel
```

An abbreviated output to fit the book page is next. Notice that this time we are installing two packages—mssql-tools and unixODBC-devel:

```
Loaded plugins: langpacks, product-id, search-disabled-repos
Resolving Dependencies
--> Running transaction check
---> Package mssql-tools.x86_64 0:14.0.6.0-1 will be installed
---> Package unixODBC-devel.x86_64 0:2.3.1-11.el7 will be installed
--> Finished Dependency Resolution
```

```
Dependencies Resolved
Installing:
Package mssql-tools unixODBC-devel
Arch x86_64 x86_64
Version 14.0.6.0-1 2.3.1-11.el7
Repository packages-microsoft-com-prod rhui-rhel-7-server-rhui-rpms
Size 249 k 55 k
Transaction Summary
Install  2 Packages

Total download size: 304 k
Installed size: 435 k
Is this ok [y/d/N]: y
Downloading packages:
(1/2): mssql-tools-14.0.6.0-1.x86_64.rpm
(2/2): unixODBC-devel-2.3.1-11.el7.x86_64.rpm
Running transaction check
Running transaction test
Transaction test succeeded
Running transaction
The license terms for this product can be downloaded from
http://go.microsoft.com/fwlink/?LinkId=746949 and found in
/usr/share/doc/mssql-tools/LICENSE.txt . By entering 'YES',
you indicate that you accept the license terms.
Do you accept the license terms? (Enter YES or NO)
YES
   Installing : mssql-tools-14.0.6.0-1.x86_64
   Installing : unixODBC-devel-2.3.1-11.el7.x86_64
   Verifying  : unixODBC-devel-2.3.1-11.el7.x86_64
   Verifying  : mssql-tools-14.0.6.0-1.x86_64

Installed:
   mssql-tools.x86_64 0:14.0.6.0-1
   unixODBC-devel.x86_64 0:2.3.1-11.el7
Complete!
```

Now we can connect to SQL Server using the Linux version of the familiar `sqlcmd` command-line tool:

```
/opt/mssql-tools/bin/sqlcmd -U sa
Password:
```

Run the following:

```
SELECT @@VERSION
GO
```

This is what I get with my current release:

```
Microsoft SQL Server 2017 (RTM-CU2) (KB4052574) - 14.0.3008.27 (X64)
        Nov 16 2017 10:00:49
        Copyright (C) 2017 Microsoft Corporation
        Developer Edition (64-bit) on Linux (Red Hat Enterprise Linux
Server 7.4 (Maipo))
```

Inspecting the /opt/mssql-tools/bin directory will also show you the familiar bcp (bulk copy program) utility, which is used to import data from data files into SQL Server.

So far, we have been able to connect from inside the virtual machine. Could we connect from a SQL Server client outside the virtual machine? We could try using SQL Server Management Studio (SSMS) on Windows, connecting to the listed public IP address.

NOTE

At this point, you may need to install SQL Server Management Studio, preferably the latest version, which you can download from https://docs.microsoft.com/en-us/sql/ssms/download-sql-server-management-studio-ssms. As of this writing, the latest version is 17.3.

Trying to connect now will show a familiar message:

> Cannot connect to 40.112.137.60. Additional information. A network-related or instance-specific error occurred while establishing a connection to SQL Server. The server was not found or was not accessible. Verify that the instance name is correct and that SQL Server is configured to allow remote connections. (provider: Named Pipes Provider, error: 40 – Could not open a connection to SQL Server) (Microsoft SQL Server, Error: 53). The network path was not found.

The virtual machine needs to be configured to allow SQL Server remote connections. We were able to connect before using SSH as this protocol TCP port is configured by default, as you can see next, but connections to the SQL Server port, and basically anything else, need to be explicitly configured.

To configure your new virtual machine to accept SQL Server connections, open the Microsoft Azure Portal and go to Virtual Machines. Select your virtual machine, in this case sqlonlinux; click Networking; select the only available network interface in this example; and then select Network Security Group and Inbound Security Rules. You will see a configuration similar to the one shown in Figure 1-9, where only SSH on TCP port 22 is enabled by default. This was the reason we were able to connect from outside the virtual machine previously.

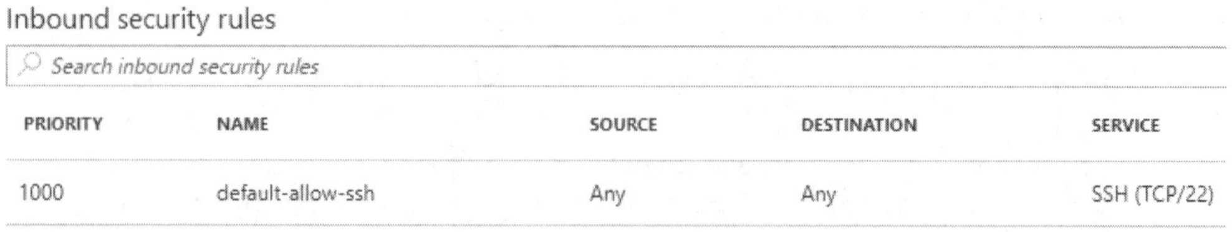

Inbound security rules

PRIORITY	NAME	SOURCE	DESTINATION	SERVICE
1000	default-allow-ssh	Any	Any	SSH (TCP/22)

Figure 1-9   *Inbound security rules*

We need to configure a new inbound rule on the network security group. We want to add a new rule to allow SQL Server connections using TCP port 1433. Click Add and change the configuration as shown in Figure 1-10. Type a name such as **MSSQL** and select MS SQL on the Service drop-down list. Protocol and Port Range will be automatically configured to TCP and 1433, respectively.

Leave the other fields set to their default values and click OK. For completeness, these are the definitions as shown on the Azure portal:

▶ **Priority**   Rules are processed in priority order; the lower the number, the higher the priority. We recommend leaving gaps between rules—100, 200, 300, and so on—so that it's easier to add new rules without having to edit existing rules.

▶ **Source**   The source filter can be Any, an IP address range, or a default tag. It specifies the incoming traffic from a specific source IP address range that will be allowed or denied by this rule.

▶ **Service**   The service specifies the destination protocol and port range for this rule. You can choose a predefined service, such as RDP or SSH, or provide a custom port range. In our case, there is a predefined service, MS SQL, which already specifies the TCP protocol and port 1433.

▶ **Protocol**   You can provide a single port, such as 80, or a port range, such as 1024-65535. This specifies on which ports incoming traffic will be allowed or denied by this rule. Enter an asterisk (*) to allow traffic from clients connecting on any port.

Click OK to finish the configuration. Refreshing the content shown in Figure 1-10 will now show both SSH and MS SQL services, using the TCP ports 22 and 1433, respectively. Only for Red Hat Enterprise Linux, you also have to open up port 1433 on the firewall. On Linux, run the following commands

```
$ sudo firewall-cmd --zone=public --add-port=1433/tcp --permanent
$ sudo firewall-cmd --reload
```

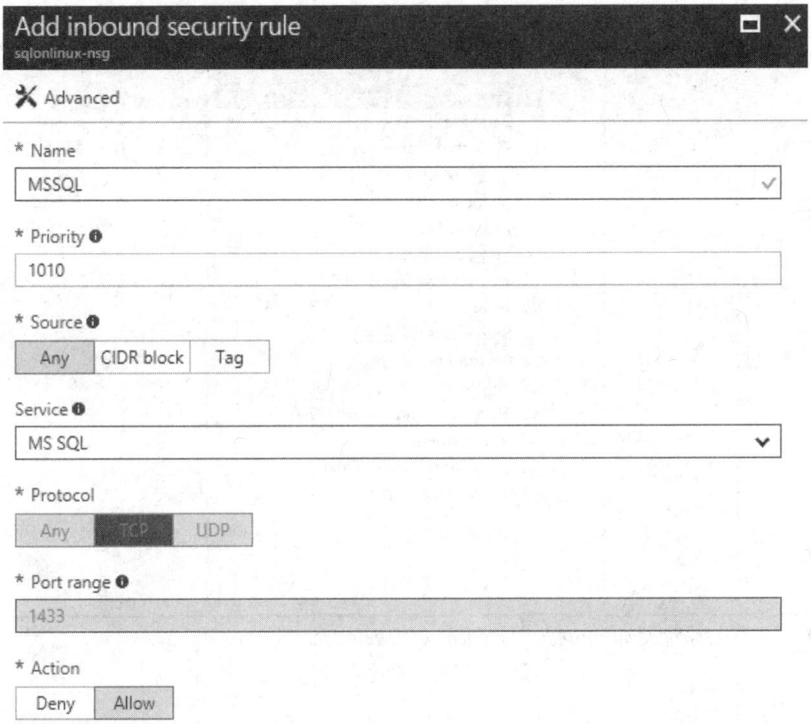

Figure 1-10 *Adding a rule to accept SQL Server connections*

Now you can connect from SQL Server Management Studio on Windows or any other SQL Server client outside the virtual machine, including applications on a large number of programming languages or frameworks such as .NET, Java, Python, and so on.

If you are accustomed to connecting using Windows authentication, as I am, keep in mind that for now you need to use the only login available at the moment, sa, and the password provided earlier. For example, Figure 1-11 shows Object Explorer from my current connection using SQL Server Management Studio.

Let's go back to our Linux SSH connection to create a couple of databases and explore where the database files are stored in the file system. Connect to the SQL Server instance using `sqlcmd`, as explained earlier, and create your first database by running the next statement:

```
CREATE DATABASE demo
GO
```

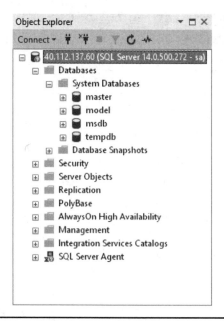

Figure 1-11 *SQL Server Management Studio connected to a Linux instance*

So you now have your first user database in Linux. Where could it be located? There are a few ways to figure that out. Try the following:

```
USE demo
GO
SELECT name, filename FROM sysfiles
GO
```

Here's the information returned:

```
name            filename
demo            /var/opt/mssql/data/demo.mdf
demo_log        /var/opt/mssql/data/demo_log.ldf
```

The default data location in Linux is /var/opt/mssql/data. This is the equivalent of the familiar C:\Program Files\Microsoft SQL Server\MSSQL14.MSSQLSERVER\ MSSQL\DATA in Windows. The location can be changed with the ms-conf utility as discussed in Chapter 4.

Run the following backup statement to find the default location of backup files:

```
BACKUP DATABASE demo TO DISK = 'demo.bak'
GO
Processed 304 pages for database 'demo', file 'demo' on file 1.
```

```
Processed 3 pages for database 'demo', file 'demo_log' on file 1.
BACKUP DATABASE successfully processed 307 pages in 0.182 seconds (13.178 MB/sec).
```

You should be able to see the backup files at /var/opt/mssql/data/demo.bak (assuming you have the proper permissions). Similarly, the system databases files are at the following locations:

- ► /var/opt/mssql/data/master.mdf
- ► /var/opt/mssql/data/mastlog.ldf
- ► /var/opt/mssql/data/model.mdf
- ► /var/opt/mssql/data/modellog.ldf
- ► /var/opt/mssql/data/msdbdata.mdf
- ► /var/opt/mssql/data/msdblog.ldf
- ► /var/opt/mssql/data/tempdb.mdf
- ► /var/opt/mssql/data/templog.ldf

Note that, as with a default Windows installation, both data and transaction log files reside on the same directory, /var/opt/mssql, which also contains a log directory, which is also the same as in Windows; it is used to store the SQL Server error log files, trace files created by the default trace, and extended events system_health files. This should not be confused with the location for database transaction log files. Spend some time inspecting the structure and files located both on /var/opt/mssql and /opt/mssql.

Finally, there are several ways to move or copy your Windows databases and data to Linux. For now, I can show you how to copy a Windows database backup file quickly and perform a database restore in Linux.

First, we need a way to copy the database backup file from Windows to our Linux virtual machine. Once of these choices is to install the PuTTY scp client on Windows, which you can download from www.putty.org. (The scp stands for secure copy and it is a utility used to copy files between computers.)

Once scp is installed, run the following:

```
C:\Data\pscp AdventureWorks2014.bak bnevarez@13.91.94.234:.
Using keyboard-interactive authentication.
Password:
AdventureWorks2014.bak | 81128 kB | 2617.0 kB/s | ETA: 00:00:00 | 100%
```

This will take a couple of minutes and will copy the database backup file to your home directory in Linux. In my case, the file ended at /home/bnevarez/AdventureWorks2014 .bak.

Next, to avoid issues with permissions, use the following command to copy the backup file to /var/opt/mssql/data:

```
sudo cp /home/bnevarez/AdventureWorks2014.bak /var/opt/mssql/data
```

Run the next restore statement, which specifies the location of the backup file and the new location for the created database files:

```
RESTORE DATABASE AdventureWorks2014 FROM DISK =
'/var/opt/mssql/data/AdventureWorks2014.bak'
WITH MOVE 'AdventureWorks2014_Data' TO
'/var/opt/mssql/data/AdventureWorks2014_Data.mdf',
MOVE 'AdventureWorks2014_Log' TO '/var/opt/mssql/data/AdventureWorks2014_Log.ldf',
MOVE 'AdventureWorks2014_mod' TO '/var/opt/mssql/data/AdventureWorks2014_mod'
```

You can optionally restore the database with SQL Server Management Studio, where you only have to browse to the location of the backup file and the database file locations will be handled automatically. The database will be restored as AdventureWorks2014, and you will be able to query it in exactly the same way you would have done it in Windows.

At this point, you may need the basic statements to start, restart, and stop SQL Server. More details about `systemctl` will be covered in Chapter 3.

To stop SQL Server, run the following statement:

```
sudo systemctl stop mssql-server
```

To start SQL Server, run the following:

```
sudo systemctl start mssql-server
```

To restart SQL Server, run the following:

```
sudo systemctl restart mssql-server
```

Installing Additional Components

This section covers how to install the SQL Server Agent, SQL Server Full-Text Search, and SQL Server Integration Services, which are provided in separate packages: mssql-server-agent, mssql-server-fts, and mssql-server-is, respectively. We will follow the same procedure for Red Hat Enterprise Server using the yum utility.

To install SQL Server Agent, run the following commands (again, output formatted to fit the book):

```
sudo yum install mssql-server-agent
Loaded plugins: langpacks, product-id, search-disabled-repos
Resolving Dependencies
--> Running transaction check
```

```
---> Package mssql-server-agent.x86_64 0:14.0.500.272-2 will be updated
---> Package mssql-server-agent.x86_64 0:14.0.900.75-1 will be an update
--> Finished Dependency Resolution
Dependencies Resolved
Updating:
Package mssql-server-agent
Arch x86_64
Version 14.0.900.75-1
Repository packages-microsoft-com-mssql-server
Size 1.5 M
Transaction Summary
Upgrade  1 Package
Total download size: 1.5 M
Is this ok [y/d/N]: y
Downloading packages:
Delta RPMs disabled because /usr/bin/applydeltarpm not installed.
mssql-server-agent-14.0.900.75-1.x86_64.rpm | 1.5 MB  00:00:00
Running transaction check
Running transaction test
Transaction test succeeded
Running transaction
  Updating   : mssql-server-agent-14.0.900.75-1.x86_64  1/2
Please restart mssql-server to enable Microsoft SQL Server Agent.
  Cleanup    : mssql-server-agent-14.0.500.272-2.x86_64  2/2
  Verifying  : mssql-server-agent-14.0.900.75-1.x86_64  1/2
  Verifying  : mssql-server-agent-14.0.500.272-2.x86_64  2/2
Updated:
  mssql-server-agent.x86_64 0:14.0.900.75-1
Complete!
```

As hinted in the installation, you will need to restart SQL Server after the SQL Server Agent is installed:

```
sudo systemctl restart mssql-server
```

To install SQL Server Full-Text Search, run the following yum command:

```
sudo yum install -y mssql-server-fts
Loaded plugins: langpacks, product-id, search-disabled-repos
Resolving Dependencies
--> Running transaction check
---> Package mssql-server-fts.x86_64 0:14.0.500.272-2 will be updated
---> Package mssql-server-fts.x86_64 0:14.0.900.75-1 will be an update
--> Finished Dependency Resolution
Dependencies Resolved
Updating:
```

```
Package mssql-server-fts
Arch x86_64
Version 14.0.900.75-1
Repository packages-microsoft-com-mssql-server
Size 228 M
Transaction Summary
Upgrade  1 Package
Total download size: 228 M
Downloading packages:
Delta RPMs disabled because /usr/bin/applydeltarpm not installed.
mssql-server-fts-14.0.900.75-1.x86_64.rpm  | 228 MB  00:00:03
Running transaction check
Running transaction test
Transaction test succeeded
Running transaction
  Updating    : mssql-server-fts-14.0.900.75-1.x86_64  1/2
Please restart mssql-server to enable Microsoft SQL Server Full Text Search.
  Cleanup     : mssql-server-fts-14.0.500.272-2.x86_64  2/2
  Verifying   : mssql-server-fts-14.0.900.75-1.x86_64  1/2
  Verifying   : mssql-server-fts-14.0.500.272-2.x86_64  2/2
Updated:
  mssql-server-fts.x86_64 0:14.0.900.75-1
```

Again, you will need to restart SQL Server after SQL Server Full-Text Search has been installed.

To install SQL Server Integration Services, run the following command:

```
sudo yum install -y mssql-server-is
Loaded plugins: langpacks, product-id, search-disabled-repos
packages-microsoft-com-mssql-server | 2.9 kB  00:00:00
Resolving Dependencies
--> Running transaction check
---> Package mssql-server-is.x86_64 0:14.0.900.75-1 will be installed
--> Finished Dependency Resolution
Dependencies Resolved
Installing:
Package mssql-server-is
Arch x86_64
Version 14.0.900.75-1
Repository packages-microsoft-com-mssql-server
Size 175 M
Transaction Summary
Install  1 Package
Total download size: 175 M
Installed size: 836 M
```

```
Downloading packages:
mssql-server-is-14.0.900.75-1.x86_64.rpm  | 175 MB  00:00:02
Running transaction check
Running transaction test
Transaction test succeeded
Running transaction
  Installing : mssql-server-is-14.0.900.75-1.x86_64  1/1
Please run 'sudo /opt/ssis/bin/ssis-conf setup'
to complete the setup of Microsoft SQL Server Integration Service
  Verifying  : mssql-server-is-14.0.900.75-1.x86_64  1/1
Installed:
  mssql-server-is.x86_64 0:14.0.900.75-1
Complete!
```

Finally, as hinted on the install output, run the following command to configure SQL Server Integration Services, and again select 2 to choose the free Developer edition:

```
sudo /opt/ssis/bin/ssis-conf setup
The license terms for this product can be downloaded from:
https://go.microsoft.com/fwlink/?LinkId=852741&clcid=0x409
The privacy statement can be viewed at:
https://go.microsoft.com/fwlink/?LinkId=853010&clcid=0x409
Do you accept the license terms? [Yes/No]:Yes
Choose an edition of SSIS:
  1) Evaluation (free, no production use rights, 180-day limit)
  2) Developer (free, no production use rights)
  3) Express (free)
  4) Web (PAID)
  5) Standard (PAID)
  6) Enterprise (PAID)
  7) I bought a license through a retail sales channel and have a product key to
enter.
Details about editions can be found at
https://go.microsoft.com/fwlink/?LinkId=852748&clcid=0x409
Use of PAID editions of this software requires separate licensing through a
Microsoft Volume Licensing program.
By choosing a PAID edition, you are verifying that you have the appropriate
number of licenses in place to install and run this software.
Enter your edition(1-7): 2
Only user in 'ssis' group can run 'dtexec' on Linux. Do you want to add current
user into 'ssis' group? [Yes/No]:No
Please run 'sudo usermod -aG ssis <user name>' and logout to reload the group
information.
SSIS telemetry service is now running.
Setup has completed successfully.
```

There is no need to restart SQL Server at this time. It is also recommended that you update the PATH environment variable by running the following command:

```
export PATH=/opt/ssis/bin:$PATH
```

NOTE

For details about permanently updating the PATH environment variable, see Chapter 3.

Installing on Ubuntu

You've seen the entire process of installing and configuring SQL Server 2017 using Red Hat Enterprise Linux. Let's now install SQL Server on Ubuntu. After this I'll focus only on what is different compared with the previous Red Hat installation. Let's start by creating a virtual machine running Ubuntu.

Open the Microsoft Azure virtual machines portal. In the Search field, enter **Ubuntu**. This will show you a few results. Select Ubuntu Server 16.04 LTS. Every Linux installation must have at least 3.25GB of memory for a SQL Server 2017 installation, but at the moment any virtual machine image on the gallery has at least that much memory, so this should not be a problem. You need to be careful with this, however, if you are creating the virtual machine using other methods or if you're installing the operating system software yourself.

Follow the steps described in the "Creating a Virtual Machine" section earlier in the chapter. Once you have a virtual machine running and you are able to connect to it, run the following statements to get the public repository GPG keys (more on this in a moment):

```
curl https://packages.microsoft.com/keys/microsoft.asc | sudo apt-key add -
```

Next, run the following statements to register the SQL Server Ubuntu repository:

```
curl https://packages.microsoft.com/config/ubuntu/16.04/mssql-server-2017.list |
sudo tee /etc/apt/sources.list.d/mssql-server.list
```

As with Red Hat Enterprise Linux, this was the cumulative update repository. The GDR repository is at https://packages.microsoft.com/config/ubuntu/16.04/mssql-server-2017-gdr.list, and the preview repository is at https://packages.microsoft.com/config/ubuntu/16.04/mssql-server.list.

Finally, run the following commands to install SQL Server:

```
sudo apt-get update
sudo apt-get install -y mssql-server
```

After this point, you can configure SQL Server in the same way as before by running the following, accepting the license terms, selecting the free Developer addition, and providing a strong sa password:

```
sudo /opt/mssql/bin/mssql-conf setup
```

You'll see something similar to the following output:

```
The license terms for this product can be downloaded from
http://go.microsoft.com/fwlink/?LinkId=746388
and found in /usr/share/doc/mssql-server/LICENSE.TXT.

Do you accept the license terms? [Yes/No]:Yes

Choose an edition of SQL Server:
  1) Evaluation (free, no production use rights, 180-day limit)
  2) Developer (free, no production use rights)
  3) Express (free)
  4) Web (PAID)
  5) Standard (PAID)
  6) Enterprise (PAID)
  7) I bought a license through a retail sales channel and have a product key to
enter.

Details about editions can be found at
https://www.microsoft.com/en-us/sql-server/sql-server-2016-editions

Use of PAID editions of this software requires separate licensing through a
Microsoft Volume Licensing program.
By choosing a PAID edition, you are verifying that you have the appropriate
number of licenses in place to install and run this software.

Enter your edition(1-7): 2
Enter the SQL Server system administrator password:
Confirm the SQL Server system administrator password:
Configuring SQL Server...

This is an evaluation version.  There are [170] days left in the evaluation period.
Created symlink from /etc/systemd/system/multi-user.target.wants/mssql-
server.service to /lib/systemd/system/mssql-server.service.
Setup has completed successfully. SQL Server is now starting.
```

Installing client tools is also different from Red Hat Enterprise Linux. Start by importing the public repository GPG keys if you have not done so when you installed SQL Server in the previous step:

```
curl https://packages.microsoft.com/keys/microsoft.asc | sudo apt-key add -
```

Run the next step to register the Ubuntu repository:

```
curl https://packages.microsoft.com/config/ubuntu/16.04/prod.list | sudo tee
/etc/apt/sources.list.d/msprod.list
```

Now we are ready to update the sources list and to install both the mssql-tools and the unixODBC developer packages:

```
sudo apt-get update
sudo apt-get install mssql-tools unixodbc-dev
```

Now we can connect to the SQL Server instance same as before:

```
/opt/mssql-tools/bin/sqlcmd -U sa
```

In this case, running `SELECT @@VERSION` returns the following:

```
Microsoft SQL Server 2017 (RTM-CU2) (KB4052574) - 14.0.3008.27 (X64)
        Nov 16 2017 10:00:49
        Copyright (C) 2017 Microsoft Corporation
        Developer Edition (64-bit) on Linux (Ubuntu 16.04.3 LTS)
```

Follow the same steps shown earlier to connect from outside the virtual machine. Basically, you will need to configure a new inbound rule on the network security group to allow SQL Server connections using the TCP port 1433.

As I did with Red Hat Enterprise Server, I will now cover how to install SQL Server Agent, SQL Server Full-Text Search, and SQL Server Integration Services for Ubuntu.

To install SQL Server Agent, run the following command:

```
sudo apt-get install mssql-server-agent
```

To install SQL Server Full-Text Search, run the following command:

```
sudo apt-get install -y mssql-server-fts
```

After you install these components, you will need to restart SQL Server:

```
sudo systemctl restart mssql-server
```

Finally, to install and configure SQL Server Integration Services, run the following statements:

```
sudo apt-get install -y mssql-server-is
sudo /opt/ssis/bin/ssis-conf setup
```

There is no need to restart SQL Server this time. As mentioned earlier, it is also recommended at this time that you update the PATH environment variable by running the following command:

```
export PATH=/opt/ssis/bin:$PATH
```

NOTE

For details about permanently updating the PATH *environment variable see Chapter 3.*

Installing on SUSE Linux Enterprise Server

Now let's use the same process with SUSE Linux Enterprise Server. Again, open the Microsoft Azure virtual machines portal. Enter **SLES** for SUSE Linux Enterprise Server in the Search field, and you will see a few choices. Select the recommended version and service pack. I am using SLES 12 SP2.

As with the previous installations, remember that every Linux installation must have at least 3.25GB of memory to run SQL Server 2017. Follow the steps described in the "Creating a Virtual Machine" section earlier.

Once you have a virtual machine and you are able to connect to it, start by downloading the SQL Server SLES repository configuration file. Run the following commands:

```
sudo zypper addrepo -fc https://packages.microsoft.com/config/sles/12/mssql-
server-2017.repo
sudo zypper --gpg-auto-import-keys refresh
```

Same as the previous Linux distributions mentioned, this was the cumulative update repository. The GDR repository is at https://packages.microsoft.com/config/sles/12/mssqlserver-2017-gdr.repo, and the preview repository is at https://packages.microsoft.com/config/sles/12/mssql-server.repo.

Next, run the following command to install SQL Server:

```
sudo zypper install mssql-server
```

Configure SQL Server the same way you did earlier using the mssql-conf utility:

```
sudo /opt/mssql/bin/mssql-conf setup
```

Finally, install the SQL Server client tools. Use the following steps to install the mssql-tools package on SUSE Linux Enterprise Server. Add the SQL Server repository to zypper:

```
sudo zypper addrepo -fc https://packages.microsoft.com/config/sles/12/prod.repo
sudo zypper --gpg-auto-import-keys refresh
```

Install mssql-tools with the unixODBC developer package:

```
sudo zypper install mssql-tools unixODBC-devel
```

Connect as usual using the sqlcmd command-line utility:

```
/opt/mssql-tools/bin/sqlcmd -U sa
```

Running SELECT @@VERSION this time shows the following:

```
Microsoft SQL Server 2017 (RTM-CU2) (KB4052574) - 14.0.3008.27 (X64)
        Nov 16 2017 10:00:49
        Copyright (C) 2017 Microsoft Corporation
        Developer Edition (64-bit) on Linux (SUSE Linux Enterprise Server 12 SP2)
```

Follow the same steps indicated earlier to connect from outside the virtual machine. You will need to configure a new inbound rule on the network security group to allow SQL Server client connections using the TCP port 1433.

As I did with Red Hat Enterprise Server and Ubuntu, I will next cover how to install SQL Server Agent, SQL Server Full-Text Search, and SQL Server Integration Services on SUSE Linux Enterprise Server. To install SQL Server Agent, run the following command:

```
sudo zypper install mssql-server-agent
```

To install SQL Server Full-Text Search, run the following command:

```
sudo zypper install mssql-server-fts
```

After you install these components, you will need to restart SQL Server:

```
sudo systemctl restart mssql-server
```

Finally, as of this writing SQL Server Integration Services is not yet available for SUSE Linux Enterprise Server.

Running SQL Server on Docker

Docker is a software technology that provides containers as an additional layer of abstraction and automation to the virtualization technologies we are very familiar with. Docker can run on the Linux, Windows, or Mac OS operating systems.

A fundamental difference between using SQL Server on Docker and the previous Linux installations is that Docker will run a preexisting SQL Server 2017 image. The currently available image is an installation of SQL Server 2017 on Ubuntu 16.04. But keep in mind that this Ubuntu SQL Server 2017 image can run on any operating system that supports Docker containers.

To run SQL Server 2017 on Docker, you will first need a Docker installation. Because there might be different ways to configure Docker, in this exercise I will show Docker on an Ubuntu virtual machine.

For example, to run Docker on my previous Ubuntu virtual machine image, I use the following:

```
$ docker
```

And I get the following response:

```
The program 'docker' is currently not installed. You can install it by typing:
sudo apt install docker.io
```

So I followed the recommendation and ran the following:

```
sudo apt install docker.io
```

NOTE

SQL Server 2017 requires 3.25GB of memory on Docker, so make sure the host is configured with at least 4GB of memory. This was a common problem I found on some default Docker installations.

Next, we need to download the SQL Server 2017 image by running the following:

```
sudo docker pull microsoft/mssql-server-linux:2017-latest
```

Here is some output in my installation:

```
Using default tag: latest
latest: Pulling from microsoft/mssql-server-linux:2017-latest
aed15891ba52: Pull complete
773ae8583d14: Pull complete
d1d48771f782: Pull complete
```

```
cd3d6cd6c0cf: Pull complete
8ff6f8a9120c: Pull complete
1fd7e8b10447: Pull complete
bd485157db89: Pull complete
273a1970ce9c: Pull complete
fe20b2602177: Pull complete
086b69c4d68d: Pull complete
Digest: sha256:38346f8beba690c99f7ff35b11118df3c0731a77784a25e3165eec5f592a1498
Status: Downloaded newer image for microsoft/mssql-server-linux:2017-latest
```

Next we are ready to run the SQL Server container image on Docker, executing the next statement while specifying an appropriate sa login password:

```
docker run -e 'ACCEPT_EULA=Y' -e 'MSSQL_SA_PASSWORD=password' -p
1421:1433 --name sqlonlinux -d microsoft/mssql-server-linux:2017-latest
```

For this example, port 1421 has to be available on the host computer. We cannot use the host port 1433 because we are already running an instance of SQL Server there (installed in a previous exercise). The second port, 1433, will be the port on the container.

Validate that the SQL Server 2017 container is running by executing the following:

```
sudo docker ps -a
```

The output will show something similar to this, where you can validate the STATUS information to verify that SQL Server container is effectively running:

```
CONTAINER ID        IMAGE                                COMMAND
CREATED             STATUS              PORTS            NAMES
3770544f5e6d        microsoft/mssql-server-linux    "/bin/sh -c /opt/mssq"
44 seconds ago      Up 35 seconds       0.0.0.0:1433->1433/tcp    sqlonlinux
```

If you have SQL Server client tools on the same server, you can connect directly to the new installation. Or you can install them as described earlier for the Ubuntu Linux distribution. Note that only client tools are required, because you will be connecting to a SQL Server image running in a Docker container.

You should be able to connect as indicated earlier. For example, you can use the following command using the host port 1421:

```
/opt/mssql-tools/bin/sqlcmd -U sa -H localhost,1421
```

This time @@VERSION will return

```
Microsoft SQL Server 2017 (RTM-CU2) (KB4052574) - 14.0.3008.27 (X64)
        Nov 16 2017 10:00:49
        Copyright (C) 2017 Microsoft Corporation
        Developer Edition (64-bit) on Linux (Ubuntu 16.04.3 LTS)
```

Here's a quick explanation of several parameters used for the container. To confirm your acceptance of the end-user licensing agreement:

```
-e "ACCEPT_EULA=Y"
```

To specify the sa password:

```
-e "SA_PASSWORD=<password>"
```

Remember the sa login password policy requirements mentioned earlier. A problem with this password will be a bit more complicated to troubleshoot because you need to look at the SQL Server error log.

To specify the port mapping—the first value is the TCP port on the host environment and the second the TCP port on the container:

```
-p 1421:1433
```

To specify the SQL Server container image:

```
-d microsoft/mssql-server-linux
```

To specify a custom name for the container:

```
--name sqlonlinux
```

Optionally you can connect to the container and run the client tools from there. For example, you can use the following command, which runs an interactive Bash shell inside the container, where e69e056c702d is the container ID shown earlier on the Docker ps command. The docker exec command is used to run a command in a running container:

```
$ sudo docker exec -it e69e056c702d "bash"
```

After running the command, you will receive a bash prompt, #, where you can run the sqlcmd client as usual. Note that this time, we don't need to specify a port since we are inside the container, which was configured to listen to the default SQL Server port 1433:

```
root@e69e056c702d:/#/opt/mssql-tools/bin/sqlcmd -U sa
```

Follow the same steps indicated earlier to connect from outside the virtual machine. Basically, we will need to configure a new inbound rule on the network security group to allow SQL Server connections using the host TCP port, in this example, 1421.

Finally, here a few basic Docker commands, just to get you started. In any of the following cases you can use the container ID or the provided name.

To stop one or more running containers:

```
$ sudo docker stop 05f247e0d59c
```

Or

```
$ sudo docker stop sqlonlinux
```

To start one or more stopped containers:

```
$ sudo docker start 05f247e0d59c
```

Or

```
$ sudo docker start sqlonlinux
```

To restart a container:

```
$ sudo docker restart 05f247e0d59c
```

When you no longer need the container, you can remove it using the rm option:

```
$ sudo docker rm 05f247e0d59c
```

Note that you should stop the container before trying to remove it, unless you also specify the -f option.

To troubleshoot problems with a container, you can look at the SQL Server error log using the following command:

```
$ sudo docker logs 05f247e0d59c
```

Uninstalling SQL Server

Removing SQL Server is essentially the same procedure for all the Linux distributions, and it involves using the appropriate package manager utility that we have used previously in the chapter. First, stop the SQL Server instance as indicated earlier.

To remove SQL Server on Red Hat Enterprise Linux, run the following:

```
sudo yum remove mssql-server
```

To remove SQL Server on Ubuntu, run the following:

```
sudo apt-get remove mssql-server
```

To remove SQL Server on SUSE Linux Enterprise Server, run the following:

```
sudo zypper remove mssql-server
```

In any of the listed Linux distributions, if you need to remove all the databases after uninstalling SQL Server, run the following:

```
sudo rm -rf /var/opt/mssql/
```

Summary

This chapter covered installing SQL Server on Linux and provided you with enough information to get started using the product as quickly as possible. It covered how to install and configure SQL Server in a preexisting Linux installation, which could be either a virtual machine on Microsoft Azure or Amazon Web Services or your own Linux installation. You learned how to install SQL Server on Red Hat Enterprise Linux, SUSE Linux Enterprise Server, and Ubuntu and how to configure an image of SQL Server on a Docker container.

If you've followed the instructions in this chapter, you will have a SQL Server up and running and will be ready to cover most advanced topics, such as configuring SQL Server on Linux for high availability and disaster recovery or covering the new query processing and security features. Chapter 2 covers architecture decisions, how SQL Server works on Linux, how SQL Server interacts with the operating system, and other related topics.

Chapter 2

How SQL Server on Linux Works

In This Chapter

Most SQL Server users will be surprised to learn that SQL Server was actually born on the Unix platform, first ported to OS/2 and later to the Windows NT operating system. So in its early days, SQL Server was in fact a multiplatform technology. SQL Server was originally written by Sybase and released for OS/2 and Windows NT in an agreement with Microsoft. After its business relationship with Sybase ended, Microsoft secured the code base of the database engine and decided to make SQL Server a Windows-only technology, which remained the case for more than two decades.

A second important architecture feature for the future Linux implementation was the development of SQL Operating System (SQLOS), which was written for the SQL Server 2005 release. SQLOS was created to exploit the newly available hardware and to provide the database engine with more specialized services than a standard operating system could afford. SQLOS is also the SQL Server application layer responsible for managing all operating system resources, such as nonpreemptive scheduling, memory and buffer management, I/O functions, resource governance, exception handling, and extended events. SQLOS was never intended to be a platform-independent solution. Porting SQL Server to other operating systems was not in the plan during the SQLOS development.

In an astonishing announcement in March 2016, Microsoft surprised the industry by declaring that SQL Server would be available on the Linux platform sometime in 2017. After that moment, it seems that the industry expected a real port that compiled the SQL Server C++ code base into a native Linux application. Microsoft later indicated that this version would be named SQL Server 2017 and would be available on Red Hat Enterprise Linux, Ubuntu, and SUSE Linux Enterprise Server, in addition to Docker containers. Docker itself runs on multiple platforms, which means that it would be possible to run the SQL Server Docker image on Linux, Mac, and Windows.

But when the first parts of the beta version of the software, called a Community Technology Preview (CTP), were released in November 2016, we were in for another surprise: instead of a port, SQL Server was able to run on Linux thanks to some virtualization technologies based on Drawbridge, the software result of a Microsoft project completed just a few years earlier.

Microsoft soon released more information about how SQL Server on Linux works; its architecture includes several components such as the Drawbridge technology, a revamped SQLOS, and the SQL Platform Abstraction Layer (SQLPAL), the layer that enabled Microsoft to bring Windows applications to Linux. SQL Server 2017 was finally released in October 2017.

This chapter covers some SQL Server history with different operating systems and explains some of the details about how SQL Server on Linux works. This includes describing the interaction between SQL Server and the operating system, decisions regarding its architecture, its software implementation, and other related topics.

The Sybase Years

Microsoft SQL Server was born indirectly as part of an agreement between IBM and Microsoft to develop OS/2, the operating system that was planned to be the successor of MS-DOS. Before the release of this operating system, IBM added a database product to its version of OS/2, so Microsoft needed a database product as well. Microsoft turned to a new company, Sybase, to license its database product. The original agreement between Sybase and Microsoft was to port its database engine, DataServer, originally developed for Unix platforms, to the OS/2 operating system.

Later in the process, to appeal to the large dBASE community, a marketing and distribution deal was also signed with Ashton-Tate, and the final product was named Ashton-Tate/Microsoft SQL Server, which was eventually released in May 1989. It's interesting to note that Sybase, the company that wrote the original software, was not included in the product name.

The SQL Server database engine was ported to OS/2 from the Unix source code, and Ashton-Tate/Microsoft SQL version 1.0 debuted in OS/2 in May 1989. The agreement with Ashton-Tate did not last long, however, and the product was soon renamed Microsoft SQL Server; its first version under this name, version 1.1, shipped in the summer of 1990.

OS/2 was created as a replacement for MS-DOS, but the market was in for a huge surprise. Instead of moving from MS-DOS to OS/2, users were moving to Windows 3.0. Windows 3.0 had been an unexpected huge success in the computer industry. So it was essential for SQL Server to support Windows as a client as well. To achieve this, Microsoft provided tools for developers to create Windows applications that could connect to SQL Server. (Note that Windows was not an immediate success either, as the first two versions of the software were mostly ignored.)

At that time, Microsoft was also working on an operating system kernel, originally intended to be used on OS/2, but that later became a new operating system called Windows NT, which was released in 1993. For Microsoft, the obvious next step was to port SQL Server to Windows NT.

Suddenly the SQL Server team in Microsoft was faced with the dilemma of simultaneously developing versions for both OS/2 and Windows NT; some of the issues faced with this development would be revisited many years later for the Linux release. The team was faced with a new set of problems: they needed to add an abstraction layer to hide the differences in the operating systems, they'd need major reengineering for both versions of SQL Server, or they'd take a lowest common-denominator approach and not fully use the services or features of either system.

The decision was to keep SQL Server as a Windows NT–only technology, even when at the time it was a new operating system with no installed user base. So this time, SQL Server version 4.2 for OS/2 was ported to Windows NT. Because there was no need to be concerned about portability to other operating systems or creating an abstraction layer, the team could focus on doing the best possible job for only one operating system, Windows NT. It was decided that the goals of portability were in conflict with the goal of creating the best possible software for Windows NT. The final product, SQL Server for Windows NT, would then be more than a port from the OS/2 code, because it required rewriting the kernel of SQL Server, the part of the software that interacts with the operating system.

The initial release, Windows NT 3.1, was shipped on July 27, 1993, and was written in C, C++, and assembly language. (There was no version 1.0 or 2.0.) The first beta version of SQL Server for Windows NT was released in October 1992. SQL Server 4.21a, released in 1993, was the first version to run on Windows. This was the last full port of SQL Server, because Microsoft got the rights for the 4.21a code base and, as mentioned earlier, later changes of the product would focus only on Windows NT without consideration of any future possibility of porting back to Unix or any other operating system.

In those early days, Microsoft was competing with Sybase, which was releasing System 10 for Windows NT. Sybase System 10 was designed in a more portable manner and as a consequence could not perform as well as SQL Server, which was designed, written, and optimized exclusively for Windows NT. In April 1994, Microsoft and Sybase announced the end of their development agreement, and each decided to develop its own SQL Server products. The last version of SQL Server for OS/2, SQL Server 4.2B, was released in 1993.

Although no additional major development happened during the following releases, at least for the purposes of this story, Microsoft would rearchitect the entire database engine and include a brand-new query processor for its SQL Server 7.0 release, which shipped in 1998.

Although the first version of SQL Server was version 1.X, there was no version 2.0 or 3.0. Later, Microsoft would also skip version 5.0, moving from version 4.2 to release 6.0. Finally, instead of using version 8.0 for the SQL Server 2000 release, Microsoft would use a new company-wide naming standard for many of its products, which continues to this day, with SQL Server 2017, although their internal version numbers, which can be returned by using the @@VERSION function, still shows the original version number. For example, SQL Server 2000 was version 8, and the full build name for RTM (release to manufacturing) was 8.00.194. The current version, SQL Server 2017, is version 14.0, and the current software RTM-CU2 shows 14.0.3008.27.

NOTE

For more about the history of SQL Server, at least until SQL Server 2000, read the first chapter of the Inside Microsoft SQL Server *books by Kalen Delaney and Ron Soukup, which can also be found online at the bottom of https://www.sqlserverinternals.com/resources.*

SQLOS

As mentioned, SQLOS was another very important development for the future Linux implementation. SQLOS was a new operating system layer whose purpose was to provide the database engine with performance and scalability improvements by exploiting the new available hardware capabilities and providing the database engine with more specialized services than the general ones an operating system can offer.

SQLOS was first available on the SQL Server 2005 release. Although in part SQLOS was created to remove or abstract away the operating system dependencies, it was not originally intended to provide platform independence or portability, or to help in porting the database engine to other operating systems. Its first purpose was to exploit the new available hardware capabilities, including Symmetric Multithreading (SMT) and multi-CPU configuration with multiple cores per socket systems, computers with very large amounts of memory, non-uniform memory access (NUMA) systems, and support for hot memory and CPU add-ons and removals. Database engines could benefit from these new hardware and hardware trends.

SQLOS also became the SQL Server application layer responsible for managing all operating system resources, and it was responsible for managing nonpreemptive scheduling, memory and buffer management, I/O functions, resource governance, exception handling, deadlock detection, and extended events. SQLOS performs these functions by making calls to the operating system on behalf of other database engine layers or, as in the cases of scheduling, by providing services optimized for the specific needs of SQL Server. The SQLOS architecture is shown in Figure 2-1.

The main architecture design decision behind SQLOS replaced some of the available operating system services. Operating system services are general-purpose services and are sometimes inappropriate for database engine needs, because they do not scale well. Instead of using generic scheduling facilities for any process, scheduling can be optimized and tailored to the specific needs of a database engine, in this case, SQL Server. The main difference between the two is that a Windows scheduler is a preemptive scheduler, while with SQL Server, the decision was to use a cooperative scheduler (aka nonpreemptive scheduler). This implementation improves scalability, because having threads yield voluntarily is more efficient than involving the Windows kernel to prevent a single thread from monopolizing a processor.

The most important objects on SQLOS are memory and CPU nodes, schedulers, and tasks. Schedulers and tasks are easily visible and well known to the SQL Server user through the use of dynamic management views (DMVs) such as sys.dm_os_schedulers and sys.dm_os_tasks. In SQL Server, each user request is an operating system thread, and when a client connects, it is assigned to a specific scheduler. Schedulers are handled at the SQLOS level, which also handles tasks and workers, among other functions. For example, the SQL Server task execution process is shown in Figure 2-2. SQL Server schedulers were introduced with SQL Server 7, but that version still relied on the Windows scheduling facilities.

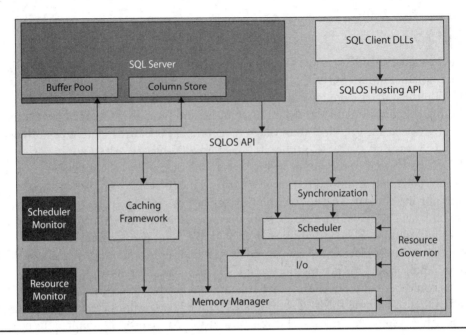

Figure 2-1   *SQLOS architecture*

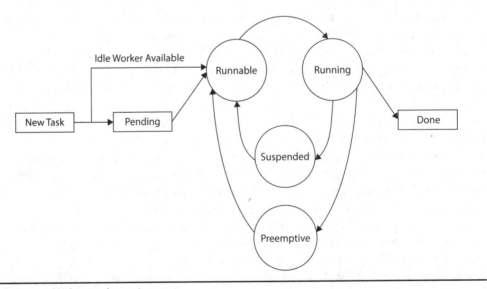

Figure 2-2   *SQL Server task execution process*

SQL Server will also detect and work with the then-new NUMA systems. SQL Server 2000 Service Pack 4 included limited support for NUMA systems. Full NUMA support was added when SQLOS was released with SQL Server 2005. Software NUMA is automatically configured starting with SQL Server 2014 Service Pack 4 and SQL Server 2016 (some support was also possible before but required manually editing the Windows registry). Starting with these versions of the database engine, whenever SQL Server detects more than eight physical cores per NUMA node or socket at startup, software NUMA nodes will be created automatically by default.

SQLOS was never intended to be a platform-independent solution, but rather a way to provide purpose-built operating system services to the database engine for performance and scalability with the SQL Server 2017 release.

NOTE

For more details about SQLOS, read the paper "A New Platform Layer in SQL Server 2005 to Exploit New Hardware Capabilities and Their Trends" by Slava Oks, at https://blogs.msdn.microsoft.com/slavao/2005/07/20/platform-layer-for-sql-server/. In addition, in the paper "Operating System Support for Database Management," Michael Stonebraker examines whether several operating system services are appropriate for support of database management functions such as scheduling, process management, interprocess communication, buffer pool management, consistency control, and file system services. You can use your favorite search engine to find this research paper online.

The Industry Changes

In March 2016 at the Data Driven event in New York, Microsoft surprised the entire technology community by announcing that SQL Server would be released on the Linux platform. In November of that year, at the Microsoft Connect() event in the same city, it announced that the first bits of the technology, the first CTP of the then-named SQL Server vNext, was available for download. At the same event, the Linux Foundation, a nonprofit organization advancing professional open-source management for mass collaboration, announced that Microsoft had joined the organization as a platinum member.

The SQL Server on Linux announcement mentioned that this release would include almost all the features of SQL Server for Windows. Among the features not included for this release were transactional replication, merge replication, Stretch DB, Polybase, distributed query with third-party connections, system extended stored procedures, file tables, CLR assemblies with the EXTERNAL_ACCESS or UNSAFE permission set, database mirroring, and buffer pool extension. Also some services such as SQL Server Browser Service, SQL Server R Services, StreamInsight, SQL Server Analysis

Services, Reporting Services, Data Quality Services, and Master Data Services would not be available on the current release. In addition, only SQL Server default instances (as opposed to named instances) would be available on Linux. You can see the entire and current list of unsupported features and services at https://docs.microsoft.com/en-us/sql/linux/sql-server-linux-release-notes.

Several other announcements impacted this SQL Server release as well. During the same Microsoft Connect() event, the first service pack for SQL Server 2016 was announced. Usually a service pack is not a big deal, but this one was different. Microsoft stated that starting with this service pack, all programmability features would be available on all editions of SQL Server. Features such as In-Memory OLTP, columnstore indexes, database snapshots, compression, partitioning, Always Encrypted, Row-Level Security, Dynamic Data Masking, and Change Data Capture, among others, would be available on all the editions of SQL Server, from the free Express edition to Standard and Enterprise. Obviously, this impacted SQL Server on Linux as well, because it applied to every SQL Server release after SQL Server 2016 Service Pack 1.

In November 2014, Microsoft announced that it would open-source the full server-side .NET Core stack and that the open-source .NET would be expanded to run on Linux and Mac OS X in addition to Windows. Visual Studio Community 2013 was also announced as a new, free, and fully featured edition of Visual Studio. SQL Server Developer edition, which is not meant to be run in production environments, was also made available for free according to a separate announcement in March 2016.

Finally, on August 18, 2016, Microsoft announced that it would open-source PowerShell and make it available on Linux. PowerShell is a task-automation command-line shell and scripting language built on the .NET Framework. As I started my career in the Unix world, even before Windows NT, PowerShell for me was just like a Unix shell. In a similar way, Microsoft made available Bash shell on Windows as part of a component called the Windows Subsystem for Linux (WSL). A *shell* is a user interface to access operating system services, and in the case of Unix, it uses a command-line interface. It is called a shell because it is a layer around the operating system kernel. I will cover more about Unix shells in the next chapter.

Project Helsinki

There are reports that Microsoft had been contemplating porting SQL Server to Unix and Linux as early as the 2000s. One example is the article "Porting Microsoft SQL Server to Linux" at https://hal2020.com/2011/07/27/porting-microsoft-sql-server-to-linux/, by Hal Berenson, who retired from Microsoft as a distinguished engineer and general manager. Also, in an interview with Rohan Kumar, general manager of Microsoft's Database Systems group, he mentioned that there were a couple of discussions in the past about porting SQL Server to Linux, but such a project was not approved. For more details of the interview, see https://techcrunch.com/2017/07/17/how-microsoft-brought-sql-server-to-linux/.

More recently, starting around 2015, there was a new attempt to port—or in this case to release—SQL Server on Linux. This was called Project Helsinki. The following were the project objectives of releasing SQL Server on Linux:

▶ It would cover almost all the SQL Server features available on the Windows version. Current exceptions were documented earlier in this chapter.

▶ It would offer at least the same security level as the Windows version.

▶ It would offer at least the same performance as the Windows version.

▶ It would ensure compatibility between Windows and Linux.

▶ It would provide a Linux-native experience—for example, installation using packages.

▶ It would keep the continued fast pace of innovation in the SQL Server code base, making sure that new features would appear on both platforms simultaneously.

If you have followed the history of SQL Server so far, you may wonder, since SQL Server was born on the Unix platform and later ported to OS/2 and Windows, why not port it back to Linux? Truth is, however, that after two decades as a Windows-only technology, the code base had diverted hugely from its Unix origins.

Nevertheless, porting during this project was still a consideration. Porting the application from one operating system to another would require using the original source code, making the required changes so it would work on the new system, and compiling it to run as a native application. Porting SQL Server to Linux, however, would require the review of more than 40 million lines of C++ code to make changes so it would work on Linux. According to the Microsoft team, this would be an enormous project and would face the following challenges:

▶ With more than 40 million lines of C++ code, porting would take years to complete.

▶ During the porting project, the code will still be changing. New features, updates, and fixes are performed all the time. Catching up with the current code base was a serious challenge.

In addition, not all operating system dependencies are handled by SQLOS. SQL Server makes a huge number of Windows calls outside, too. After more than two decades of SQL Server being used on the Windows platform only, the product had a large number of references to Windows libraries, which fall into the following three categories:

- ▶ NT kernel (ntdll.dll)
- ▶ Win32 libraries
- ▶ Windows application libraries

The SQL Server team listed the last category, Windows application libraries, as the one with more complex dependencies. Some of these Windows application libraries were Microsoft XML Core Services (MSXML), the Common Language Runtime (CLR), components written in Component Object Model (COM), the use of the Microsoft Distributed Transaction Coordinator (MSDTC), and the interaction of the SQL Server Agent with many Windows subsystems. It was mentioned that porting even something like SQLXML would take a significant amount of time to complete.

So the team, according to several posts and interviews mostly by Slava Oks, partner group engineering manager at the SQL Server team, was considering alternative choices to porting in order to complete the project in a faster way, or at least in a reasonable amount of time. This is where Drawbridge came to the rescue.

A Virtualization Surprise

Although the original Microsoft announcements did not mention whether SQL Server on Linux was going to be a port, the entire technology community assumed it would be, and everybody expected that SQL Server was going to be a native Linux application. It also seems that the first sources reporting that SQL Server on Linux was not a port, but instead was using some sort of virtualization technology came from outside Microsoft.

SQL Server CTP 1 was released on November 16, 2016, and just two days later an article at *The Register* indicated that SQL Server on Linux was not a native Linux application but was instead using the Drawbridge application sandboxing technology. The article stated that Drawbridge references could be found on the installation, for example, at the /opt/mssql/lib/system.sfp library, which could be easily confirmed.

NOTE

You can still read the article, "Microsoft Linux? Microsoft Running Its Windows' SQL Server Software on Linux: Embrace, Extend, er, Enter," at www.theregister.co.uk/2016/11/18/microsoft_running_windows_apps_on_linux.

I sensed at the time that the SQL Server community had mixed reactions to this news. It may have been the disappointment that SQL Server was not going to be a native Linux application, but it later also turned into curiosity, and everybody wanted to know how it worked and how Microsoft was able to run a very complex application such as SQL Server on a different platform without a code port. There was also the initial concern of whether this Linux implementation would offer the same performance as its Windows counterpart.

Drawbridge

Drawbridge was a Microsoft Research project that created a prototype of a new form of virtualization for application sandboxing based on a library OS version of Windows. Drawbridge was created to reduce the virtualization resource overhead drastically when hosting multiple virtual machines in the same hardware, something similar to what Docker would do later. Drawbridge was a 2011 project, while Docker was released as open source in March 2013. Drawbridge, according to Microsoft, was one of many research projects that provided valuable insights into container technology.

In simple terms, Drawbridge took the Windows kernel to run it in user mode in a process to create a high-density container that could run Windows applications. So it was basically taking the entire operating system, Windows, in user mode. The original intention was to use Drawbridge to host small applications in Windows Azure. At the same time, Microsoft starting testing running Drawbridge in other operating systems so they could use this technology as a container to run a Windows application on another platform. One of those platforms tested was Linux.

NOTE

You can find more details about Drawbridge on the Microsoft Research page at www.microsoft.com/en-us/research/project/drawbridge/.

Looking for a Shortcut

It is interesting to learn how the decision was made to use Drawbridge. Drawbridge was used to run small Windows applications on an operating system called Midori. Midori is an operating system Slava Oks help to write, and during a specific project implementation, there was the requirement for Midori to run some Windows applications. Though Midori did not directly have such capability, Drawbridge was suggested as a possible solution. Within a few months, developers had the required Windows applications running in Midori using Drawbridge.

Later, when confronted with the problem of running SQL Server on Linux, someone suggested using Drawbridge to run a Windows application such as SQL Server on another platform, in this case, Linux. Problem was, SQL Server is not a simple Windows application, so the idea originally was not taken too seriously. However, Drawbridge was tested on a few operating systems, and it was learned that a member of the Drawbridge team, Andrew Baumann, already had a working prototype of Drawbridge on Linux partially up and running.

Using Drawbridge, the SQL Server team was able to boot SQL Server on Linux within 30 days of starting the project. Obviously, this was just a prototype, but it showed that this was feasible and that the entire project could be achieved without porting. In this way, the team could focus on testing that all the functionality was there and that everything worked. It also gave the team the possibility and advantage of starting work on the remaining parts of the project, including features that would be intrinsically different on a Linux platform, such as high availability, disaster recovery, security, and performance.

The Drawbridge architecture, as shown in Figure 2-3, offered the following components:

▶ **A library OS that was capable of hosting other Windows components**   For example, using library OS, it was possible to implement MSXML, CLR, and other functionality, which was essential to bring all SQL Server features to the Linux release.

▶ **A picoprocess**   This is a process-based isolation container with a minimal kernel API surface. This part of Drawbridge was not used in the SQL Server project.

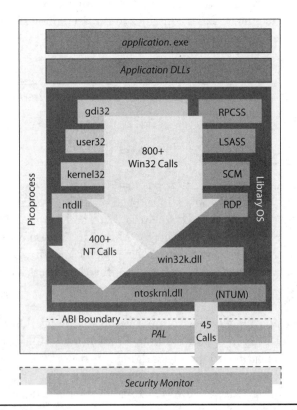

Figure 2-3   *Drawbridge architecture*

Since the Microsoft Research project was complete and there was no support for Drawbridge, the team also took ownership of the Drawbridge code base—and, in fact, they owned the code for all the components involved in the project, including the Linux host extension, which I cover next. Finally, it is also interesting to note that by using these technologies, in theory, Microsoft could bring any other Windows application to Linux without doing a port.

SQLPAL

Although for some SQL Server users, it may seem like SQLOS already provided the abstraction functionality to move SQL Server to another platform, that was not the case with Linux. Though SQLOS was more about services and optimizing for new hardware than abstraction, Drawbridge provided the abstraction that was needed. Marrying these two technologies was the appropriate solution. In fact, the Drawbridge library OS component provided the required functionality. (The second component, the picoprocess, was not required for the project.) The SQLPAL architecture is depicted in Figure 2-4, which also includes a host extension layer that was added on the bottom of SQLOS to help SQLPAL interact with the operating system. Host extension is the operating system–specific component that maps calls from inside SQLPAL to the real operating system calls.

Remember, of course, that this did not mean that completing this project was just a matter of running the current SQL Server Windows executable file on Drawbridge and fixing a few bugs. There was still a large amount of work to do.

As mentioned, earlier in the history of SQL Server, back when the developer team was debating whether to continue releasing the product on both OS/2 and Windows NT, it was evident that some platform abstraction layer (PAL) needed to be created.

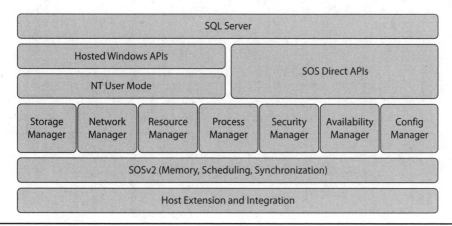

Figure 2-4 *SQLPAL architecture*

No PAL was created at that time, however, because the decision was to continue SQL Server as a Windows-only platform. This did not happen when SQLOS was released, as it was not part of the original design.

But now, many years later, when the team faced the dilemma again, a PAL was created to abstract the calls and libraries from the underlying operating system. SQLPAL was created to separate all operating system- or platform-specific code in one layer while keeping the rest of the SQL Server code base operating-system agnostic.

After months of testing SQL Server on Linux, the product offered some duplication of services, as shown in Figure 2-5. As you can see, all components, SQLOS, library OS, and the Linux host extension implemented duplicated services such as object management, memory management, trading and scheduling, synchronization, and I/O services.

The final architecture needed only single components instead of duplications, however. This was the birth of SQLPAL. The decision was made to keep most of SQLOS, make SQLOS the core, and use some parts of both the Drawbridge library OS and the Linux host extension. The final SQL Server system architecture is depicted in Figure 2-6.

Finally, Figure 2-7 shows the process model when SQL Server is running on Linux. SQL Server runs in a Linux process. The Linux host extension is a native Linux application that first loads and initializes SQLPAL. SQLPAL then starts SQL Server.

Technologies	SOS	Library OS	Host Extension
Object Management	✓	✓	✓
Memory Management	✓	✓	✓
Threading/Scheduling	✓	✓	✓
Synchronization	✓	✓	✓
I/O (Disk, Network)	✓	✓	✓

Figure 2-5   *Functionality overlap*

System Architecture

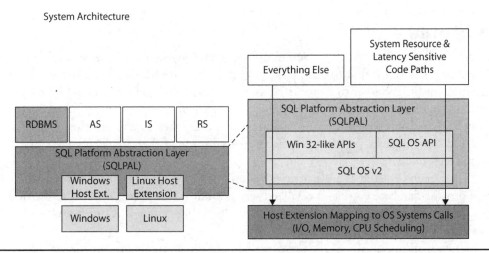

Figure 2-6   *SQL Server system architecture*

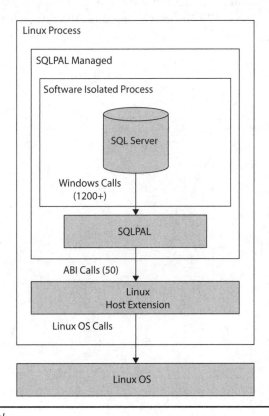

Figure 2-7   *Process model*

Summary

Even if you are an expert SQL Server user and have worked with the technology for years, you may think that this database engine has always been a Windows-exclusive technology. SQL Server in fact started as a multiplatform technology, and its roots actually go back to an operating system called OS/2 and even to Unix. To understand how SQL Server came to the Linux platform and Docker containers, this chapter covered some historic perspectives that mirrored some of the same challenges that were faced today.

SQLOS was created as a platform layer designed to exploit new hardware capabilities and provide database engine–specialized services, but it was never designed to provide platform independence or portability to other operating systems. SQLOS was used again, however, for the Linux release.

When working on the SQL Server on Linux project, the team considered a code port, but since this would be an enormous project that would take years to complete, other solutions were considered, including using the Microsoft Research project Drawbridge. Drawbridge and SQLOS were used on the final release of SQL Server on Linux implementation.

Chapter 3

Linux for the SQL Server Professional

In This Chapter

The primary purpose of this chapter is to help you get started with Linux, but it also covers some more advanced topics and system monitoring tools. A traditional SQL Server book would not cover how to use an operating system or its administration. This book is an exception, however, because SQL Server users have been working with the Windows platform since the beginning, and most are not familiar with Linux. The information in this chapter may be extremely useful to help with the transition from the Windows platform to Linux.

This chapter is not intended to provide much information to the Linux administrator, but I hope it helps SQL Server professionals get started with Linux. As he or she would when administering the Windows platform, the SQL Server administrator should work with related professionals such as system or storage administrators to help achieve optimum results, especially when configuring and administering production environments.

First of all, Linux is an operating system based on Unix. Unix was originally conceived and implemented in 1969 and later rewritten in the C language, with its first version publicly released in 1973. There have been a large number of Unix implementations throughout the years, including some successful commercial versions such as System V, Sun Solaris, IBM AIX, and Hewlett Packard HP-UX.

In 1991, Linus Torvalds, looking to create a free operating system as a hobby, wrote and published Linux. Currently Linux reportedly includes more than 18 million lines of source code. As with Unix, Linux has many distributions. This huge number of implementations, with incompatibilities and lack of standardization, has been considered a weakness of this operating system. Linux is open source, while Unix is mostly proprietary software (only a few versions of Unix have been free or open sourced, such as BSD).

NOTE

Writing this chapter brought back some memories. I used to teach Unix system administration in a university back in the 1990s, and this is my first time writing a tutorial since then. I first heard about Linux in a personal computing magazine back in the early days and immediately went to download it onto a few 3½-inch floppy disks and installed it. Not many people knew about Linux or even had access to the Internet in those days. I also worked with all the most popular Unix implementations including AIX, Sun Solaris, and HP-UX.

Getting Started

If you made it this far, you are probably at least familiar with the most basic Linux commands such as `ls`, `cd`, `more`, `md`, and `ps`. You also may know that Linux commands are case-sensitive and usually in lowercase. For example, typing `ls` works as expected, but typing LS or Ls does not. Let's review some basic commands in this section and then move to more advanced ones later in the chapter.

When you open a new session, you are always running a shell (more on that later—for now think about opening an MS-DOS command prompt session in Windows). Unix traditionally provides different shells such as Bourne, C, or Korn Shell. In Red Hat Enterprise Linux, the default is Bash (for Bourne-again shell), one of the most popular shells in Linux distributions. You are also defined a default startup directory, which is your home directory.

NOTE

This book uses the Courier font to show the commands to execute, and in some cases, the output follows. The command you have to type will usually be the first line and starts with the shell prompt, such as $ or #.

Use the man (manual) command, mentioned in Chapter 1, to see the Linux documentation or online reference manuals. For example, to look for documentation of the ps command, you can use

```
$ man ps
```

You will see something similar to Figure 3-1.

To exit the man page, press Q for quit. To learn more about the man command, you would use man itself—for example, type the following:

```
$ man man
```

Use man -k to search for the man page descriptions for keywords and display any matches. For example, to find information about shells, you could use this:

```
$ man -k shell
```

Also, if you are accustomed to the style of the SQL Server documentation (where at the end of a topic, similar commands are mentioned), if you don't find what you are looking for or if you want more information, look for a "SEE ALSO" section with additional commands or man pages:

```
SEE ALSO
        pgrep(1), pstree(1), top(1), proc(5)
```

Another important concept is the path, defined by the $PATH variable. Same as with Windows, $PATH enables you to define the directories containing executable code

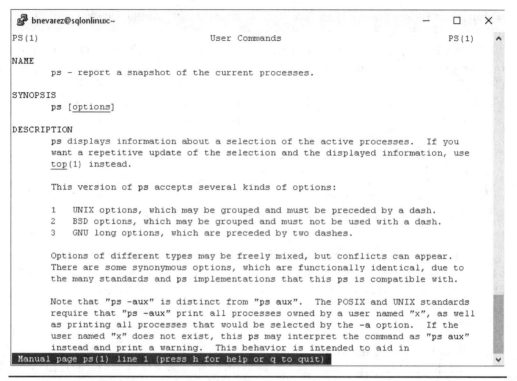

Figure 3-1 *The ps man page*

so you can run a program without specifying its file location. In my default installation, I have the following:

```
$ echo $PATH
/usr/local/bin:/usr/bin:/usr/local/sbin:/usr/sbin:/home/bnevarez/.local/bin:
/home/bnevarez/bin
```

I can include a new directory, if needed. For example, trying to execute the SQL Server sqlcmd utility in a default installation will show the following:

```
$ sqlcmd
-bash: sqlcmd: command not found
```

Try the following command to add the /opt/mssql-tools/bin directory to the current $PATH variable. Notice the separator is the colon (:) character:

```
$ PATH=$PATH:/opt/mssql-tools/bin
```

Then you can verify the updated value of the variable by running this command:

```
$ echo $PATH

/usr/local/bin:/usr/bin:/usr/local/sbin:/usr/sbin:/home/bnevarez/.local/bin:
/home/bnevarez/bin:/opt/mssql-tools/bin
```

You will now be able to execute sqlcmd without having to worry about its location in the file system. Now, this path change is just for the current session; if you disconnect and connect again, the changes will be lost. To make this change permanent, you need to update your profile file, which for the Bash shell is named .bash_profile. Notice the following lines inside the file:

```
PATH=$PATH:$HOME/.local/bin:$HOME/bin
export PATH
```

Open the file and edit the following line as shown:

```
PATH=$PATH:$HOME/.local/bin:$HOME/bin:/opt/mssql-tools/bin
```

NOTE

There are several ways to edit files in Linux. The traditional Unix way is to use the vi editor, which may be complicated to use for new Linux users. There is also the Vim (Vi Improved) editor. Covering vi is beyond the scope of this chapter, but you should be able to find a tutorial online to learn how to use any of these editors.

Files and Directories

I will start this section by showing you how to manage and navigate directories. First, to display your current directory, use the pwd (print working directory) command:

```
$ pwd
/home/bnevarez
```

NOTE

Some Unix commands may have awkward names, such as pwd, which may be an abbreviation of a word or words describing what they do. I will be using parentheses to show what the command stands for, if needed. In some other cases, such as with find or sort, its description will be obvious.

You can navigate to any directory you have access to by using the cd (change directory) command. For example, to move to the SQL Server databases file directory, you could use the following:

```
cd /var/opt/mssql/data
```

If you tried the MS-DOS `chdir` command, you may have noticed that it does not work here. Using `cd` without a directory moves you back to your home directory, which is defined by the `$HOME` variable:

```
$ cd
$ pwd
/home/bnevarez
$ echo $HOME
/home/bnevarez
```

You can also use the tilde (~) symbol as a shortcut for your home directory, which may be useful when you want to run a command or script while you are in some other directory without having to specify the full file path. For example, the following commands create a backup directory in your home directory and then try to list the contents of the same directory even if you are working in the /tmp directory:

```
$ cd /tmp
$ mkdir ~/backup
$ touch ~/backup/file1
$ ls ~/backup
```

As with Windows, you can also use relative paths. For example, use the following command to start in your current directory and change to apps/dir1:

```
$ cd apps/dir1
$ pwd
/home/bnevarez/apps/dir1
```

You can use a dot (.) to refer to your current directory and two dots (..) to refer to the parent directory of the current directory. For example, use the following command to move two levels up the directory hierarchy structure:

```
# pwd
/var/opt/mssql/data
# cd ../..
# pwd
/var/opt
```

Assuming you have the required permissions, you can also create and remove directories using the `mkdir` (make directories) and `rmdir` (remove empty directories) commands. Interesting to note is that, unlike the `cd` command, the Windows `md` and `rd` commands will not work.

```
$ mkdir mydir
$ cd mydir
$ cd ..
$ rmdir mydir
```

No surprises here if you are familiar with these commands on the old MS-DOS or Windows command prompt. The first command creates the directory mydir; the second command changes the current directory to the directory just created and then changes to the previous directory by going one level back. Finally, the directory is removed.

The `rmdir` command can remove only empty directories, however. Trying the following will return an error message:

```
$ mkdir mydir
$ touch mydir/file1
$ rmdir mydir
rmdir: failed to remove 'mydir': Directory not empty
```

In the next section, I will show you how to remove nonempty directories using the `rm` command. You could also manually remove each file and directory inside this directory, which, although time consuming, in some cases may be beneficial—for example, to avoid deleting something you may need.

To list the contents of a directory, use the `ls` (list) command. As with many Unix commands, `ls` has a large number of options, so make sure you use the man documentation if you need more details. Most typical use is as `ls` or `ls -l`. For example, the following `ls -l` command on the /var/opt/mssql/data directory will list the current SQL Server database files:

```
$ ls -l /var/opt/mssql
total 53336
-rw-r-----. 1 mssql mssql  4653056 Aug 24 03:22 master.mdf
-rw-r-----. 1 mssql mssql  2097152 Aug 24 03:22 mastlog.ldf
-rw-r-----. 1 mssql mssql  8388608 Aug 24 03:22 modellog.ldf
-rw-r-----. 1 mssql mssql  8388608 Aug 24 03:22 model.mdf
-rw-r-----. 1 mssql mssql 15400960 Aug 24 03:17 msdbdata.mdf
-rw-r-----. 1 mssql mssql   786432 Aug 24 03:17 msdblog.ldf
-rw-r-----. 1 mssql mssql  8388608 Aug 24 03:17 tempdb.mdf
-rw-r-----. 1 mssql mssql  8388608 Aug 24 03:22 templog.ldf
```

You can see a lot of interesting information about the listed file, including file type and permissions, shown as `-rw-r-----` (more details on permissions later in this chapter), the number of links to the file, the user owner, the group owner, the size in bytes, the last date the file was modified, and the filename.

Displaying the size in bytes for very large files can be difficult to read, so you can also try both the `-l` and `-h` (human readable) options. They will show the previous size bytes value 15400960 as 15M. Size units are reported as K, M, G, T, P, E, Z, and Y for kilobytes, megabytes, gigabytes, terabytes, petabytes, exabytes, zettabytes, and yottabytes, respectively (though I don't think anyone is using some of those extremely large file sizes just yet).

NOTE

Although the amount of data generated worldwide is increasing rapidly, units such as exabytes, zettabytes, and yottabytes are still huge. In comparison, the maximum database size allowed in SQL Server is 524,272 terabytes, which is very large even for current standards.

Some other useful ls options are -a (or --all) and -A (or --almost-all), which are used to include hidden files on the list. The only difference is that the latter does not include the named . and .. entries, which represent the current and parent directories, respectively. A Unix file starting with a dot (.) is considered a hidden file.

Files

Almost everything in Unix is a file, and, unlike Windows, Linux does not use a file extension in the filename. (The file command can be used to determine what kind of file it is, although this will be rarely needed.) You can perform basic file manipulation by using the cp (copy), mv (move), and rm (remove) commands.

Use cp to copy files and directories. The following makes a copy of file1 and names it file2:

```
$ cp file1 file2
```

You can also use -r (or -R or --recursive) to copy directories recursively. For example, the following statements create a couple of files inside the dir1 directory and copy the dir1 directory and its contents to the backup directory:

```
$ mkdir dir1
$ touch dir1/file1
$ touch dir1/file2
$ mkdir backup
$ cp -r dir1 backup
```

Use the mv command to move files and directories. Or use it to rename files and directories. The next commands create a new dir2 directory and move file1 from directory dir1 to dir2:

```
$ mkdir dir2
$ mv dir1/file1 dir2
```

The following command renames file2 to file3:

```
$ mv file2 file3
```

The following example is similar to the previous cp example, but this time it moves the entire directory dir1 and its contents to the backup directory. Note that no recursive option is needed:

```
$ mkdir dir1
$ touch dir1/file1
$ touch dir1/file2
$ mkdir backup
$ mv dir1 backup
```

Use the rm command to remove files and directories. The following example removes the file named file1:

```
$ rm file1
```

I showed you the rmdir command to remove directories. But if the directory is not empty and you use this command, you will get the "directory not empty" error message. Use rm with -r (or -R or --recursive) to remove directories and their contents recursively:

```
$ rmdir dir1
rmdir: failed to remove 'dir1': Directory not empty
$ rm -r dir1
```

Using -i to prompt before removal could be useful in some cases to protect against some mistakes. The -f option, on the other hand, forces the removal and does not prompt for user input. It is common to use both -r and -f to delete a directory and its entire contents, but you need to be extremely cautious about their use:

```
$ rm -rf dir1
```

The following example deletes all the files in the current directory, while being prompted on each one:

```
$ rm -i *
rm: remove regular file 'file1'? y
rm: remove regular empty file 'file2'? y
```

Use the touch command to change file timestamps or update the file access and modification times to the current time. It is also commonly used to create empty files:

```
$ touch file1
```

The find command is very useful; its purpose is to search for files in a directory hierarchy. find also has a large number of parameters and choices, so make sure to check the documentation if you have some specific needs. For example, you may be wondering where the sqlcmd utility is located. Here's how to find it:

```
$ find / -name sqlcmd
/opt/mssql-tools/bin/sqlcmd
```

You'll need the required permissions for the folders you specify, or you may get the following message for one or more directories:

```
find: '/root': Permission denied
```

Optionally, you can use the -iname option for a case-insensitive search. To find the files modified in the last 50 days, use the -mtime option, as in the following example:

```
$ find / -mtime 50
```

Similar to -mtime, use the -atime command to report the files that have been accessed on a specified number of days:

```
$ find / -atime 7
```

Use the -type option to find a specific type of file, which can be b (block), c (character), d (directory), p (named pipe), f (regular file), l (symbolic link), and s (socket). Use the -empty option to find empty files or directories:

```
$ find /tmp -type f -empty
```

You can also find files owned by a specific user:

```
$ find / -user bnevarez
```

The find command is extremely flexible and can also be used to perform an operation or execute a command on the files found. For example, the following command changes the permissions on all the files encountered (chmod is explained later in the chapter in the "Permissions" section):

```
$ find . -type f -perm 0777 -print -exec chmod 644 {} \;
```

The next example removes the files found:

```
$ find . -type f -name "*.txt" -exec rm -f {} \;
```

The next command searches for a string within the files found:

```
$ find . -type f -exec grep -i 'text' {} \;
```

In these three cases, find is using the -exec option, which enables you to execute a command for each filename found. The string { } is replaced by the current filename being processed. Use the optional -print to print the filename found; it is useful to have a quick indication of the work performed. Executed commands must end with \; (a backslash and semicolon).

Finally, find is also commonly used to find information and send it to another command for additional processing. More on than later in this section, where I cover piping and redirection.

You can use a few Linux commands to show information from a file, such as cat (concatenate), more, less, tail, or head. The cat command is the simplest to use to display small files:

```
$ cat file1
```

Both the more and less commands enable you to read a file or some other input with additional choices. For example, you can navigate one page at a time allowing forward and backward movement or search for text:

```
$ man ps > file1
$ more file1
$ less file1
```

Once you open a file, you can press the SPACEBAR or F to move forward, press B to go backward one page, or press Q to quit.

Use the tail command to output the last part of a file, which can be used to inspect the latest data on a changing file:

```
$ tail file1
```

Use the head command to output the first part of a file:

```
$ head file1
```

Use the diff (difference) command to see the differences between two files. This will report the differences between both files, or nothing will be returned if the files are the same.

```
$ diff file1 file2
```

If nothing is returned (and that seems confusing), you can use the -s option to get a confirmation when the files are the same:

```
$ diff -s file1 file2
Files file1 and file2 are identical
```

Use the `sort` command to sort lines of text files. For example, assuming file1 has a list of items, running the following command will return the list sorted:

```
$ sort file1
```

This will sort to the standard output, but if you want to keep the sorted list, you may save it to a file, like in the following example:

```
$ sort file1 > file2
```

Finally, you can use the `file` command to determine the file type. Here's an example:

```
$ file /opt/mssql/lib/system.sfp
/opt/mssql/lib/system.sfp: data
```

The Unix File System

Another new experience for first-time Linux users coming from the Windows world is the Unix file system. First of all, Unix uses no drive letters, such as C:, D:, or E:. If you are familiar with Windows mount points, introduced with Windows 2000, you may have an idea of how a Unix file system looks. A Unix file system is defined as one rooted tree hierarchy of directories. The root of the entire tree is denoted as *root* or */* and every additional directory starts from there. New volumes can be mounted as a directory in this tree structure. Traditionally a Unix file system includes the following directories:

- ▶ **/bin**   Directory for binaries; may be a link to /usr/bin
- ▶ **/dev**   Directory for devices
- ▶ **/etc**   (etcetera) Directory for system configuration files and system databases
- ▶ **/home**   User home directories
- ▶ **/lib**   Directory for libraries
- ▶ **/mnt**   (mount) Empty directory used as a temporary mount point
- ▶ **/opt**   Directory for locally installed software
- ▶ **/proc**   Directory for processes
- ▶ **/sbin**   Directory for system binaries
- ▶ **/root**   Root user home directory
- ▶ **/sys**   Directory for system hardware and operating system information
- ▶ **/tmp**   Directory for temporary files

▶ **/usr** User directory, traditionally hosted user home directories; also hosts additional binaries and libraries

▶ **/var** Directory for files that may change frequently such as system log files, mail spools, or print jobs

NOTE

As you may remember from Chapter 1, SQL Server software was installed in the /opt directory, while the databases were placed in /var/opt.

SQL Server on Linux works on XFS or EXT4 file systems; other file systems, such as BTRFS, are not currently supported. To print your file system type, use the `df -T` or `cat /etc/fstab` command.

Use the `mount` command to mount a file system, for example, when you have a new disk partition. Use `umount` to unmount a file system. Running `mount` without any option will list all the current mount points.

You can also use the `lsblk` command to list the block devices or disks available in the system; this output is easier to read than the output using `mount`. Here is an example on my system:

```
$ lsblk
NAME    MAJ:MIN RM  SIZE RO TYPE MOUNTPOINT
fd0      2:0    1    4K  0 disk
sda      8:0    0   32G  0 disk
├─sda1   8:1    0  500M  0 part /boot
└─sda2   8:2    0 31.5G  0 part /
sdb      8:16   0    7G  0 disk
└─sdb1   8:17   0    7G  0 part /mnt/resource
```

The most important columns are the Name, Size, and Type of the device and their mount point.

Use the `lscpu` command to display information about the Linux system CPU architecture. Here is some partial output on my system from a Windows Azure virtual machine:

```
$ lscpu
Architecture:          x86_64
CPU op-mode(s):        32-bit, 64-bit
Byte Order:            Little Endian
CPU(s):                1
On-line CPU(s) list:   0
Thread(s) per core:    1
```

```
Core(s) per socket:     1
Socket(s):              1
NUMA node(s):           1
Vendor ID:              GenuineIntel
CPU family:             6
Model:                  63
Model name:             Intel(R) Xeon(R) CPU E5-2673 v3 @ 2.40GHz
Stepping:               2
CPU MHz:                2394.447
BogoMIPS:               4788.89
Hypervisor vendor:      Microsoft
Virtualization type:    full
L1d cache:              32K
L1i cache:              32K
L2 cache:               256K
L3 cache:               30720K
NUMA node0 CPU(s):      0
```

Additional Commands

The ps (process status) command is one of the most useful Unix commands and has a large variety of options. Use it to see the current processes running in the system. Let's start with the most basic ps command, which will return only the processes running in the current session:

```
$ ps
  PID TTY          TIME CMD
 2315 pts/0    00:00:00 bash
 3820 pts/0    00:00:00 ps
```

The columns returned are PID (process ID), the terminal associated with the process, the cumulated CPU time, and the executable name. This example shows only the current shell and the ps process itself. You will usually need to specify some parameters to see system-wide information. Here's a common one:

```
$ ps -ef
UID         PID  PPID  C STIME TTY          TIME CMD
root          1     0  0 03:05 ?        00:00:03 /usr/lib/systemd/systemd --switched-
root --system --deserialize 2
1
root          2     0  0 03:05 ?        00:00:00 [kthreadd]
root          3     2  0 03:05 ?        00:00:00 [ksoftirqd/0]
root          7     2  0 03:05 ?        00:00:00 [migration/0]
```

Use option -e to select all the processes and -f to add columns. These additional columns are UID, PPID, C, and STIME, which are the user ID, parent process ID, CPU usage, and time when the process started, respectively. In addition, -f includes the command arguments, if any. Use options -A and –a to select all the processes in the system. Keep in mind that ps provides a snapshot of the system at the time the command is executed. For real-time information, you could also use the top and htop commands, which I cover in the "System Monitoring" section later in this chapter.

Several other options are useful as well. Let's try a few.

Use -u to display processes by a specific user:

```
# ps -f -u mssql
UID         PID  PPID  C STIME TTY          TIME CMD
mssql       857    1   0 Sep02 ?        00:00:00 /opt/mssql/bin/sqlservr
mssql       939   857  0 Sep02 ?        00:18:18 /opt/mssql/bin/sqlservr
```

Use -C to select the processes for a specific executable file:

```
# ps -f -C sqlservr
UID         PID  PPID  C STIME TTY          TIME CMD
mssql       857    1   0 Sep02 ?        00:00:00 /opt/mssql/bin/sqlservr
mssql       939   857  0 Sep02 ?        00:18:19 /opt/mssql/bin/sqlservr
```

It is also popular to use the BSD syntax to show every process in the system, as shown next. Notice that no dash (–) is required in this case:

```
$ ps aux
```

The ps command offers incredible flexibility. For example, you can specify which columns to list using the -o option:

```
$ ps -e -o pid,uname,pcpu,pmem,comm
```

This example will list process ID, user ID, CPU usage, memory usage, and command name. For the entire list of possible columns, see the man documentation.

You can sort by one or more columns, in ascending or descending order, where + means increasing, which is the default, and - means decreasing. As with the -o option, you can see the entire list of available columns in the documentation using this command:

```
$ ps aux --sort=-pcpu
```

You can limit the previous output to a specific number of processes by sending it to the head command, which outputs the first part of it. In the following example, we use the head -n option to specify only ten lines:

```
$ ps aux --sort=-pcpu | head -n 10
```

You can use the watch command to run the same ps command periodically and display its current output. In this case, watch uses the -n option interval in seconds:

```
watch -n 1 'ps aux --sort=pcpu | head -10'
```

Press CTRL-C to stop the previous command.

Finally, use the –forest (or f, not to be confused with -f) option to display the process tree:

```
$ ps -f --forest -C sqlservr
UID         PID  PPID  C STIME TTY         TIME CMD
mssql       857    1   0 Sep02 ?       00:00:00 /opt/mssql/bin/sqlservr
mssql       939   857  0 Sep02 ?       00:30:35 \_ /opt/mssql/bin/sqlservr
```

This output shows that the sqlservr process PID 857 spawned a second copy of the process with PID 939. You can also correlate using the PPID or parent process ID: PID 939 has PPID 857.

Use the grep (global regular expression parser) command to return lines matching a pattern or basically to search text and regular expressions in the provided input. Let's create a text file for our next examples. The next command saves the documentation of the grep command itself into a file named file1:

```
$ man grep > file1
```

Let's try our first search looking for the word "variables":

```
$ grep variables file1
```

In my case, it returned seven lines.

By default, a search is case-sensitive. A commonly used option to change this is –i (or --ignore-case) to ignore case distinctions:

```
$ grep -i variables file1
```

This example returns the previous output, plus one more line with the word in all uppercase.

Use the -v option (or --invert-match) to return all the lines that do not contain the indicated text:

```
$ grep -v variables file1
```

Use single quotes to include spaces:

```
$ grep 'preceding item' file1
```

Add `-n` to include the line number in addition to the line text:

```
$ grep -n 'preceding item' file1
```

Use the `-E` option (or the `egrep` command) to search for multiple patterns at a time:

```
$ grep -E 'variables|item' file1
```

You can also use regular expressions to search for text. For example, the following command will search for either "egrep" or "fgrep" on the just created file1:

```
$ grep [ef]grep file1
```

This expression means search for either "e" or "f" followed by "grep."

You can use numbers, too. The following command will search for four digits inside file1:

```
$ grep '[0-9][0-9][0-9][0-9]' file1
```

If you try a search on binary files, such as in the next example, by default, you'll get the following response only:

```
$ grep Drawbridge /opt/mssql/lib/system.sfp
Binary file /opt/mssql/lib/system.sfp matches
```

One choice is to use the `-a` option to process a binary file as if it were text. The following will perform the desired search:

```
$ grep -a Drawbridge /opt/mssql/lib/system.sfp
Dependency.Drawbridge
[Dependency.Drawbridge]
Name=Drawbridge
[Drawbridge.OS]
```

Finally, `grep` also includes the behavior of both `egrep` (extended `grep`) and `fgrep` (fixed-string `grep`), which are now deprecated but still available for backward-compatibility. (For more details about regular expressions, see the `grep` documentation.)

Use the `kill` command to terminate a process. You need to specify the process ID as in the following example:

```
$ kill 2886
```

You can also specify `kill -9` (SIGKILL signal) as a last resort when terminating a process that cannot be terminated otherwise:

```
$ kill -9 2886
```

Basically, `kill` is used to signal processes. By default, `kill` sends the SIGTERM signal, which tells the process to exit gracefully. If the process is coded properly, it will call its own exit routines, shut down gracefully, and clean up its internal resources. Using `kill -9` will send the SIGKILL signal, which will kill the process without calling its exit routines.

NOTE

Do not use the `kill` command to stop a service, including SQL Server. To see the proper way to stop, start, or restart a service, see the section "Services Management" later in this chapter.

Use the `who` and `whoami` commands to display information about the current logged-in user:

```
$ who
bnevarez pts/0        2017-08-24 03:09 (cpe-108-185-252-80.socal.res.rr.com)
```

Use the `date` command to print the system date. Or use it to set the system date:

```
$ date
Sat Aug 26 23:05:46 UTC 2017
```

You can use the `wc` (word count) utility to count lines, words, and bytes for each specified file. For example, on the previously created file1, I get the following output:

```
$ wc file1
  504  4259 32263 file1
```

Another very helpful command is `history`. Use it to display the history of commands recently executed, which can be useful when you want to type the same command again. The `history` command provides an easy way to move through the history of commands, optionally edit them, and execute them again—for example, using keyboard arrows to move up and down. Here's a partial output in my system:

```
$ history
313 whoami
314 ps
315 ps -ef | grep sqlservr
316 cat /etc/redhat-release
```

A specific command can also be executed using the ! symbol and the history line number, as in the following case:

```
$ !315
```

Sometimes you may need to find the version of Red Hat Enterprise Linux. You can see it by opening the /etc/redhat-release file:

```
# cat /etc/redhat-release
Red Hat Enterprise Linux Server release 7.3 (Maipo)
```

Finally, you can use the clear command to clear the terminal screen and the passwd command to update a user password.

Building a Command

It is very common in Unix environments to use commands built from one or more commands using *piping* or *redirection*. This is typically the result of one command producing some output to be processed by another command. Output is usually redirected from one command to another using the pipe symbol (|). Output can also be redirected to other devices or files using the > and >> symbols.

Let's start by looking at some examples. The following command saves the output of ps into a file named ps_output:

```
$ ps > ps_output
```

Using > always creates a new file, overwriting an existing file if needed. You can use >> to add the output to an existing file. Running the following command will add the new output to the existing file:

```
$ ps >> ps_output
```

Using 2> redirects the standard error output to a file. For example, you may have standard error output mixed with normal output, which may be difficult to read. A common case is using find and getting the permission denied error on multiple directories:

```
$ find / -name sqlcmd
...
find: '/root': Permission denied
/opt/mssql-tools/bin/sqlcmd
```

You could try something like the following command, which returns a clean output with only the information you need:

```
$ find / -name sqlcmd 2> errors
/opt/mssql-tools/bin/sqlcmd
```

You may choose to inspect the created file later. Or, better yet, you may want to discard the errors if you do not need to see them by sending the standard error output to the null device, a concept that also exists in Windows:

```
$ find / -name sqlcmd 2> /dev/null
/opt/mssql-tools/bin/sqlcmd
```

Using < sends the content of a file as the input to a command:

```
$ wc < file1
  984   6282 49072
```

You can send the content of one file as the input to a command and send its output to yet another file:

```
$ wc < file1 > file2
```

It is very common to use the pipe symbol to build complex commands by sending the output of one command as the input to another. For example, it is typical to start with a ps -ef command. This may return more than 100 lines, one for each process. I list here just a few examples:

```
$ ps -ef
UID        PID  PPID  C STIME TTY          TIME CMD
root         1     0  0 03:05 ?        00:00:03 /usr/lib/systemd/systemd --switched-
root --system --deserialize 2
1
root         2     0  0 03:05 ?        00:00:00 [kthreadd]
root         3     2  0 03:05 ?        00:00:00 [ksoftirqd/0]
root         7     2  0 03:05 ?        00:00:00 [migration/0]
```

You could next send the output as the input to another command—for example, grep, followed by a string to search for. Here is the desired output:

```
ps -ef | grep sqlservr
mssql        857     1  0 Sep02 ?        00:00:00 /opt/mssql/bin/sqlservr
mssql        939   857  0 Sep02 ?        00:31:22 /opt/mssql/bin/sqlservr
bnevarez 19685 16111  0 07:36 pts/0     00:00:00 grep --color=auto sqlservr
```

Permissions

Use root or superuser permissions only when performing system administration activities and as minimally as possible. As expected, making mistakes as the root user can create catastrophic failures, especially on a production system. The sudo command enables a permitted user to execute a command as either the superuser or another user, according to the defined security policy. Multiple examples using sudo to execute a command as superuser were provided in Chapter 1, where I covered the installation and configuration of SQL Server. Here's one example used in that chapter:

```
$ sudo /opt/mssql/bin/mssql-conf setup
[sudo] password for bnevarez:
```

You could also switch to superuser using the sudo su command, as shown next:

```
$ sudo su
[sudo] password for bnevarez:
#
```

The root prompt is #. When you're finished executing the administrative tasks, execute exit or press CTRL-D.

Now let's cover file permissions. We'll start with the default permissions for creating a file. Run the following statements:

```
$ touch file3
$ ls -l
total 0
-rw-rw-r--. 1 bnevarez bnevarez    0 Aug 24 06:26 file3
```

The default permissions in Linux are defined by a permissions mask called umask, which can also be changed to anything you need. Permissions are r (read), w (write), and x (execute), and they correspond to the owner, group, and other (meaning anyone else who is not the owner or is not in the group).

> **NOTE**
>
> The first character is the file type and usually is a dash (-) for a regular file or d for a directory. As introduced earlier with the find command, there are also five special file types that use b for block file, c for character, p for named pipe, l for a symbolic link, and s for a socket.

Use the chmod (change mode) command to change the mode bits of a file, where u is user, g is group, and o is other. Use the symbol + to grant the permission and - to revoke it.

```
$ chmod o+w file3
$ ls -l
total 0
-rw-rw-rw-. 1 bnevarez bnevarez 0 Aug 24 06:26 file3
$ chmod g-w file3
$ ls -l
total 0
-rw-r--rw-. 1 bnevarez bnevarez 0 Aug 24 06:26 file3
```

In this example, o+w grants the write permission to other and g-w revokes the write permission to the group.

You can also change multiple permissions at a time:

```
$ chmod u-x,g+w,o-w file3
```

This example removes execute permission from the user, assigns write permissions to the group, and removes write permissions from other.

An alternative method to work with permissions is to use the octal permission representation, as shown in the following example:

```
$ chmod 567 file3
$ ls -l
total 0
-r-xrw-rwx. 1 bnevarez bnevarez 0 Aug 24 06:26 file3
```

You can define any combination of permissions with just three digits, but using this method may be more complicated for the beginner. Basically, this octal representation uses 4 for read, 2 for write, and 1 for execute, and you can add these values to assign more than one permission at a time. For example, to give read permission you'd use the value 4, to give write you'd use 2, to give both read and write you'd add both values to get 6, to give read and execute you'd add both values to get 5, and to give all three permissions you'd add all three values to get 7. It is also possible to remove all the permissions. You can see a chart with all the possible permissions in Figure 3-2.

```
$ chmod 000 file1
$ ls -l
----------. 1 bnevarez bnevarez 32263 Sep  4 22:07 file1
```

The same permissions apply to directories in which *read* means that the user can list the contents of the directory, *write* means that the user can create or delete files or other directories, and *execute* means that the user can navigate through the directory.

- 3 bits- Used to represent permissions
- $2^3 = 8$ possible permissions, 0 through 7

Read	Write	Execute		
4	2	1	Octal	Permission
0	0	0	0	No access
0	0	1	1	Execute
0	1	0	2	Write
0	1	1	3	Write and execute
1	0	0	4	Read
1	0	1	5	Read and execute
1	1	0	6	Read and write
1	1	1	7	Full control

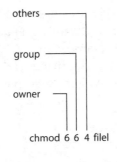

Figure 3-2   *Octal notation*

In addition to changing the permissions of a file or directory, you can use the following commands to change its owner and group. Use chown (change owner) to change the file or directory owner and chgrp (change group) to change its group. For example, the following commands are executed as root:

```
# chown root file3
# ls -l
total 0
-r-xrw-rwx. 1 root bnevarez 0 Aug 24 06:26 file3
```

The next example uses chgrp to change the group to mssql:

```
chgrp mssql file3
# ls -l
total 0
-r-xrw-rwx. 1 root mssql 0 Aug 24 06:26 file3
```

Bash Shell

As mentioned in Chapter 1, a shell is a user interface used to access operating system services, and in the case of Unix, most of you will use a shell as a command-line interface. It is called a shell because it is a layer around the operating system kernel. Most popular Unix shells used throughout the years include the Bourne, C, and Korn shells. Most Linux distributions use the Bourne-Again shell, or Bash, as is the case with Red Hat Enterprise Linux, Ubuntu, and SUSE Linux Enterprise Server.

Unix and Linux sometimes have a GUI similar to that of Windows. However, there has never been a standard, and those interfaces could differ greatly from one Unix or Linux distribution to another. Although learning such GUIs could be useful, using command-line commands and scripts is essential for working with Linux.

Let's discuss some basics about working with a Linux shell. The SHELL variable will return the full pathname to the current shell:

```
$ echo $SHELL
/bin/bash
```

Similar to Windows, you can use wildcards in Linux. It is possible to use the asterisk symbol (*) to represent zero or more characters and the question mark symbol (?) to represent a single character. You can also use brackets ([ ]) to represent a range of characters—for example [0-9] or [a-e] to include any number between "0" and "9" or any letter between "a" and "e," respectively. As an example, assuming that you create the following four files, the ls command will list anything starting with "b" or "c" plus "123":

```
$ touch a123; touch b123; touch c123; touch d123
$ ls [bc]123
b123   c123
```

NOTE

As you noticed from the first line, you can submit multiple commands in the same line if they are separated by a semicolon.

Although most Unix commands are provided as executable files on the file system, some could be provided by the shell as well. In some cases, even the same command could be provided by both. For example, the pwd command could be provided by the shell or by the operating system as an executable file. Usually the shell version supersedes the latter. Consider the following:

```
$ pwd --version
-bash: pwd: --: invalid option
pwd: usage: pwd [-LP]
```

This shows the shell version, which complains that only the choices -L and -P are allowed.

Now try the following to execute the pwd version located on /usr/bin. Notice that, this time, the -version option is allowed:

```
$ /usr/bin/pwd --version
pwd (GNU coreutils) 8.22
Copyright (C) 2013 Free Software Foundation, Inc.
License GPLv3+: GNU GPL version 3 or later <http://gnu.org/licenses/gpl.html>.
This is free software: you are free to change and redistribute it.
There is NO WARRANTY, to the extent permitted by law.
Written by Jim Meyering.
```

It is also very common to change the Linux prompt instead of just simply $ to include some information, like the hostname you are connected to. This is usually defined on the .bash_profile configuration file or in some other script or variable defined or called inside it. For example, my current prompt is defined as follows:

```
$ echo $PS1
[\u@\h \W]\$
```

where \u is the username, \h is the hostname, and \W is the current working directory. In my case, the following would be displayed next if, for example, I am currently on the directory dir1 and my hostname is sqlonlinux:

```
[bnevarez@sqlonlinux dir1]$
```

You can update your prompt by assigning a new value to the PS1 variable, if needed.

NOTE

.bash_profile is the profile filename used by the Bash shell. Other shells will use different filenames.

Finally, scripting is a very common method to perform system administration tasks. Scripting would take an entire chapter or book on its own, so I will not cover it here. But let's create a "hello, world" script in case you want to get started. Create a new file called hello, with the following two lines:

```
#!/bin/bash
echo "hello, world"
```

Try to execute the script by typing its name. You may get a couple of errors before you can make it work:

```
$ hello
-bash: hello: command not found
$ ./hello
-bash: ./hello: Permission denied
$ chmod u+x hello
$ ./hello
hello, world
```

First, the current directory is not included in the current `$PATH` environment variable, so the second time I used `./hello` to specify the script location explicitly. The second issue was that by default the file did not have execute permissions, so I granted those, too. Finally, I was able to execute the script.

NOTE

The tradition to use a "hello, world" program as the very first program people write when they are new to a language was influenced by an example in the seminal book The C Programming Language *by Brian Kernighan and Dennis Ritchie (Prentice Hall, 1978).*

Services Management

As introduced in Chapter 1, systemd is an init, or initialization system, used in Linux distributions to manage system processes that will run as daemons until the system is shut down. systemd has several utilities, such as systemctl, which you can use to start, restart, or stop a service or to show runtime status information.

Chapter 1 also covered the basics of systemctl, including how to start, stop, and restart a service using the following syntax:

```
systemctl start name-service
systemctl stop name-service
systemctl restart name-service
```

More specifically, the chapter covered the following commands:

- ▶ **Stop SQL Server** `sudo systemctl stop mssql-server`
- ▶ **Start SQL Server** `sudo systemctl start mssql-server`
- ▶ **Restart SQL Server** `sudo systemctl restart mssql-server`

This section covers some additional systemctl choices. A very useful option is `status`, which you can use as shown in the following example:

```
$ systemctl status mssql-server
```

You will get an output similar to the following, plus the latest ten lines of the SQL Server error log (not shown here). Technically, it returns the last ten lines from the journal, counting from the most recent ones.

```
ql-server.service - Microsoft SQL Server Database Engine
Loaded: loaded (/usr/lib/systemd/system/mssql-server.service; enabled; vendor preset: disabled)
Active: active (running) since Wed 2017-08-30 03:54:52 UTC; 7s ago
  Docs: https://docs.microsoft.com/en-us/sql/linux
in PID: 63997 (sqlservr)
CGroup: /system.slice/mssql-server.service
        ├─63997 /opt/mssql/bin/sqlservr
        └─63999 /opt/mssql/bin/sqlservr
```

Notice that the `status` option provides a lot of valuable information, such as whether the service is loaded or not, the absolute path to the service file (in this case, /usr/lib/systemd/system/mssql-server.service), the process ID of the service process, whether the service is running, and how long it has been running.

Use the `is-active` option to return whether the service is active or not:

```
# systemctl is-active mssql-server
Inactive
```

Use the `try-restart` option to try to restart a service, but only if it is running. In any of both cases, it will return silently.

```
# systemctl try-restart mssql-server
```

You can also use the service file extension as in the following case:

```
# systemctl start mssql-server.service
```

To display the status of all the services in the system, use the `list-units` option:

```
# systemctl list-units --type service
```

My system returns 48 service units. Here's a partial list:

```
UNIT                       LOAD   ACTIVE SUB     DESCRIPTION
auditd.service             loaded active running Security Auditing Service
chronyd.service            loaded active running NTP client/server
mssql-server.service       loaded active running Microsoft SQL Server Database Engine
NetworkManager.service     loaded active running Network Manager
rsyslog.service            loaded active running System Logging Service
waagent.service            loaded active running Azure Linux Agent
LOAD   = Reflects whether the unit definition was properly loaded.
ACTIVE = The high-level unit activation state, i.e. generalization of SUB.
SUB    = The low-level unit activation state, values depend on unit type.
48 loaded units listed. Pass --all to see loaded but inactive units, too.
To show all installed unit files use 'systemctl list-unit-files'.
```

The output shows the name of the unit, description, and whether it is loaded and active.

Use the `reload` option to reload a service configuration without interrupting the service. It does not apply to all the services including SQL Server.

```
# systemctl reload mssql-server.service
Failed to reload mssql-server.service: Job type reload is not applicable for unit
mssql-server.service.
See system logs and 'systemctl status mssql-server.service' for details.
```

Use the `enable` option to enable a service so it can be started automatically at boot time:

```
# systemctl enable mssql-server
Created symlink from /etc/systemd/system/multi-user.target.wants/mssql-
server.service to /usr/lib/systemd/system/mssql-server.service.
```

You can also do the opposite and `disable` a service so it does not start automatically at boot time:

```
# systemctl disable mssql-server
Removed symlink /etc/systemd/system/multi-user.target.wants/mssql-server.service.
```

A disabled service can be started manually using the `start` option.

You can also use systemd on a remote computer using the following syntax:

```
systemctl --host username@hostname command
```

Here's an example:

```
systemctl --host bnevarez@sqlonlinux status mssql-server
```

This would require that the sshd service be running on the remote computer.

Finally, in addition to many other features, you can use systemctl to shut down the system, shut down and reboot the system, or shut down and power off the system. The required commands, respectively, are shown next:

```
# systemctl halt
# systemctl reboot
# systemctl poweroff
```

This is similar to using the shutdown, halt, poweroff and reboot commands which, depending on the options provided, can also be used to shut down, shut down and reboot, or shut down and power off the system.

Software Management

Chapter 1 gave you a quick introduction to package managers to provide basic information on how to install SQL Server software. A package managing system is a collection of utilities used to install, upgrade, configure, and remove packages or distributions of software or to query information about available packages. There are several package management systems, and the chapter briefly covered some package management utilities such as yum, apt, and zypper, which we used with Red Hat Enterprise Linux, Ubuntu, and SUSE Linux Enterprise Server, respectively. This section covers yum in more detail. You can easily find similar choices in the documentation for the apt or zypper utilities.

The RPM Package Manager (RPM) is a packaging system used by several Linux distributions, including Red Hat Enterprise Linux. The yum package manager is written in Python and is designed to work with packages using the RPM format. Yum requires superuser privileges to install, update, or remove packages.

In Chapter 1, we used yum to install the SQL Server package mssql-server by running the following command:

```
yum install -y mssql-server
```

Let's continue with additional topics, starting with updating packages. During the SQL Server beta deployment process, it was common to upgrade regularly to new CTP or RC packages. You could check which installed packages had updates available by running the command

```
yum check-update
```

NOTE

CTPs (Community Technology Previews) and RCs (Release Candidates) are versions of SQL Server used during the beta program before the final software was released. The final release, which is the only version that can be used in a production environment, is the RTM (release to manufacturing) version.

Depending on your system, you may see a long list of entries. For example, this is what I get from a fresh Microsoft Azure virtual machine, which seems to have an old version of SQL Server:

```
msodbcsql.x86_64                13.1.9.0-1       packages-microsoft-com-prod
mssql-server.x86_64             14.0.900.75-1    packages-microsoft-com-mssql-server
mssql-server-agent.x86_64       14.0.900.75-1    packages-microsoft-com-mssql-server
mssql-server-fts.x86_64         14.0.900.75-1    packages-microsoft-com-mssql-server
mssql-tools.x86_64              14.0.6.0-1       packages-microsoft-com-prod
```

The second row, for example, shows the package mssql-server, architecture x86_64, and the available version in this case is 14.0.900.75-1. It also shows the repository in which the package is located: packages-microsoft-com-mssql-server. The current version provided by my new virtual machine is SQL Server vNext CTP 2.0 14.0.500.272, so, obviously, the recommendation by yum is a newer version.

Let's install the latest recommended version. Stop your SQL Server instance and run the following command to update the mssql-server package:

```
sudo yum update mssql-server
```

Part of the interesting output follows (formatted to fit this book):

```
Resolving Dependencies
---> Package mssql-server.x86_64 0:14.0.500.272-2 will be updated
---> Package mssql-server.x86_64 0:14.0.900.75-1 will be an update
--> Finished Dependency Resolution
Dependencies Resolved
Package: mssql-server
Arch x86_64
Version   14.0.900.75-1
Repository: packages-microsoft-com-mssql-server
Size: 165 M
Upgrade  1 Package
```

After this command was completed, my software version was successfully updated to SQL Server 2017 RC2 14.0.900.75. If you update your SQL Server version, be sure to update the remaining SQL Server–related packages as well or run the check-update command again to validate that they are up to date:

```
yum update msodbcsql
yum update mssql-server-agent
yum update mssql-server-fts
yum update mssql-tools
```

If you already have the latest version of the software, you will see something similar to this:

```
yum update mssql-tools
Loaded plugins: langpacks, product-id, search-disabled-repos
No packages marked for update
```

You could also update packages that have security updates available—though, at the time of writing, no security updates have been released:

```
yum update --security
```

Use the yum info command to display information about a specific package. Here's an example:

```
yum info mssql-server
Installed Packages
Name        : mssql-server
Arch        : x86_64
Version     : 14.0.900.75
Release     : 1
Size        : 870 M
Repo        : installed
From repo   : packages-microsoft-com-mssql-server
Summary     : Microsoft SQL Server Relational Database Engine
License     : Commercial
Description : The mssql-server package contains the Microsoft SQL Server Relational Database Engine.
```

The package version matches the version build returned by SQL Server—for example, using the @@VERSION function.

Finally, to remove a package, you can run the following:

```
$ sudo yum remove mssql-server
```

Use the list all option to list information on all installed and available packages. Commands that return a large amount of data usually allow an expression similar to the following example to limit the data returned:

```
yum list all mssql*
Loaded plugins: langpacks, product-id, search-disabled-repos
Installed Packages
mssql-server.x86_64         14.0.900.75-1      @packages-microsoft-com-mssql-server
mssql-tools.x86_64          14.0.6.0-1         @packages-microsoft-com-prod
Available Packages
mssql-server-agent.x86_64   14.0.900.75-1      packages-microsoft-com-mssql-server
mssql-server-fts.x86_64     14.0.900.75-1      packages-microsoft-com-mssql-server
mssql-server-ha.x86_64      14.0.900.75-1      packages-microsoft-com-mssql-server
mssql-server-is.x86_64      14.0.900.75-1      packages-microsoft-com-mssql-server
```

Optionally, you can also list all the packages in all yum repositories available to install:

```
# yum list available mssql*
```

Finally, use the `search` command when you have some information about the package but do not know the package name:

```
# yum search mssql
Loaded plugins: langpacks, product-id, search-disabled-repos
N/S matched: mssql
mssql-server.x86_64 : Microsoft SQL Server Relational Database Engine
mssql-server-agent.x86_64 : Microsoft SQL Server Agent
mssql-server-fts.x86_64 : Microsoft SQL Server Full Text Search
mssql-server-ha.x86_64 : High Availability support for Microsoft SQL Server Relational Database Engine
mssql-server-is.x86_64 : Microsoft SQL Server Integration Service
mssql-tools.x86_64 : Tools for Microsoft(R) SQL Server (R)
```

NOTE

For more details and options, consult the yum documentation, which you can access via the `man yum` *command.*

Disk Management

Let's review a few commands that can provide information about the file system disk space usage. The `df` (disk free) command is a very useful utility to display file system disk space usage. Here is the output I get on my default Microsoft Azure Red Hat Enterprise Linux virtual machine:

```
$ df
File system     1K-blocks     Used Available Use% Mounted on
/dev/sda2       33025276  5131540  27893736  16% /
devtmpfs         1751724        0   1751724   0% /dev
tmpfs            1761320        0   1761320   0% /dev/shm
tmpfs            1761320   172316   1589004  10% /run
tmpfs            1761320        0   1761320   0% /sys/fs/cgroup
/dev/sda1         508580   146088    362492  29% /boot
/dev/sdb1        7092664  2129404   4579932  32% /mnt/resource
tmpfs             352264        0    352264   0% /run/user/1000
```

The listed information is self-explanatory and includes the file system name, the total size in 1KB blocks, the used space and available disk space, the used percentage, and the file system mount location.

Use -h to print sizes in human-readable format—for example, using K, M, or G for kilobytes, megabytes, and gigabytes, respectively.

```
$ df -h
File system      Size  Used Avail Use% Mounted on
/dev/sda2        32G   4.9G   27G  16% /
```

Add totals using the --total option:

```
$ df -h --total
File system      Size  Used Avail Use% Mounted on
/dev/sda2        32G   4.9G   27G  16% /
devtmpfs        1.7G      0  1.7G   0% /dev
tmpfs           1.7G      0  1.7G   0% /dev/shm
tmpfs           1.7G   177M  1.6G  11% /run
tmpfs           1.7G      0  1.7G   0% /sys/fs/cgroup
/dev/sda1       497M   143M  354M  29% /boot
/dev/sdb1       6.8G   2.1G  4.4G  32% /mnt/resource
tmpfs           345M      0  345M   0% /run/user/1000
total            46G   7.3G   39G  16% -
```

Finally, use -T to display the file system type:

```
$ df -h -T
File system      Type      Size  Used Avail Use% Mounted on
/dev/sda2        xfs       32G   4.9G   27G  16% /
devtmpfs         devtmpfs  1.7G      0  1.7G   0% /dev
tmpfs            tmpfs     1.7G      0  1.7G   0% /dev/shm
tmpfs            tmpfs     1.7G   177M  1.6G  11% /run
tmpfs            tmpfs     1.7G      0  1.7G   0% /sys/fs/cgroup
/dev/sda1        xfs       497M   143M  354M  29% /boot
/dev/sdb1        ext4      6.8G   2.1G  4.4G  32% /mnt/resource
tmpfs            tmpfs     345M      0  345M   0% /run/user/1000
```

Use the du (disk usage) command to display disk usage per file. Here is an example using the -h human readable output on /var/opt/mssql, summarized for space:

```
$ du -h
9.4M    ./.system
53M     ./data
12M     ./log
4.0K    ./secrets
0       ./FTData/FilterData
204K    ./FTData
73M     .
```

System Monitoring

System monitoring is also one of those topics that would require an entire chapter of its own. In this section, I'll show you some basic commands to get you started. Earlier in the chapter, you learned about the ps command, which displays the current process information in the system. You also learned about top and htop.

The top command shows information about system processes in real time. A sample output is shown in Figure 3-2. To exit the top command, press Q.

Here's a quick summary of the information provided by the top command:

▶ The first line shows information about the system uptime, or how long the system has been running; the current number of users; and the system load average over the last 1, 5, and 15 minutes. This line contains the same information displayed with the uptime command.

▶ The second line shows, by default, information about system tasks, including running, sleeping, and stopped tasks or tasks in a zombie state.

▶ The third line shows information about CPU usage.

```
bnevarez@sqlonlinux:~                                          —    □    ×
top - 06:12:11 up 9 min,  1 user,  load average: 0.10, 0.16, 0.10
Tasks: 110 total,   1 running, 109 sleeping,   0 stopped,   0 zombie
%Cpu(s):  0.0 us,  0.2 sy,  0.0 ni, 99.8 id,  0.0 wa,  0.0 hi,  0.0 si,  0.0 st
KiB Mem :  7135564 total,  4730232 free,   978132 used,  1427200 buff/cache
KiB Swap:  2097148 total,  2097148 free,        0 used.  5878120 avail Mem

  PID USER      PR  NI    VIRT    RES    SHR S  %CPU %MEM     TIME+ COMMAND
 2586 mssql     20   0 3116060 745028   5656 S   1.3 10.4   0:05.66 sqlservr
    1 root      20   0  128092   6728   3976 S   0.0  0.1   0:03.48 systemd
    2 root      20   0       0      0      0 S   0.0  0.0   0:00.00 kthreadd
    3 root      20   0       0      0      0 S   0.0  0.0   0:00.13 ksoftirqd/0
    5 root       0 -20       0      0      0 S   0.0  0.0   0:00.00 kworker/0:0H
    6 root      20   0       0      0      0 S   0.0  0.0   0:00.11 kworker/u128:0
    7 root      rt   0       0      0      0 S   0.0  0.0   0:00.07 migration/0
    8 root      20   0       0      0      0 S   0.0  0.0   0:00.00 rcu_bh
    9 root      20   0       0      0      0 S   0.0  0.0   0:00.22 rcu_sched
   10 root      rt   0       0      0      0 S   0.0  0.0   0:00.07 watchdog/0
   11 root      rt   0       0      0      0 S   0.0  0.0   0:00.00 watchdog/1
   12 root      rt   0       0      0      0 S   0.0  0.0   0:00.05 migration/1
   13 root      20   0       0      0      0 S   0.0  0.0   0:00.05 ksoftirqd/1
   17 root      20   0       0      0      0 S   0.0  0.0   0:00.00 kdevtmpfs
   18 root       0 -20       0      0      0 S   0.0  0.0   0:00.00 netns
   19 root      20   0       0      0      0 S   0.0  0.0   0:00.00 khungtaskd
   20 root       0 -20       0      0      0 S   0.0  0.0   0:00.00 writeback
   21 root       0 -20       0      0      0 S   0.0  0.0   0:00.00 kintegrityd
   22 root       0 -20       0      0      0 S   0.0  0.0   0:00.00 bioset
   23 root       0 -20       0      0      0 S   0.0  0.0   0:00.00 kblockd
   24 root       0 -20       0      0      0 S   0.0  0.0   0:00.00 md
   25 root      20   0       0      0      0 S   0.0  0.0   0:00.15 kworker/0:1
```

Figure 3-3 *The top command*

► The next section consists of two lines showing memory information.

► The last section, which uses most of the screen real estate, lists the current processes running in the system.

By default, `top` lists the following columns, all of which are also available with the `ps` command:

► **PID**   Process ID

► **USER**   Username

► **PR**   Scheduling priority of the task

► **NI**   The nice value of the task; this Unix concept is related to the priority of the task and defines which process can have more or less CPU time than other processes

► **VIRT**   Virtual memory size

► **RES**   Resident memory size

► **SHR**   Shared memory size

► **S**   Process status, which could be R (running), S (sleeping), T (stopped by job control signal), t (stopped by the debugger during trace), Z (zombie), or D (uninterruptible sleep)

► **%CPU**   CPU usage

► **%MEM**   Memory usage

► **TIME**   CPU time

► **COMMAND**   Command or program name

NOTE

For more details about the `top` command, see the man documentation.

Optionally you can use `htop`, a variant of `top` that is becoming increasingly popular. The `htop` command is not included with Red Hat Enterprise Linux and must be installed separately.

NOTE

For more details about `htop` see http://hisham.hm/htop.

Use the `free` command to display the amount of free and used memory in the system. Here's a sample of output I got from my test system:

```
$ free
              total        used         free       shared  buff/cache   available
Mem:        3522640     1111924      1145904         8476     1264812     2069696
Swap:       2097148           0      2097148
```

The values returned include total installed memory, used memory, free memory, shared memory, memory used by kernel buffers, memory used by the page cache, and memory available for starting new applications without swapping.

Finally, you should be aware of the Unix cron facility, which is used to execute scheduled commands, and the `crontab` command, which is used to maintain crontab files for individual users. You can think of cron as something similar to Windows Task Scheduler. Although the availability of the SQL Server Agent on the Linux platform makes it less likely that you'll need to use the Linux cron, you still may require it for some maintenance scenarios.

Summary

The chapter covered all the basic Linux commands required to get started, including managing files and directories and their permissions, along with a few more advanced topics including system monitoring. The chapter is not intended for the system administrator, but is intended to help the SQL Server administrator work with Linux. As he or she would with the Windows platform, the SQL Server administrator should work with related professionals such as system or storage administrators to help achieve optimum results, especially for production implementations.

Software management knowledge will be an essential skill for the SQL Server administrator because it will be required to install and upgrade a SQL Server instance. Service management will also be important to understand because it will provide the same functionality provided in the Windows world, including using the SQL Server Configuration Manager utility. The chapter closes with a variety of Linux commands related to file and disk management and system monitoring.

Chapter 4

SQL Server Configuration

In This Chapter

This chapter on configuring SQL Server in a Linux environment is divided into three main topics: using the mssql-conf utility to configure SQL Server, which is required in Linux environments; using Linux-specific kernel settings and operating system configurations; and using some traditional SQL Server configurations for both Windows and Linux installations.

The first section covers the mssql-conf utility, which includes some of the functionality available with the SQL Server Configuration Manager tool for Windows, including configuring network ports or configuring SQL Server to use specific trace flags. In addition, mssql-conf can be used to configure initialization and setup of SQL Server, set up the system administrator password, set the collation of the system databases, set the edition of SQL Server, and update a configuration setting. The second part of the chapter covers some Linux kernel settings, which can be used to improve the performance of SQL Server, as well as some operating system configurations such as transparent huge pages. The third section of the chapter covers some of the most popular SQL Server configuration settings, and most of the section applies both to Windows and Linux implementations.

NOTE

For additional information on configuring SQL Server for high performance, see my book High Performance SQL Server *(Apress, 2016).*

The mssql-conf Utility

Chapter 1 briefly covered the mssql-conf utility, where it was used to install and configure SQL Server. This chapter covers this tool in more detail. Let's start with a scenario in which you create a virtual machine with SQL Server already installed. In this scenario, you are required to perform only two operations: set a system administrator (sa) password and start SQL Server.

Here is the execution and output of the first of these steps on a newly created virtual machine with Red Hat Enterprise Linux:

```
$ sudo /opt/mssql/bin/mssql-conf set-sa-password
 [sudo] password for bnevarez:
Enter the SQL Server system administrator password:
Confirm the SQL Server system administrator password:
Configuring SQL Server...

The system administrator password has been changed.
Please run 'sudo systemctl start mssql-server' to start SQL Server.
```

After you set the system administrator password, start your SQL Server instance by running the following statement:

```
$ sudo systemctl start mssql-server
```

To run mssql-conf, you must have the proper permissions, either superuser or as a user with membership in the mssql group. If you try running mssql-conf without the right permissions, you'll get an error:

```
/opt/mssql/bin/mssql-conf
.is program must be run as superuser or as a user with membership in the mssql group.
```

The available arguments of the mssql-conf utility are shown next:

```
/opt/mssql/bin/mssql-conf
 age: mssql-conf [-h] [-n]  ...
 sitional arguments:

   setup         Initialize and setup Microsoft SQL Server
   set           Set the value of a setting
   unset         Unset the value of a setting
   list          List the supported settings
   traceflag     Enable/disable one or more traceflags
   set-sa-password
                 Set the system administrator (SA) password
   set-collation Set the collation of system databases
   validate      Validate the configuration file
   set-edition   Set the edition of the SQL Server instance

 tional arguments:
 -h, --help      show this help message and exit
 -n, --noprompt  Does not prompt the user and uses environment variables or defaults.
```

As suggested in the preceding output, you can use the mssql-conf utility to perform several configuration options, such as initialize and set up SQL Server, set the sa password (as shown earlier), set the collation of the system databases, enable or disable one or more trace flags, set the edition of SQL Server, and assign the value of a setting. This means that the mssql-conf utility can be used to change a configuration setting in two different ways: using an mssql-conf option such as `traceflag` or `set-sa-password`, or changing a configuration setting such as `memory.memorylimitmb`. To list the supported configuration settings, use the following command:

```
/opt/mssql/bin/mssql-conf list
```

These are the current supported settings:

- **coredump.captureminiandfull** Capture both mini and full core dumps

- **coredump.coredumptype** Core dump type to capture: mini, miniplus, filtered, full

- **filelocation.defaultbackupdir** Default directory for backup files

- **filelocation.defaultdatadir** Default directory for data files

- **filelocation.defaultdumpdir** Default directory for crash dump files

- **filelocation.defaultlogdir** Default directory for log files

- **hadr.hadrenabled** Allow SQL Server to use availability groups for high availability and disaster recovery (availability groups are covered in Chapter 7)

- **language.lcid** Locale identifier for SQL Server to use (such as 1033 for US - English)

- **memory.memorylimitmb** SQL Server memory limit (megabytes)

- **network.forceencryption** Force encryption of incoming client connections

- **network.ipaddress** IP address for incoming connections

- **network.kerberoskeytabfile** Kerberos keytab file location

- **network.tcpport** TCP port for incoming connections

- **network.tlscert** Path to certificate file for encrypting incoming client connections

- **network.tlsciphers** Transport Layer Security (TLS) ciphers allowed for encrypted incoming client connections

- **network.tlskey** Path to private key file for encrypting incoming client connections

- **network.tlsprotocols** TLS protocol versions allowed for encrypted incoming client connections

- **sqlagent.databasemailprofile** SQL Agent Database Mail profile name

- **sqlagent.errorlogfile** SQL Agent log file path

- **sqlagent.errorlogginglevel** SQL Agent logging level bitmask: 1=Errors, 2=Warnings, 4=Info

- **telemetry.customerfeedback** Telemetry status

- **telemetry.userrequestedlocalauditdirectory** Directory for telemetry local audit cache

To set the SQL Server memory limit, for example, you can use the memory
.memorylimitmb setting, as shown next:

```
/opt/mssql/bin/mssql-conf set memory.memorylimitmb 51200
SQL Server needs to be restarted in order to apply this setting. Please
run 'systemctl restart mssql-server.service'.
```

As with any of the mssql-conf changes, you will need to restart SQL Server to apply
the changes:

```
systemctl restart mssql-server.service
```

By default, SQL Server, only when running on Linux, can use up to 80 percent of
the physical memory available on the server. But in some cases, such as in a server with
a large amount of memory, this default may not be appropriate, leaving some memory
unused. Let's say, for example, that you have 512GB of memory on a dedicated
database server. With the default 80 percent allocated to SQL Server, it would leave
more than 100GB for the operating system. A large part of that memory could be
allocated to SQL Server as well.

In a similar way, to set the default SQL Server data directory, you can use the
filelocation.defaultdatadir setting as shown next, assuming the directory exists:

```
/opt/mssql/bin/mssql-conf set filelocation.defaultdatadir /data/sql
SQL Server needs to be restarted in order to apply this setting. Please run
'systemctl restart mssql-server.service'.
```

In this specific case, you would also need to grant the proper permissions to the
mssql group and user to the data directory:

```
chown mssql /data/sql
chgrp mssql /data/sql
```

You can also change the default directory for the transaction log files using the
filelocation.defaultbackupdir setting. To set the default directory for backup
files in a similar way, you can use the following:

```
/opt/mssql/bin/mssql-conf set filelocation.defaultbackupdir /data/backups
SQL Server needs to be restarted in order to apply this setting. Please run
'systemctl restart mssql-server.service'.
```

As with the data directory, you need to grant the proper permissions to the mssql group and user, as shown earlier.

To change the port used by SQL Server, you can use the `network.tcpport` setting, as shown next. The first case shows an error when a port is already in use, followed by a successful execution:

```
# /opt/mssql/bin/mssql-conf set network.tcpport 1436
Validation error on setting 'network.tcpport'
Port '1436' is already in use. Please use another port
# /opt/mssql/bin/mssql-conf set network.tcpport 1435
SQL Server needs to be restarted in order to apply this setting. Please run
'systemctl restart mssql-server.service'.
```

After making such a configuration change, you will have to specify the port number every time you need to connect to the Linux instance, because there is no SQL Server Browser service on Linux to resolve it. The SQL Server Browser service on Windows would run on UDP port 1434, automatically listen for connections intended for instances running on nondefault ports, and provide the correct port to the client. For example, to connect from SQL Server Management Studio or the sqlcmd utility to use port 1435 as defined previously, you could use the following format, in which our server hostname is sqlonlinux. Make sure the TCP/IP ports are properly configured, as indicated in Chapter 1.

```
/opt/mssql-tools/bin/sqlcmd -U sa -S sqlonlinux,1435
```

Finally, to enable or disable SQL Server trace flags, you can use the `traceflag` option, as shown next:

```
# /opt/mssql/bin/mssql-conf traceflag 3226 1222 on
SQL Server needs to be restarted in order to apply this setting. Please run
'systemctl restart mssql-server.service'.
```

As shown, you can enable or disable more than one trace flag at a time if you specify a list separated by spaces.

NOTE

Trace flag 3226 is used to suppress successful backup operation entries in the SQL Server error log and in the system event log. Some other very popular trace flags, such as 2371, 1117, and 1118, which are always recommended, are no longer required in SQL Server 2016 or later because their behavior is now part of the product. These trace flags are explained later in this chapter.

You can disable the trace flags using the `off` parameter, as shown next:

```
# /opt/mssql/bin/mssql-conf traceflag 1222 off
```

Similarly, you can unset a value to go back to the default configuration. For example, the change to TCP port 1435 can be reverted back to the default 1433 by running the following mssql-conf command:

```
/opt/mssql/bin/mssql-conf unset network.tcpport
```

As usual, with every configuration change, you will need to restart the SQL Server instance for the changes to take effect.

Finally, to enable availability groups on your SQL Server instance, you can run the following command. Availability groups, high availability, and disaster recovery will be covered in more detail in Chapter 7.

```
/opt/mssql/bin/mssql-conf set hadr.hadrenabled  1
SQL Server needs to be restarted in order to apply this setting. Please run
'systemctl restart mssql-server.service'.
```

You can see the current configured settings by viewing the contents of the /var/opt/ mssql/mssql.conf file, as shown next, which includes only the nondefault values. As such, a setting not included in this file is using the default value:

```
more /var/opt/mssql/mssql.conf
```

Here's an example with a few changes performed earlier:

```
# more /var/opt/mssql/mssql.conf
[EULA]
accepteula = Y

[traceflag]
traceflag0 = 3226

[filelocation]
defaultdatadir = /data/sql
defaultbackupdir = /data/sql

[sqlagent]
databasemailprofile = test
```

```
[network]
tcpport = 1435

[memory]
memorylimitmb = 51200

[hadr]
hadrenabled = 1
```

Using Variables

Another way to change SQL Server configuration settings is to use variables. Following are the current variables available as defined in the SQL Server documentation:

- ▶ **ACCEPT_EULA** Accept the SQL Server license agreement when set to any value (for example, Y).

- ▶ **MSSQL_SA_PASSWORD** Configure the SA user password.

- ▶ **MSSQL_PID** Set the SQL Server edition or product key. Possible values include Evaluation, Developer, Express, Web, Standard, and Enterprise. You can also specify a product key, which must be in the form of #####-#####-#####-#####-#####, where # is a number or letter.

- ▶ **MSSQL_LCID** Set the language ID to use for SQL Server. For example, 1036 is French.

- ▶ **MSSQL_COLLATION** Set the default collation for SQL Server. This overrides the default mapping of language id (LCID) to collation.

- ▶ **MSSQL_MEMORY_LIMIT_MB** Set the maximum amount of memory (in MB) that SQL Server can use. By default it is 80 percent of the total physical memory.

- ▶ **MSSQL_TCP_PORT** Configure the TCP port that SQL Server listens on (default 1433).

- ▶ **MSSQL_IP_ADDRESS** Set the IP address. Currently, the IP address must be IPv4 style (0.0.0.0).

- ▶ **MSSQL_BACKUP_DIR** Set the default backup directory location.

- ▶ **MSSQL_DATA_DIR** Change the directory where the new SQL Server database data files (.mdf) are created.

- ▶ **MSSQL_LOG_DIR** Change the directory where the new SQL Server database log (.ldf) files are created.

▶ **MSSQL_DUMP_DIR**   Change the directory where SQL Server will deposit the memory dumps and other troubleshooting files by default.

▶ **MSSQL_ENABLE_HADR**   Enable availability groups.

For example, when you configure SQL Server using /opt/mssql/bin/mssql-conf setup, you need to specify at least the SQL Server edition and the system administrator password, and accept the SQL Server license agreement. You can use the following command to perform a similar unattended configuration:

```
sudo ACCEPT_EULA='Y' MSSQL_PID='Developer' MSSQL_SA_PASSWORD='specify_
password' /opt/mssql/bin/mssql-conf setup
The license terms for this product can be found in
/usr/share/doc/mssql-server or downloaded from:
https://go.microsoft.com/fwlink/?LinkId=855862&clcid=0x409
The privacy statement can be viewed at:
https://go.microsoft.com/fwlink/?LinkId=853010&clcid=0x409
Configuring SQL Server...
Setup has completed successfully. SQL Server is now starting.
```

You need to stop SQL Server before running the preceding command or you will get a reminder to "run sudo systemctl stop mssql-server."

You'll also use variables when creating SQL Server container images on Docker, as explained in Chapter 1. For example, the following command creates a SQL Server container image passing three environment variables:

```
docker run -e 'ACCEPT_EULA=Y' -e MSSQL_PID='Developer' -e 'MSSQL_SA_
PASSWORD=password' -p 1421:1433 --name sqlonlinux
-d microsoft/mssql-server-linux:2017-latest
```

In this case, the –e option is used to set any environment variable in the container. The other options used may look obvious by now and were also explained in Chapter 1.

Linux Settings

Database professionals working with some other databases in Unix environments such as Oracle may be aware of specific kernel settings or some operating system configurations required for a database server. Configuring SQL Server on Linux is pretty much like configuring it on Windows, and not much Linux-specific configuration is required.

However, a few configuration settings can help provide better performance for SQL Server in Linux, and this section describes them. Although I cover how to implement these recommendations in the most common scenarios, you may need to look at your specific Linux distribution documentation for more details on their configuration.

Kernel Settings

Microsoft recommends several CPU- and disk-related Linux kernel settings for a high-performance configuration. Table 4-1 shows the recommended CPU settings.

Red Hat Enterprise Linux provides predefined performance tuning profiles that can help you configure these and other kernel settings automatically. Predefined performance tuning profiles have been designed to enhance performance for specific use cases, but you can also create your own profiles. For this particular case, I'll use a predefined profile named throughput-performance to configure the previously listed settings automatically.

I can use the tuned-adm tool to activate any available tuning profile. For example, for my newly create Red Hat Enterprise Linux virtual machine, I can use the `active` option to see the current active profile:

```
# tuned-adm active
Current active profile: virtual-guest
```

I can list the available profiles, which also specifies the active profile:

```
# tuned-adm list
```

My list shows the following:

- ▶ **balanced**   General nonspecialized tuned profile
- ▶ **desktop**   Optimize for the desktop use case
- ▶ **latency-performance**   Optimize for deterministic performance at the cost of increased power consumption

Setting	Value	More Information
CPU frequency governor	Performance	See the cpupower command.
ENERGY_PERF_BIAS	Performance	See the x86_energy_perf_policy command.
min_perf_pct	100	See your documentation on intel p-state.
C-States	C1 only	See your Linux or system documentation on how to ensure C-States is set to C1 only.

Table 4-1   *Recommended Settings for CPU-Related Linux Kernel*

▶ **network-latency**   Optimize for deterministic performance at the cost of increased power consumption; focused on low latency network performance

▶ **network-throughput**   Optimize for streaming network throughput; generally necessary only on older CPUs or 40G+ networks

▶ **powersave**   Optimize for low power consumption

▶ **throughput-performance**   Broadly applicable tuning that provides excellent performance across a variety of common server workloads

▶ **virtual-guest**   Optimize for running inside a virtual guest

▶ **virtual-host**   Optimize for running KVM guests

Finally, to configure Linux to use the throughput-performance profile, I can use the following command:

```
# tuned-adm profile throughput-performance
```

I can then validate that it is, in fact, the active profile:

```
# tuned-adm active
Current active profile: throughput-performance
```

NOTE

For more details about the performance tuning profiles, see the Red Hat Enterprise Linux documentation at https://access.redhat.com/documentation/en-us/red_hat_enterprise_linux or consult your Linux distribution documentation.

Table 4-2 shows the recommended disk settings.

Setting	Value	More Information
disk readahead	4096	See the `blockdev` command.
sysctl settings	kernel.sched_min_granularity_ns = 10000000 kernel.sched_wakeup_granularity_ns = 15000000 vm.dirty_ratio = 40 vm.dirty_background_ratio = 10 vm.swappiness =10	See the `sysctl` command.

Table 4-2   *Recommended Disk Settings for Linux Kernel*

The `sysctl` command enables you to configure kernel parameters at runtime. It basically reads and modifies the attributes of the system kernel. Linux exposes `sysctl` as a virtual file system at /proc/sys.

To see the value of a kernel attribute or variable, you can use `sysctl` followed by the variable name, as shown next. These are my defaults on a newly created virtual machine for the disk settings described earlier, typing a command per variable:

```
$ sysctl kernel.sched_min_granularity_ns
kernel.sched_min_granularity_ns = 10000000
$ sysctl kernel.sched_wakeup_granularity_ns
kernel.sched_wakeup_granularity_ns = 15000000
$ sysctl vm.dirty_ratio
vm.dirty_ratio = 30
$ sysctl vm.dirty_background_ratio
vm.dirty_background_ratio = 10
$ sysctl vm.swappiness
vm.swappiness = 30
```

As you can see, two values do not follow the Microsoft recommended values. To change a `sysctl` setting, you can use the –w option, as shown next:

```
$ sudo sysctl -w vm.dirty_ratio=40
vm.dirty_ratio = 40
$ sudo sysctl -w vm.swappiness=10
vm.swappiness = 10
```

Note that you cannot include a space, which may be allowed with other commands, or you will get the following error messages:

```
# sysctl -w vm.dirty_ratio = 40
sysctl: "vm.dirty_ratio" must be of the form name=value
sysctl: malformed setting "="
sysctl: "40" must be of the form name=value
```

You can display all values of kernel settings currently available in the system by using –a or --all, which will return a very large number of entries. An example is shown in Figure 4-1.

```
$ sysctl --all
```

NOTE

For more details about `sysctl`, *see the man documentation.*

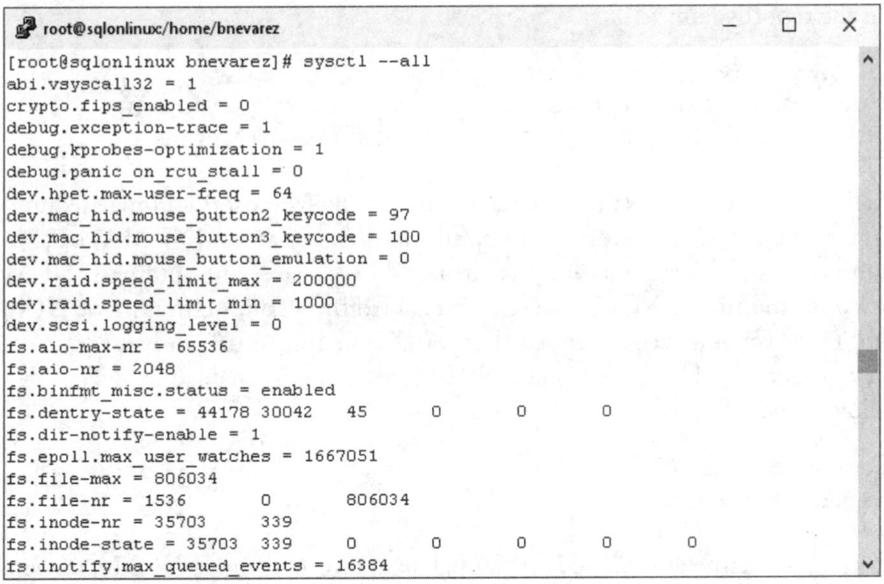

```
root@sqlonlinux/home/bnevarez                                    —   □   ✕
[root@sqlonlinux bnevarez]# sysctl --all
abi.vsyscall32 = 1
crypto.fips_enabled = 0
debug.exception-trace = 1
debug.kprobes-optimization = 1
debug.panic_on_rcu_stall = 0
dev.hpet.max-user-freq = 64
dev.mac_hid.mouse_button2_keycode = 97
dev.mac_hid.mouse_button3_keycode = 100
dev.mac_hid.mouse_button_emulation = 0
dev.raid.speed_limit_max = 200000
dev.raid.speed_limit_min = 1000
dev.scsi.logging_level = 0
fs.aio-max-nr = 65536
fs.aio-nr = 2048
fs.binfmt_misc.status = enabled
fs.dentry-state = 44178 30042      45       0       0       0
fs.dir-notify-enable = 1
fs.epoll.max_user_watches = 1667051
fs.file-max = 806034
fs.file-nr = 1536       0       806034
fs.inode-nr = 35703     339
fs.inode-state = 35703  339      0       0       0       0       0
fs.inotify.max_queued_events = 16384
```

Figure 4-1   *Partial sysctl --all output*

You can use the `blockdev` command to set the disk readahead property. For example, I will start with a report of all the devices in my system:

```
# blockdev --report
RO    RA    SSZ   BSZ   StartSec          Size   Device
rw    256   512   4096         0          4096   /dev/fd0
rw    8192  512   4096         0    17179869184  /dev/sdb
rw    8192  512   4096       128    17178755072  /dev/sdb1
rw    8192  512   4096         0    34359738368  /dev/sda
rw    8192  512   512       2048      524288000  /dev/sda1
rw    8192  512   512    1026048    33834401792  /dev/sda2
```

The RA column in the report is the block device readahead buffer size. You can use the `--getra` and `--setra` options to print and set the readahead configuration, respectively. In both cases, it is in 512-byte sectors.

```
# blockdev --getra /dev/sdb
8192
# blockdev --setra 4096 /dev/sdb
```

Run the report again:

```
# blockdev --report
RO    RA   SSZ   BSZ   StartSec         Size   Device
rw  4096   512  4096          0   17179869184   /dev/sdb
```

Finally, two additional settings are recommended by Microsoft and may require a configuration change: the automatic nonuniform memory access (NUMA) balancing for multinode NUMA systems and the virtual address space. The automatic NUMA balancing for multinode NUMA systems is enabled by default on multinode NUMA systems. However, it is recommended that you disable this setting in Linux.

You can validate whether automatic NUMA balancing is enabled by default by using the following command:

```
$ sysctl kernel.numa_balancing
kernel.numa_balancing = 1
```

You can disable the automatic NUMA balancing for multinode NUMA systems by using the `sysctl` command, as shown next:

```
$ sudo sysctl -w kernel.numa_balancing=0
kernel.numa_balancing = 0
```

NOTE

Nonuniform memory access (NUMA) is a hardware memory design used in multiprocessing, where memory access time depends on the memory location relative to the processor.

The second setting is the virtual address space; the default value of 64K may not be enough for a SQL Server installation. It is recommended that you change it to 256K, as shown next:

```
$ sysctl vm.max_map_count
vm.max_map_count = 65530
$ sudo sysctl -w vm.max_map_count=262144
vm.max_map_count = 262144
```

As you can guess, the default value for `vm.max_map_count` is 65530. A better value for SQL Server is the maximum limit of 256K, or 262144.

Transparent Huge Pages

Linux manages memory in pages of 4096 bytes, which means that just 1MB of memory requires 256 such pages. When you're managing large amounts of memory in

Linux, increasing the page size becomes a very important consideration. *Transparent huge pages* is an abstraction layer that uses large size pages, such as 2MB and 1GB sizes, and automates most of the aspects of creating and managing these large pages.

Transparent huge pages is enabled by default on most Linux distributions, and it is recommended that you leave it enabled when using SQL Server. Check your Linux documentation to validate whether transparent huge pages is enabled. For example, you can perform such validation on Red Hat Enterprise Linux using the following command:

```
# more /sys/kernel/mm/transparent_hugepage/enabled
[always] madvise never
```

Your current configuration setting is returned in brackets; in this case, you can see that transparent huge pages is enabled.

NOTE

Check your Linux documentation if you also need to enable transparent huge pages.

Swap File

Similar to Windows, Linux swap space can be used when the available memory is full. Inactive pages in memory are moved to the swap space when no more physical memory is available. As in Windows, swap space is not a replacement for memory because it is usually on disk and is slower than normal memory.

NOTE

See your Linux documentation for more details about configuring swap space.

To get started, you can use the swapon command to enable or disable devices and files for paging and swapping. Use the swapon -s command to display a swap usage summary by device; this is equivalent to looking at the information on /proc/swaps, as shown in the next two statements:

```
more /proc/swaps
lename                          Type         Size       Used    Priority
nt/resource/swapfile            file         2097148 0         -1
swapon -s
lename                          Type         Size       Used    Priority
nt/resource/swapfile            file         2097148 0         -1
```

Last Accessed Date/Time

A final operating system recommendation is to disable the last accessed date/time timestamp at the file system level. This timestamp, also known as atime, incurs a performance penalty, because it records when each file was last accessed, basically generating write activity for every read operation. You can disable the updating of this information to improve performance. Keep in mind, however, that the atime attribute may be required by some applications, so consider disabling it only for file systems used by SQL Server.

To disable the last accessed date/time timestamp at the file system level, you can edit the /etc/fstab file—although directly editing a Linux configuration file may seem like a very advanced task for a SQL Server professional. Edit the file to add the noatime attribute to the associated mount options of the required file system. The fstab file contains a line per each file system and includes information such as the device name, the mount directory, the file system type, and the associated mount options.

In the following example, the only defined mount option is defaults:

```
UUID=99cf66df-2fef-4aad-b226-382883643a1c /                    xfs
defaults        0 0
UUID=7c473048-a4e7-4908-bad3-a9be22e9d37d /boot                xfs
defaults        0 0
```

After editing the file, the mount options now show defaults,noatime:

```
UUID=99cf66df-2fef-4aad-b226-382883643a1c /                    xfs
defaults,noatime      0 0
UUID=7c473048-a4e7-4908-bad3-a9be22e9d37d /boot                xfs
defaults,noatime      0 0
```

Finally, you can use the remount option of the mount command to reload the file system information. This option will attempt to remount an already-mounted file system:

```
# mount -o remount /
```

SQL Server Configuration

This section offers an introduction to the most important SQL Server configuration settings. Most of what is covered here applies both to Windows and Linux installations. I discussed how to configure SQL Server memory in the mssql-conf section earlier in the chapter. In this section, I will start describing a Linux behavior that you should be aware of while configuring the memory available on your Linux installation.

Linux Out-of-Memory Killer

If you're a SQL Server administrator familiar with the Windows world, you need to be aware of a Linux kernel behavior: when a server is running low in memory, the kernel starts killing processes to free up memory and stay operational. This behavior, controlled by a mechanism called the Out-of-Memory Killer (OOM Killer), is in principle an optimization designed for the kernel to use the memory allocated by applications in a better way. Because many applications allocate their memory up front and usually do not utilize all the memory allocated, the Linux kernel was designed to make memory usage more efficient by having the ability to overcommit memory, allocating more memory than it actually has physically available.

Under this design, an obvious problem will occur when applications really do use all the memory allocated. For a SQL Server implementation, SQL Server will be the application using most of the memory and is therefore likely to be the killed process.

If the SQL Server process is killed and you know there is the possibility of a memory problem, start by looking at the Linux system logs at /var/log/messages. The OOM Killer algorithm, documented at https://linux-mm.org/OOM_Killer, is designed to consider several factors to estimate what is called an *OOM score*, which includes such things as trying to kill the minimum amount of processes (hopefully only one), recover a large amount of memory, and lose the minimum amount of work done.

NOTE

For an example of troubleshooting a case in which the SQL Server process was killed by the OOM Killer, see the article at https://blogs.msdn.microsoft.com/psssql/2017/10/17/how-to-safeguard-sql-server-on-linux-from-oom-killer/.

The best way to avoid the SQL Server process being killed by the Linux kernel is to configure the server memory properly, assigning the appropriate amount of memory for SQL Server, the operating system, and possibly any other process running on the same server. You can allocate the required amount of memory to SQL Server by using the mssql-conf tool, as explained earlier in this chapter. In addition, properly configuring a swap file, as indicated earlier, can help. You can view the available memory for SQL Server in the error log at instance startup, as shown next:

```
12/20/2017 5:12:16 AM Server Detected 6374 MB of RAM. This is an
informational message; no user action is required.
```

tempdb Configuration

Correctly configuring tempdb has been a performance consideration for all the versions of SQL Server for as long as I can remember. SQL Server 2016 brought some improvements such as the ability to create multiple data files automatically during the product setup based on the number of available processors on the system, or the new default tempdb configuration, which integrates the behavior of trace flags 1117 and 1118. Because SQL Server on Linux does not currently have the ability to create multiple tempdb data files during setup automatically, manually configuring this remains an important configuration requirement.

tempdb has been largely related to a classic performance problem: tempdb contention. The creation of a large number of user objects in a short period of time can contribute to latch contention of allocation pages. The main kind of tempdb contention is called DML (Data Modification Language) contention, as it relates to queries that modify data, mostly due to INSERT, UPDATE, and DELETE operations on temporary tables. A second type of contention, DDL (Data Definition Language) contention, although not common, is also possible in some heavy use scenarios. DDL contention is related to queries that create or alter objects that impact the system catalogs, as opposed to user data.

Every time a new object has to be created in tempdb, which is usually a temporary table with at least one row inserted, two new pages must be allocated from a mixed extent and assigned to the new object. One page is an Index Allocation Map (IAM) page and the second is a data page. During this process, SQL Server also has to access and update the very first Page Free Space (PFS) page and the very first Shared Global Allocation Map (SGAM) page in the data file. Only one thread can change an allocation page at a time, requesting a latch on it. When there is high activity and a large number of temporary tables are being created and dropped in tempdb, contention between the PFS and SGAM pages is possible. Remember that this is not an I/O problem, because allocation pages in this case are already in memory. Obviously, this contention impacts the performance of the processes creating those tables because they have to wait, and SQL Server may appear unresponsive for short periods of time. Keep in mind that although user databases have the same allocation pages, they are not likely to have a latch contention problem in allocation pages because not as many objects are created at the same time as they are created in tempdb.

The easiest way to check to determine whether you have a latch contention problem on tempdb allocation pages is to look for PAGELATCH_XX waits on the database activity. (Note that these are not the same as PAGEIOLATCH_XX waits.)

Although there is no perfect solution to the latch contention problem, because the database engine should be able to escalate and work fine as the number of operations increase, there are a few good recommendations to help you solve or minimize the problem. An obvious solution may be to minimize the number of temporary tables created in tempdb, but this may not be easy to implement because it would require code and application changes. Keep in mind that internal objects, such as the ones created by sort and hash operations, are not created explicitly by users and do not require the allocation methods discussed in this section. These internal objects can, however, create a different kind of performance problem.

The workaround to tempdb contention problems has historically been one or both of the following choices, especially prior to SQL Server 2016:

▶ Using multiple data files.

▶ Enable trace flags 1117 and 1118.

Multiple tempdb Data Files

With multiple files for tempdb, allocation bitmaps will be spread across the files, minimizing contention, because SQL Server will balance incoming requests across them. Using multiple files can help with both PFS and SGAM pages, and using trace flag 1118, as discussed in the next section, can greatly minimize the use of SGAM pages as well.

One question that has been debated for years about using multiple data files is what the optimal number of files for tempdb should be. Because applications can use tempdb in many different ways and can have different workloads, it's difficult to recommend a specific number for every scenario. Fortunately, there is a good recommendation that can work in most use cases: create one data file per logical processor available to the SQL Server instance, up to a maximum of eight files. This recommendation is now a default configuration option for tempdb when you install SQL Server 2016 or later on Windows, but it has to be manually configured for SQL Server on Linux. SQL Server creates a scheduler per each logical processor available to SQL Server, so the number of logical processors is also the maximum number of concurrent threads. Having multiple files means multiple PFS and SGAM pages, which means more allocations can occur at a time, reducing contention as threads are not waiting for one set of allocation pages.

This is a general guideline, however, and there may be cases in which high tempdb usage may still encounter contention problems. In such cases, it may be wise to create additional data files in multiples of four, up to the number of logical processors available in the system. Data files on tempdb also should be created with the same size and have the same autogrowth setting.

You can easily add more files to tempdb using SQL Server Management Studio (SSMS) or Transact-SQL, as shown in Figure 4-2.

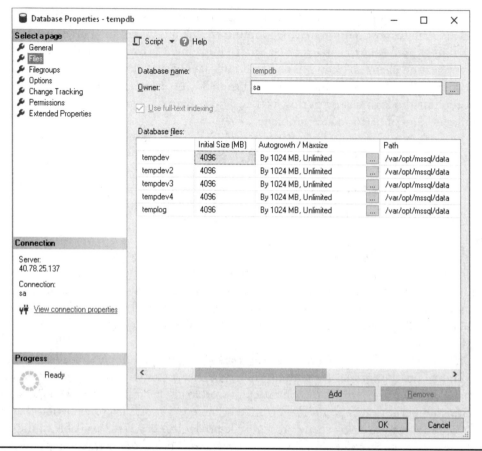

Figure 4-2 *Configuring multiple data files on tempdb*

The related Transact-SQL created by SSMS is shown here:

```
USE [master]
GO
ALTER DATABASE [tempdb] MODIFY FILE ( NAME = N'tempdev', SIZE =
4194304KB, FILEGROWTH = 1048576KB )
GO
ALTER DATABASE [tempdb] ADD FILE ( NAME = N'tempdev2', FILENAME = N'/var/
opt/mssql/data/tempdev2.ndf', SIZE = 4194304KB, FILEGROWTH = 1048576KB)
GO
ALTER DATABASE [tempdb] ADD FILE ( NAME = N'tempdev3', FILENAME = N'/var/
opt/mssql/data/tempdev3.ndf', SIZE = 4194304KB, FILEGROWTH = 1048576KB)
```

```
GO
ALTER DATABASE [tempdb] ADD FILE ( NAME = N'tempdev4', FILENAME = N'/var/
opt/mssql/data/tempdev4.ndf', SIZE = 4194304KB, FILEGROWTH = 1048576KB)
GO
ALTER DATABASE [tempdb] MODIFY FILE ( NAME = N'templog', SIZE =
4194304KB, FILEGROWTH = 1048576KB )
GO
```

Trace Flags 1117 and 1118

Because SQL Server uses SGAM pages to look for mixed extents with at least one unused page, a possible workaround to SGAM contention could be to avoid mixed extents altogether and, instead, exclusively use uniform extents. Trace flag 1118 has been available since SQL Server 2000 to do just this.

By disabling most of the single page allocations and, instead, using dedicated extents, you reduce the contention on SGAM pages. A downside with using trace flag 1118, however, is that every object will use a dedicated extent, which requires eight pages. If the object is small enough to fit in only one page, this is effectively wasting space. For example, if the object only requires 8KB of space, it will have to use 64KB, thus wasting 56KB of storage. The other downside is that this configuration takes effect at the instance level, impacting user databases as well. SGAM pages will still be used, as IAM pages will still need to be single page allocations from mixed extents, but SGAM contention most likely can be eliminated or greatly minimized. Trace flag 1117 is related to how SQL Server increases the size of database files by enabling even growth of all files in a file group.

Two additional related recommendations are to create the tempdb data files of equal size and to not rely on the autogrowth database file settings. Let's review those recommendations briefly. The recommendation to create the data files of equal size relies on the proportional fill algorithm used by SQL Server, which considers the current size of the database files, at least at the file group level. This algorithm determines in which order files are utilized and written to and spreads the allocations through the pages in a round-robin fashion. There is, however, an unfortunate behavior when files are not the same size. Instead of spreading Global Allocation Map (GAM) allocations between all the data files on a database, it would favor the largest file instead. Because of this, it is critical to configure all the data files the same size originally. Trace flag 1117 enables you to avoid this problem by growing all the tempdb files together at the same time by the configured increment. However, as in the case of trace flag 1118, trace flag 1117 applies to the entire SQL Server instance, working at the file group level on user databases. You may need to review whether it could be another issue for file groups on your user databases.

Finally, do not rely on the default autogrowth configuration, but leave it enabled with a proper file growth configuration, so it can be used as a last-resort choice. A production environment most likely will have a dedicated drive or file system for tempdb, if not a dedicated drive for data files and another for the transaction log file. If you are in this situation, simply allocate all the space possible to the tempdb files (maybe just limited by your space-available thresholds warnings so full disk notifications are not being sent). This will help avoid growing the file during production operations, causing unnecessary overhead. At the same time, it will minimize database fragmentation.

Process Affinity

Microsoft recommends that you set the process affinity for all the NUMA nodes and CPUs when SQL Server is running in a Linux operating system. You can accomplish this using the ALTER SERVER CONFIGURATION statement with the SET PROCESS AFFINITY option. You can either use CPU or NUMANODE choices, the latter being the easiest choice. Using the CPU option enables you to specify the CPU or range of CPUs to assign threads to. Using the NUMANODE option enables you to assign threads to all CPUs that belong to the specified NUMA node or range of nodes.

PROCESS AFFINITY enables hardware threads to be associated with CPUs and helps maintain an efficient Linux and SQL Server scheduling behavior. It is recommended that you set process affinity even if your system has a single NUMA node.

The following command, for example, sets the process affinity for all the NUMA nodes on a system with four nodes:

```
ALTER SERVER CONFIGURATION
SET PROCESS AFFINITY NUMANODE = 0, 3
```

Max Degree of Parallelism

One of the most important settings to configure on a new SQL Server installation, the *max degree of parallelism* option, defines the number of logical processors employed to run a single statement for parallel execution plans. Although a perfect configuration may depend on the specific workload, Microsoft has, since long ago, published a best practice recommendation that can work on most of the workloads or that can be used as a starting point.

First of all, the hardware on which SQL Server is running must be capable of running parallel queries—which means at least two logical processors are required, and this basically includes almost every server available today, including most typical configurations in virtual machines for production instances. Second, the affinity mask configuration option, which is now deprecated, or the ALTER SERVER CONFIGURATION SET PROCESS AFFINITY statement, covered earlier, must allow the use of multiple processors, which both do by default. Finally, the query processor must decide whether using parallelism can in fact improve the performance of a query, based on its estimated cost.

When a SQL Server installation is using the default max degree of parallelism value, which is 0, the database engine can decide at runtime the number of logical processors in a plan, up to a maximum of 64. Obviously, this does not mean that every parallel query would use the maximum number of processors available all the time. For example, even if your system has 64 logical processors and you are using the default configuration, it is still very possible that a query can use only 8 processors and run with eight threads. This is a decision the query processor makes at execution time.

Microsoft published an article recommending a value for the max degree of parallelism option to be the same as the number of logical processors in the server, up to a maximum of eight. You can read the article at https://support.microsoft.com/en-us/kb/2806535. Because it is very common to have eight processors or more nowadays, a value of eight is a common configuration.

Keep in mind that the listed recommendation is just a guideline, and that the article specifies that the guideline is applicable for typical SQL Server activity. In addition, depending on your workload or application patterns, some other values for this setting may be considered and thoroughly tested as well. As an example, if your SQL Server installation has 16 logical processors and a workload with a small number of queries running at the same time, a max degree of parallelism value of 16 could be your best choice. On the other hand, for a workload with a large number of queries, a value of 4 could be considered as well.

Cost Threshold for Parallelism

As mentioned in the previous section, parallelism is considered only for expensive queries, which again are defined by another configuration option, the *cost threshold for parallelism*. The cost threshold for parallelism configuration option defines the threshold at which SQL Server considers parallel plans for queries during the query optimization process.

The cost threshold for parallelism, whose default value is 5, means that parallelism would be considered by the query optimizer only if an initially created serial plan has the cost of five or more cost units. Although it is very likely that a parallel plan will be selected, when it does, this does not mean it will always be the case. For example, it is totally possible that the query optimizer initially estimates a cost of 6 for a serial plan, decides to inspect a parallel choice, and after finding a parallel plan of 6.3, decides to stick with the serial choice as the lowest cost choice is selected. But for more expensive queries, most likely a parallel plan would be produced.

It is worth clarifying that when a parallel plan is selected for execution, the execution plan itself does not define the degree of parallelism. This will be defined at runtime by the query processor.

Although the default value of 5 could be a good choice for many workloads, you may also consider increasing this value for specific scenarios. The choice of which new value to use would depend on your workload and should be thoroughly tested. If you decide to change the configuration value from 5 to 25, for example, this roughly means that all your plans with an original serial cost estimated at between 5 and 25 will no longer be considered to be parallelized and will continue as serial plans. You can choose either to research such queries to determine whether the new serial choice does not impact the execution performance, especially if those are critical queries or executed frequently, or to test your workload in general.

Statistics

This section covers statistics, which is one of the most important things that can impact query performance. In versions prior to SQL Server 2016, a very common configuration was to enable trace flag 2371 to improve the threshold use by SQL Server to update optimizer statistics automatically. Starting with this SQL Server version, this configuration was enabled by default, so the trace flag was no longer needed.

By default, SQL Server automatically creates and updates query optimizer statistics. You can change this database-level default, but doing so is almost never recommended because it would require the developer or administrator to create all the required statistics manually. Although this is possible, it doesn't make much sense, because the query optimizer can efficiently create the required statistics for you. Some other statistics will be created automatically when you create indexes for the columns involved in the index key. Manually creating statistics could be required only in a very limited number of cases, one of those being when multicolumn statistics are required. Multicolumn statistics are not created automatically by SQL Server.

Updating statistics is a little bit different. SQL Server can automatically update statistics when a specific threshold is reached. Although there are two thresholds or algorithms used to accomplish this, which I will cover in just a moment, a common problem is the size of the sample used to update the statistics object. High-performance databases may require a more proactive approach to updating statistics instead of letting SQL Server hit any of these two thresholds and using a very small sample.

The main limitation with automatic statistics update is the traditional 20 percent fixed threshold of changes required to trigger the update operation, which for large tables would require a very significant amount of changes. The second algorithm mentioned, usually enabled by using trace flag 2371, improves a bit on the threshold required to update statistics automatically, but the size of sample issue remains. The statistics update is triggered during the query optimization process when you run a query, but before it is executed. Because the update is technically part of the execution process, only a very small sample is used. Using a small sample makes sense, because you don't want to use a large sample in the middle of the query execution since it will most likely impact the execution time.

The process can be efficient for many workloads, but for more performance-demanding applications, a more proactive approach is required. This proactive approach usually means performing a scheduled maintenance job to update statistics on a regular basis. This method fixes both problems—not waiting until you hit a specific large threshold and providing a better sample size, which may include using the entire table.

In my opinion, the new algorithm is still not enough, but it is certainly better than the default threshold. The benefit of the new algorithm is with large tables, but a small sample in large tables may still be inadequate. This is why I recommend that you proactively update statistics in the first place, but leave the automatic update enabled, just in case, as a second choice.

Although there are free tools and scripts available to update statistics, even within SQL Server, creating an efficient script to perform this update is not as easy as it sounds, especially for large databases. Your script will have to deal with some or all of the following questions: Which tables, indexes, or statistics should be updated? What percent of the table should be used as the sample size? Do I need to scan the entire table? How often do I need to update statistics? Does updating statistics impact my database performance activity? Do I need a maintenance window? The answer to most of these questions will depend on the particular implementation, because there are many varying factors.

First, you have to define a point at which you will update statistics. For example, a typical solution to rebuild indexes is using the fragmentation level, and such information is available through the sys.dm_db_index_physical_stats DMV, whose documentation can be found at https://docs.microsoft.com/en-us/sql/relational-databases/system-dynamic-management-views/sys-dm-db-index-physical-stats-transact-sql. It even provides a threshold and a script to get started. This process, however, is a little bit more complicated for statistics.

Traditionally, database administrators relied on updating statistics based on the last updated date for statistics (for example, using the DBCC SHOW_STATISTICS statement or the STATS_DATE function) or older columns such as rowmodctr, available on the sys .sysindexes compatibility view, both of which have some drawbacks. If a table has not changed much in a specific period of time, those statistics may still be useful. In addition, the rowmodctr column does not consider changes for the leading statistics column, as the following solution does. Introduced only relatively recently in SQL Server 2012 (and currently in SQL Server 2008 R2 Service Pack 2 and SQL Server 2012 Service Pack 1) and later versions, you can use a new DMF, sys.dm_db_stats_properties, to return information about a specific statistics object. One of the columns, modification_ counter, returns the number of changes for the leading statistics column since the last time the statistics on the object were updated, so this value can be used to decide when to update them. The point at which to update will depend on your data and could be difficult to estimate, but at least you have better choices than before.

Along with jobs for statistics maintenance, usually there are also jobs to rebuild or reorganize indexes, which makes the choice to update statistics a bit more complicated. Rebuilding an index will update statistics with the equivalent of the full-scan option. Reorganizing an index does not touch or update statistics at all. We usually want to rebuild indexes depending on their fragmentation level, so statistics will be updated only for those indexes. We may not want the statistics job to update those statistics again. Traditionally, this has been left to your scripts, with the difficult decision about which statistics object to update and which sometimes end up updating the same object twice. As mentioned, currently this problem can be fixed or minimized by using the sys .dm_db_stats_properties DMF.

Finally, there is currently no documented method to determine whether statistics are being used by the query optimizer. Let's suppose, for example, that an ad hoc query was executed only once, which created statistics on some columns. Assuming those statistics are not used again, maintenance jobs will continue to update those statistics objects potentially as long as the columns exist.

Finally, I recommend Ola Hallengren's Maintenance Solution, available at https:// ola.hallengren.com, to implement maintenance jobs for backups, index and statistics maintenance, and consistency checks.

Standard Automatic Statistics Update

Automatically updating statistics has been available since SQL Server 7, when the query processor was rearchitected. Since then, the algorithm to update statistics automatically has not changed much; for tables with more than 500 rows, the automatic update will occur when the column modification counters (colmodctrs) or changes on statistics leading column hits 20 percent of changes plus 500.

Keep in mind that SQL Server 7 and SQL Server 2000 relied instead on the rowmodctrs, or row-level modification counters, to get the same behavior. Obviously, using rowmodctrs was not optimal if, for example, there was a statistics object on column c1, 25 percent changes on column c2, but no changes on c1; it will still trigger a statistics update on column c1, which was not needed.

A few more details about the algorithm to update statistics automatically, especially as it relates to tables with 500 rows or smaller, temporary tables, and filtered statistics, can be found in the white paper at https://msdn.microsoft.com/en-us/library/dd535534(SQL.100).aspx.

Trace Flag 2371

Trace flag 2371 was introduced with SQL Server 2008 R2 as a way to change and lower the threshold in which statistics are automatically updated, and, as with any other trace flag, it has to be manually enabled. The new algorithm will use whatever number of changes is smaller between the new formula, defined as SQRT(1000 * number of rows), and the old one using 20 percent of the size of the table. If you do the math using both formulas, you can see that the threshold changes with tables of 25,000 rows, in which both cases return the same value: 5000 changes. For example, with the default algorithm requiring 20 percent of changes, if a large table has a billion rows, it would require 200 million rows to trigger the update. Trace flag 2371 would require a smaller threshold, in this case, SQRT(1000 * 1000000000), or 1 million. SQL Server 2016 and later has the behavior of trace flag 2371 enabled by default when you use the new database compatibility level 130 or later.

Finally, as covering statistics in full detail is outside the scope of this book, I would recommend the Microsoft white paper Statistics Used by the Query Optimizer in Microsoft SQL Server 2008, which is still valid for the latest versions. You can find it at https://msdn.microsoft.com/en-us/library/dd535534(SQL.100).aspx.

Summary

This chapter covered configuring SQL Server on Linux from three different areas. First, there is no Configuration Manager on Linux, so configuring the SQL Server port or a trace flag at the server level now has to be done with the mssql-conf utility. In addition, mssql-conf can be used to configure a large variety of other settings.

It also covered several CPU- and disk-related Linux kernel settings for a high-performance configuration, in addition to some operating system–level configurations such as transparent huge pages, which can improve the performance of Linux when managing large amounts of memory.

Finally, it covered some critical SQL Server configuration settings that apply either to Windows or Linux implementations. An interesting behavior used by Linux when a server is running low in memory, the Out-Of-Memory Killer, was introduced as well.

Chapter 5

SQL Server Query Tuning and Optimization

In This Chapter

S o far, I have covered installing and configuring SQL Server on Linux and I showed you how SQL Server works on this operating system. We'll now move on to the operational part and use the technology for database queries.

The next two chapters discuss query processing and performance. This chapter is an introduction to query tuning and optimization in SQL Server. The next chapter covers many new features in SQL Server 2017, including adaptive query processing and automatic tuning. The content of both chapters applies to SQL Server on both Linux and Windows, and this chapter applies to all the currently supported versions of the product. Later chapters in the book will focus on high availability, disaster recovery, and security.

Query optimization usually refers to the work performed by the query optimizer, in which an efficient—or good enough—plan is produced. Sometimes you may not be happy with its query execution performance and may try to improve it by making changes, via query tuning. It is important to understand that the results you originally get from the query optimizer—that is, the execution plan—will greatly depend on the information you feed it, including your database design, the defined indexes, and even some configuration settings. You can impact the work performed by the query processor in many ways, which is why it is very important that you understand how you can help this SQL Server component to do a superior job. Providing quality information to the query processor will usually result in high-quality execution plans, which will also improve the performance of your databases and applications. You also need to be aware that no query optimizer is perfect, and sometimes you may not, in fact, get a good execution plan or good query performance, but other solutions may still be available.

This chapter provides an introduction to query tuning and optimization and is not intended to cover this topic in detail. For more complete coverage of this topic, read my book *Microsoft SQL Server 2014 Query Tuning & Optimization* (McGraw-Hill Education, 2014). For a focus on SQL Server performance and configuration, read my book *High Performance SQL Server: The Go Faster Book* (Apress, 2016).

Query Performance

We all have been there: A phone call notifies you of an application outage and asks you to join an urgent conference call. After joining the call, you learn that the application is so slow that the company is not able to conduct business; it is losing money and potentially customers, too. Nobody on the call is able to provide any additional information that can help you determine what the problem is. What do you do? Where do you start? And after troubleshooting and fixing the issue, how do you avoid these problems in the future?

Although an outage can occur for several different reasons, including a hardware failure and an operating system problem, as a database professional, you should be able to tune and optimize your databases proactively and be ready to troubleshoot any problem quickly. By focusing on SQL Server performance, and more specifically on query tuning and optimization, you can, first, avoid these performance problems by optimizing your databases and, second, quickly troubleshoot and fix the problems if they actually occur.

One of the best ways to learn how to improve the performance of your databases is not only to work with the technology, but to understand how the underlying technology works, how to get the most benefit from it, and even what its limitations are. The most important SQL Server component impacting the performance of your queries is the SQL Server query processor, which includes the query optimizer and the execution engine.

With a perfect query optimizer, you could just submit any query and you would get a perfect execution plan every time. And with a perfect execution engine, each of your queries would run in a matter of milliseconds. But the reality is that query optimization is a very complex problem, and no query optimizer can find the best plan all the time, or at least not in a reasonable amount of time. For complex queries, a query optimizer would need to analyze many possible execution plans. And even if a query optimizer could analyze all the possible solutions, its next challenge would be to decide which plan to choose. In other words, which of the possible solutions is the most efficient? Choosing the best plan would require estimating the cost of each solution, which again is a very complicated task.

Don't get me wrong: The SQL Server query optimizer does an amazing job and gives you a good execution plan almost all the time. But you must understand which information you need to provide to the query optimizer so it can do a good job, which may include providing the right indexes and adequate statistics, as well as defining the required constraints and providing a good database design. SQL Server even provides you with tools to help you in some of these areas, including the Database Engine Tuning Advisor (DTA) and the auto-create and auto-update statistics features. But you can still do more to improve the performance of your databases, especially when you are building high-performance applications. Finally, you need to understand the cases for which the query optimizer may not give you a good execution plan and what to do in those cases.

To help you better understand this technology, I will start with an overview of how the SQL Server query processor works. I will explain the purpose of both the query optimizer and the execution engine and how they interact with the plan cache to reuse plans as much as possible. I will also show you how to work with execution plans, which are the primary tool we will use to interact with the query processor.

Query Processor Architecture

At the core of the SQL Server database engine are two major components: the storage engine and the relational engine, also called the query processor. The storage engine is responsible for reading data between the disk and memory in a manner that optimizes concurrency while maintaining data integrity. The query processor, as the name suggests, accepts all queries submitted to SQL Server, devises a plan for their optimal execution, and then executes the plan and delivers the required results.

Queries are submitted to SQL Server using the SQL language (or Transact-SQL [T-SQL], the Microsoft SQL Server extension to SQL). Because SQL is a high-level declarative language, it only defines what data to get from the database, not the steps required to retrieve that data or any of the algorithms for processing the request. Thus, for each query it receives, the first job of the query processor is to devise a plan, as quickly as possible, that describes the best possible way (or, at the very least, an efficient way) to execute said query. Its second job is to execute the query according to that plan. Each of these tasks is delegated to a separate component within the query processor; the query optimizer devises the plan and then passes it along to the execution engine, which will actually execute the plan and get the results from the database.

The SQL Server query optimizer is a cost-based optimizer. It analyzes a number of candidate execution plans for a given query, estimates the cost of each of these plans, and selects the plan with the lowest cost of the choices considered. Indeed, given that the query optimizer cannot consider every possible plan for every query, it actually has to find a balance between the optimization time and the quality of the selected plan.

Therefore, it is the SQL Server component that has the biggest impact on the performance of your databases. After all, selecting the right or wrong execution plan could mean the difference between a query execution time of milliseconds and one of minutes, or even hours. Naturally, a better understanding of how the query optimizer works can help both database administrators and developers to write better queries and to provide the query optimizer with the information it needs to produce efficient execution plans. This chapter will demonstrate how you can use your newfound knowledge of the query optimizer's inner workings; in addition, it will give you the knowledge and tools to troubleshoot the cases when the query optimizer is not giving you a good plan.

To arrive at what it believes to be the best plan for executing a query, the query processor performs the following steps, which are also shown in Figure 5-1.

1. **Parsing and binding**   The query is parsed and bound. Assuming the query is valid, the output of this phase is a logical tree, with each node in the tree representing a logical operation that the query must perform, such as reading a particular table or performing an inner join.

2. **Query optimization**   The logical tree created in the step 1 is used to run the query optimization process, which roughly consists of the following two steps:

    a. **Generation of possible execution plans**   Using the logical tree, the query optimizer devises a number of possible ways to execute the query (that is, a number of possible execution plans). An execution plan is, in essence, a set of physical operations (such as an index seek or a nested loops join) that can be performed to produce the required result, as described by the logical tree.

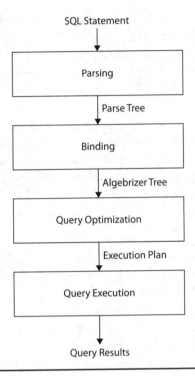

Figure 5-1 *The query processing process*

    b.   **Cost assessment of each plan**   Although the query optimizer does not generate every possible execution plan, it assesses the resource and time cost of each plan it does generate; the plan that the query optimizer deems to have the lowest cost of those it has assessed is selected and then passed along to the execution engine.

3.   **Query execution and plan caching**   The query is next executed by the execution engine according to the selected plan; the plan may be stored in memory in the plan cache.

Let us now review these operations in a bit more detail.

Parsing and Binding

Parsing and binding are the first operations performed when a query is submitted to a SQL Server instance. Parsing makes sure that the T-SQL query has a valid syntax, and it translates the SQL query into an initial tree representation: specifically, a tree of logical operators representing the high-level steps required to execute the query in question. Initially, these logical operators will be closely related to the original syntax of the query and will include such logical operations as "get data from the Customer table," "get data from the Contact table," "perform an inner join," and so on. Different tree representations of the query will be used throughout the optimization process, and this logical tree will receive different names until it is finally used to initialize a memory structure called the Memo. This memory structure will be used during the entire optimization process.

Binding is mostly concerned with name resolution. During the binding operation, SQL Server makes sure that all the object names do exist, and it associates every table and column name on the parse tree with its corresponding object in the system catalog. The output of this second process is called an algebrizer tree, which is then sent to the query optimizer.

Query Optimization

The next step is the optimization process, which is basically the generation of candidate execution plans and the selection of the best of these plans according to their cost. As already mentioned, the SQL Server query optimizer uses a cost-estimation model to estimate the cost of each of the candidate plans.

Query optimization could be also seen as the process of mapping the logical query operations expressed in the original tree representation to physical operations, which can be carried out by the execution engine. So it's actually the functionality of the execution engine that is being implemented in the execution plans being created by the query optimizer; that is, the execution engine implements a certain number of different algorithms, and it is from these algorithms that the query optimizer must choose when formulating its execution plans. It does this by translating the original logical operations into the physical operations that the execution engine is capable of performing. Execution plans show both the logical and physical operations for each operator. Some logical operations, such as sorts, translate to the same physical operation, whereas other logical operations map to several possible physical operations. For example, a logical join can be mapped to a nested loops join, merge join, or hash join physical operator. However, this is not a one-to-one operator matching and instead follows a more complicated process.

Thus, the end product of the query optimization process is an execution plan: a tree consisting of a number of physical operators that contain the algorithms to be performed by the execution engine to obtain the desired results from the database.

Generating Candidate Execution Plans

Even for relatively simple queries, there may be a large number of different ways to access the data to produce the same end result. As such, the query optimizer has to select the best possible plan from what may be a very large number of candidate execution plans. Making a wise choice is important, because the time taken to return the results to the user can vary wildly, depending on which plan is selected.

The job of the query optimizer is to create and assess as many candidate execution plans as possible, within certain criteria, to find a good enough plan, which may be, but it is not necessarily, the optimal plan. We define the search space for a given query as the set of all possible execution plans for that query, in which any possible plan in this search space returns the same results. Theoretically, to find the optimum execution plan for a query, a cost-based query optimizer should generate all possible execution plans that exist in that search space and correctly estimate the cost of each plan. However, some complex queries may have thousands, or even millions, of possible execution plans, and although the SQL Server query optimizer can typically consider a large number of candidate execution plans, it cannot perform an exhaustive search of all the possible plans for every query. If it did, the time taken to assess all of the plans would be unacceptably long and could have a major impact on the overall query execution time.

The query optimizer must strike a balance between optimization time and plan quality. For example, if the query optimizer spends a few milliseconds finding a good enough plan that executes in two or three seconds, then it doesn't make sense to try to find the perfect or most optimal plan if this is going to take one or more minutes of optimization time, plus the execution time. So SQL Server does not do an exhaustive search, but instead tries to find a suitably efficient plan as quickly as possible. As the query optimizer is working within a time constraint, there's a chance that the plan selected may be the optimal plan, but it is also likely that it may just be something close to the optimal plan.

To explore the search space, the query optimizer uses transformation rules and heuristics. The generation of candidate execution plans is performed inside the query optimizer using transformation rules, and the use of heuristics limits the number of choices considered in order to keep the optimization time reasonable. The set of alternative plans considered by the query optimizer is referred to as the *plan space*, and these plans are stored in memory during the optimization process in the Memo structure.

Assessing the Cost of Each Plan

Searching or enumerating candidate plans is just one part of the optimization process. The query optimizer still needs to estimate the cost of these plans and select the least expensive one. To estimate the cost of a plan, it estimates the cost of each physical operator in that plan, using costing formulas that consider the use of resources such as I/O, CPU, and memory. This cost estimation depends mostly on both the algorithm used by the physical operator and the estimated number of records that will need to be processed. This estimate of the number of records is known as the *cardinality estimation*.

To help with the cardinality estimation, SQL Server uses and maintains statistics that contain information describing the distribution of values in one or more columns of a table. Once the cost for each operator is calculated using estimations of cardinality and resource demands, the query optimizer will add up all of these costs to estimate the cost for the entire plan. I will cover statistics in more detail later in this chapter.

Query Execution and Plan Caching

Once the query is optimized, the resulting plan is used by the execution engine to retrieve the desired data. The generated execution plan may be stored in memory in the plan cache so it can be reused if the same query is executed again. SQL Server has a pool of memory that is used to store both data pages and execution plans. Most of this memory is used to store database pages, and it is called the *buffer pool*. A portion of this memory contains the execution plans for queries that were optimized by the query optimizer and is referred to as the *plan cache* (and was previously known as the procedure cache). The percentage of memory allocated to the plan cache or the buffer pool varies dynamically, depending on the state of the system.

Before optimizing a query, SQL Server first checks the plan cache to see if an execution plan exists for the batch. Query optimization is a relatively expensive operation, so if a valid plan is available in the plan cache, the optimization process can be skipped and the associated cost of this step, in terms of optimization time, CPU resources, and so on, can be avoided. If a plan for the batch is not found, the batch is compiled to generate an execution plan for all queries in the stored procedure, the trigger, or the dynamic SQL batch. Query optimization begins by loading all the interesting statistics. Then the query optimizer validates whether the statistics are outdated. For any outdated statistics, when using the statistics default options, it will update the statistics and will proceed with the optimization.

After a plan is found in the plan cache or a new one is created, the plan is validated for schema and data statistics changes. Schema changes are verified for plan correctness. Statistics are also verified: the query optimizer checks for new applicable statistics or outdated statistics. If the plan is not valid for any of these reasons, it is discarded and the batch or individual query is compiled again. Such compilations are known as *recompilations*. This process is summarized in Figure 5-2.

Plans may also be removed from the plan cache when SQL Server is under memory pressure or when certain statements are executed. Changing some configuration options (for example, max degree of parallelism) will clear the entire plan cache. Alternatively, some statements, such as altering a database with certain ALTER DATABASE options, will clear all the plans associated with that particular database.

It is worth noting, however, that reusing an existing plan may not always be the best solution for a given query, and some performance problems may result. For example,

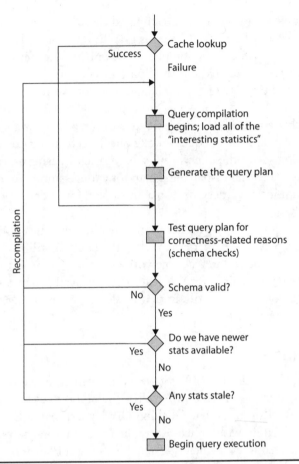

Figure 5-2 *Compilation and recompilation processes*

depending on the data distribution within a table, the optimal execution plan for a query may differ greatly depending on the parameters being used. More details about parameter-sensitive queries are covered later in the chapter in the section "Parameter Sniffing."

Execution Plans

Now that we have a foundation in the query processor and how it works its magic, it is time to consider how we can interact with it. Primarily, we will interact with the query processor through execution plans, which as I mentioned earlier are ultimately trees consisting of a number of physical operators that, in turn, contain the algorithms to produce the required results from the database.

You can request either an actual or an estimated execution plan for a given query, and either of these two types can be displayed as a graphic, text, or XML plan. Any of these three formats shows the same execution plan—the only differences are in how they are displayed and the levels of detailed information they contain.

When an estimated plan is requested, the query is not executed; the plan displayed is simply the plan that SQL Server would most probably use if the query were executed (bearing in mind that a recompile may generate a different plan at a later time). However, when an actual plan is requested, the query needs to be executed, and the plan is then displayed along with the query results. Nevertheless, using an estimated plan has several benefits, including displaying a plan for a long-running query for inspection without actually running the query, or displaying a plan for update operations without changing the database.

Live Query Statistics, a query troubleshooting feature introduced with SQL Server 2016, can be used to view a live query plan while the query is still in execution, so you can see query plan information in real time without needing to wait for the query to complete. Since the data required for this feature is also available in the SQL Server 2014 database engine, it can also work in that version if you are using SQL Server 2016 Management Studio or later.

Graphical Plans

You can display graphical plans in SQL Server Management Studio by clicking the Display Estimated Execution Plan button or the Include Actual Execution Plan button from the SQL Editor toolbar. Clicking Display Estimated Execution Plan will show the plan immediately, without executing the query, whereas to request an actual execution plan, you need to click Include Actual Execution Plan and then execute the query and click the Execution plan tab.

As an example, copy the following query to the Management Studio Query Editor, select the AdventureWorks2014 database, click the Include Actual Execution Plan button, and execute the query:

```
SELECT DISTINCT(City) FROM Person.Address
```

Then select the Execution Plan tab in the results pane. This displays the plan shown in Figure 5-3.

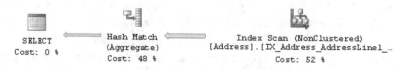

Figure 5-3 *Graphical execution plan*

NOTE

This book contains a large number of sample SQL queries, all of which are based on the AdventureWorks database. All code has been tested on SQL Server 2017 RTM. These sample databases are not included in your SQL Server installation but can be downloaded separately. In addition, the AdventureWorks sample databases are no longer provided in the SQL Server 2017 release. The latest version available, and used for this book, is AdventureWorks OLTP SQL Server 2014, which you can download from https://github.com/Microsoft/sql-server-samples/releases/tag/adventureworks. Restore the database as AdventureWorks2014. For more details on how to copy backup files to Linux and restore a database, refer to Chapter 1.

Each node in the tree structure is represented as an icon that specifies a logical and physical operator, such as the Index Scan and the Hash Aggregate operators, as shown in Figure 5-3. The first icon is a language element called the result operator, which represents the `SELECT` statement and is usually the root element in the plan.

NOTE

Beginning with SQL Server Management Studio 17.4, execution plan operator icons look a little bit different from those in all the previous versions. They should be updated by the time this book goes to press on the SQL Server documentation page at https://docs.microsoft.com/en-us/sql/relational-databases/showplan-logical-and-physical-operators-reference.

Operators implement a basic function or operation of the execution engine; for example, a logical join operation could be implemented by any of three different physical join operators: nested loops join, merge join, or hash join. Obviously, many more operators are implemented in the execution engine, and you can see the entire list at https://msdn.microsoft.com/en-us/library/ms191158(v=sql.110).aspx. Logical and physical operators' icons are displayed in blue, except for cursor operators, which are yellow, and language elements are displayed in green:

	A logical/physical operator in blue
	A language element in green
	A cursor in yellow

The query optimizer builds an execution plan, choosing from these operators, which may read records from the database, such as the Index Scan operator shown in the previous plan; or they may read records from another operator, such as the Hash Aggregate, which reads records from the Index Scan operator.

Each node is related to a parent node, connected with arrowheads, where data flows from a child operator to a parent operator, and the arrow width is proportional to the number of rows. After the operator performs some function on the records it has read, the results are output to its parent. You can hover the mouse pointer over an arrow to get more information about that data flow, displayed as a tooltip. For example, if you hover the mouse pointer over the arrow between the Index Scan and Hash Aggregate operators, shown in Figure 5-3, you can see the data flow information between these operators, as shown in Figure 5-4.

By looking at the actual number of rows, you can see that the Index Scan operator is reading 19,614 rows from the database and sending them to the Hash Aggregate operator. The Hash Aggregate operator is, in turn, performing some operation on this data and sending 575 records to its parent, which you can see by placing the mouse pointer over the arrow between the Hash Aggregate and the SELECT icon.

Basically, in this plan, the Index Scan operator is reading all 19,614 rows from an index, and the Hash Aggregate is processing these rows to obtain the list of distinct cities, of which there are 575, that will be displayed in the Results window in Management Studio. Notice also that you can see the estimated number of rows, which is the query optimizer's cardinality estimation for this operator, as well as the actual number of rows. Comparing the actual and the estimated number of rows can help you detect cardinality estimation errors, which can affect the quality of your execution plans.

To perform their job, physical operators implement at least the following three methods:

▶ **Open()**   Causes an operator to be initialized, and may include setting up any required data structures

▶ **GetRow()**   Requests a row from the operator

▶ **Close()**   Performs some cleanup operations and shuts down the operator once it has performed its role

An operator requests rows from other operators by calling their GetRow() method, which also means that execution in a plan starts from left to right. Because GetRow() produces just one row at a time, the actual number of rows displayed in the execution

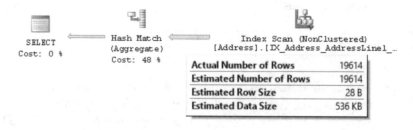

Figure 5-4   *Data flow between the Index Scan and Hash Aggregate operators*

plan is also the number of times the method was called on a specific operator, and an additional call to GetRow() is used by the operator to indicate the end of the result set. In the previous example, the Hash Aggregate operator calls the Open() method once, GetRow() 19,615 times, and Close() once on the Index Scan operator.

NOTE

For now, I will explain the traditional query-processing mode in which operators process only one row at a time. This processing mode has been used in all versions of SQL Server since SQL Server 7.0. In the next chapter, I will touch on the new batch-processing mode, introduced with SQL Server 2012, which is used by operators related to columnstore indexes.

In addition to learning more about the data flow, you can hover the mouse pointer over an operator to get more information about it. For example, Figure 5-5 shows information about the Index Scan operator. Notice that it includes, among other things, a description of the operator and data on estimated costing information, such as the

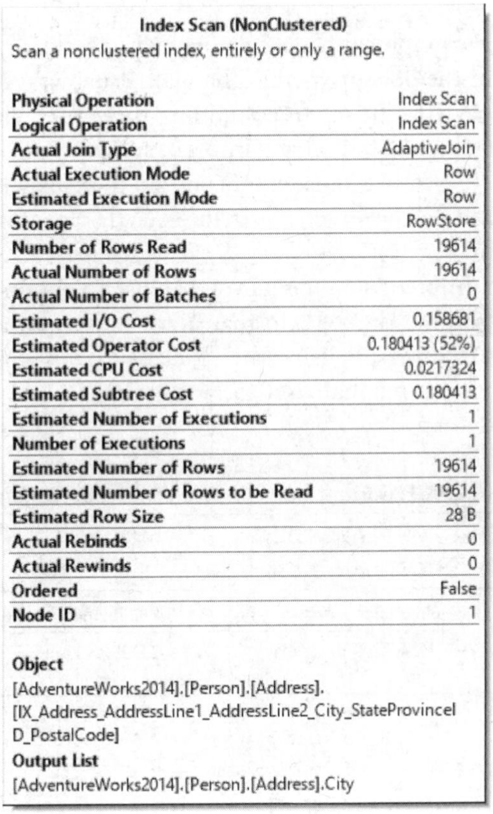

Index Scan (NonClustered)	
Scan a nonclustered index, entirely or only a range.	
Physical Operation	Index Scan
Logical Operation	Index Scan
Actual Join Type	AdaptiveJoin
Actual Execution Mode	Row
Estimated Execution Mode	Row
Storage	RowStore
Number of Rows Read	19614
Actual Number of Rows	19614
Actual Number of Batches	0
Estimated I/O Cost	0.158681
Estimated Operator Cost	0.180413 (52%)
Estimated CPU Cost	0.0217324
Estimated Subtree Cost	0.180413
Estimated Number of Executions	1
Number of Executions	1
Estimated Number of Rows	19614
Estimated Number of Rows to be Read	19614
Estimated Row Size	28 B
Actual Rebinds	0
Actual Rewinds	0
Ordered	False
Node ID	1

Object
[AdventureWorks2014].[Person].[Address].
[IX_Address_AddressLine1_AddressLine2_City_StateProvincel
D_PostalCode]
Output List
[AdventureWorks2014].[Person].[Address].City

Figure 5-5   *Tooltip for the Index Scan operator*

estimated I/O, CPU, operator, and subtree costs. It is worth mentioning that the cost is just internal cost units that are not meant to be interpreted in other units such as seconds or milliseconds.

You can also see the relative cost of each operator in the plan as a percentage of the overall plan, as shown in Figure 5-3. For example, the cost of the Index Scan is 52 percent of the cost of the entire plan. Additional information from an operator or the entire query can be obtained by using the Properties window. So, for example, choosing the SELECT icon and the Properties window from the View menu (or pressing F4) will show the properties for the entire query.

XML Plans

Once you have displayed a graphical plan, you can also easily display it in XML format. Simply right-click anywhere on the graphical execution plan window to display a pop-up menu and select Show Execution Plan XML. This will open the XML editor and display the XML plan. As you can see, you can easily switch between a graphical and an XML plan.

If needed, you can save graphical plans to a file by right-clicking and selecting Save Execution Plan As from the pop-up menu. The plan, usually saved with an .sqlplan extension, is actually an XML document containing the XML plan information, but it can be read by Management Studio back into a graphical plan. You can load this file again by selecting File | Open in Management Studio to display it immediately as a graphical plan, which will behave exactly as before. XML plans can also be used with the USEPLAN query hint.

Table 5-1 shows the different statements you can use to obtain an estimated or actual execution plan in text, graphic, or XML format. Keep in mind that when you run any of the statements listed in this table using the ON clause, it will apply to all subsequent statements until the option is manually set to OFF again.

	Estimated Execution Plan	Actual Execution Plan
Text plan	SET SHOWPLAN_TEXT SET SHOWPLAN_ALL	SET STATISTICS PROFILE
Graphic plan	Management Studio	Management Studio
XML plan	SET SHOWPLAN_XML	SET STATISTICS XML

Table 5-1 *Statements for Displaying Query Plans*

To show an XML plan directly, you can use the following commands:

```
SET SHOWPLAN_XML ON
GO
SELECT DISTINCT(City) FROM Person.Address
GO
SET SHOWPLAN_XML OFF
```

This will display a single-row, single-column (titled "Microsoft SQL Server 2005 XML Showplan") result set containing the XML data that starts with the following: `<ShowPlanXML xmlns="http://schemas.microsoft.com/ sqlserver/2004/07/showplan"`. Clicking the link will show you a graphical plan, and you can then display the XML plan using the same procedure I explained earlier.

You can browse the basic structure of an XML plan via the following exercise. A very simple query will create the basic XML structure, but in this example I show you a query that can provide two additional parts: the missing indexes and parameter list elements. Run the following query and request an XML plan in the same way we did in the previous example:

```
SELECT * FROM Sales.SalesOrderDetail WHERE OrderQty = 1
```

Collapse `<MissingIndexes>`, `<RelOp>`, and `<ParameterList>` by clicking the minus sign (–) on the left so you can easily see the entire structure. You should see something similar to Figure 5-6.

```
<?xml version="1.0" encoding="utf-16"?>
<ShowPlanXML xmlns:xsi="http://www.w3.org/2001/XMLSchema-instance" xmlns:xsd="http://www.w3.org/2001/XMLSchema"
  <BatchSequence>
    <Batch>
      <Statements>
        <StmtSimple StatementCompId="1" StatementEstRows="68460.1" StatementId="1" StatementOptmLevel="FULL" Car
          <StatementSetOptions ANSI_NULLS="true" ANSI_PADDING="true" ANSI_WARNINGS="true" ARITHABORT="true" CONC
          <QueryPlan DegreeOfParallelism="1" CachedPlanSize="32" CompileTime="4" CompileCPU="4" CompileMemory=":
            <MissingIndexes>...</MissingIndexes>
            <MemoryGrantInfo SerialRequiredMemory="0" SerialDesiredMemory="0" />
            <OptimizerHardwareDependentProperties EstimatedAvailableMemoryGrant="206667" EstimatedPagesCached=":
            <OptimizerStatsUsage>...</OptimizerStatsUsage>
            <WaitStats>...</WaitStats>
            <QueryTimeStats CpuTime="160" ElapsedTime="829" />
            <RelOp AvgRowSize="112" EstimateCPU="0.0582322" EstimateIO="0" EstimateRebinds="0" EstimateRewinds='
            <ParameterList>...</ParameterList>
          </QueryPlan>
        </StmtSimple>
      </Statements>
    </Batch>
  </BatchSequence>
</ShowPlanXML>
```

Figure 5-6   *XML execution plan*

As you can see, the main components of the XML plan are the `<StmtSimple>`, `<StatementSetOptions>`, and `<QueryPlan>` elements. These three elements include several attributes, some of which were mentioned when we discussed the graphical plan. In addition, the `<QueryPlan>` element includes other elements, such as `<MissingIndexes>`, `<MemoryGrantInfo>`, `<OptimizerHardwareDependentProperties>`, `<WaitStats>`, `<QueryTimeStats>`, `<RelOp>`, `<ParameterList>`, and others not shown in Figure 5-6, such as `<Warnings>`. A new element in SQL Server 2017, `<OptimizerStatsUsage>`, will be covered in more detail in the next chapter.

Text Plans

As shown in Table 5-1, you can use two commands to get estimated text plans: SET SHOWPLAN_TEXT and SET SHOWPLAN_ALL. Both statements show the estimated execution plan, but SET SHOWPLAN_ALL shows some additional information, including the estimated number of rows, estimated CPU cost, estimated I/O cost, and estimated operator cost. You can use the following code to display a text execution plan:

```
SET SHOWPLAN_TEXT ON
GO
SELECT DISTINCT(City) FROM Person.Address
GO
SET SHOWPLAN_TEXT OFF
GO
```

This code will actually display two result sets, the first one returning the text of the T-SQL statement. In the second result set, you see the following text plan (edited to fit the page), which shows the same Hash Aggregate and Index Scan operators displayed in Figure 5-3.

```
|--Hash Match(Aggregate, HASH:([Person].[Address].[City]), RESIDUAL …
     |--Index Scan(OBJECT:([AdventureWorks].[Person].[Address]. [IX_Address …
```

SET SHOWPLAN_ALL and SET STATISTICS PROFILE can provide more detailed information than SET SHOWPLAN_TEXT. Also, as shown in Table 5-1, you can use SET SHOWPLAN_ALL to get an estimated plan only and SET STATISTICS PROFILE to actually execute the query.

Query Troubleshooting

In the previous section, I introduced you to reading execution plans as the primary tool we will use to interact with the SQL Server query processor. Now I will show you additional basic tuning tools and techniques you can use to find out how much server resources your queries are using and to find the most expensive queries on your system.

Dynamic management views (DMVs) and dynamic management functions (DMFs) were introduced with SQL Server 2005 as great tools to diagnose problems, tune performance, and monitor the health of a server instance. Many DMVs are available, and in this section I will focus on sys.dm_exec_requests, sys.dm_exec_sessions, and sys.dm_exec_query_stats, which you can use to determine the server resources, such as CPU and I/O, used by queries running on the system. They can also be used to find the most expensive queries in your SQL Server instance.

In addition, starting with SQL Server 2016, the query store is an amazing query performance feature that can help you collect historical query and plan information along with their runtime statistics, which you can use to identify query-performance–related problems and even force an existing execution plan.

I will close this section with the SET STATISTICS TIME and SET STATISTICS IO statements, which can provide additional performance information about your queries.

sys.dm_exec_requests and sys.dm_exec_sessions

The sys.dm_exec_requests DMV can be used to display the requests currently executing on SQL Server, whereas sys.dm_exec_sessions shows the authenticated sessions on the instance. Although these DMVs include many columns, in this section, we will focus on the ones related to resource usage and query performance. You can look at the definitions of the other columns within the SQL Server documentation. Both DMVs share several columns, which are defined next:

▶ **cpu_time**   CPU time in milliseconds used by this request or by the requests in this session

▶ **total_elapsed_time**   Total elapsed time in milliseconds since the request arrived or the session was established

▶ **reads**   Number of reads performed by this request or by the requests in this session

▶ **writes**   Number of writes performed by this request or by the requests in this session

▶ **logical_reads**   Number of logical reads performed by this request or by the requests in this session

▶ **row_count**   Number of rows returned to the client by this request

Basically, sys.dm_exec_requests will show the resources used by a specific request currently executing, whereas sys.dm_exec_sessions will show the accumulated resources of all the requests completed by a session. To understand how these two DMVs collect resources' usage information, we can run the following exercise, using a query that takes at least a few seconds. Open a new query in Management Studio and get its session ID (for example, using SELECT @@SPID), but make sure you don't run anything yet, because the resource usage will be accumulated on the sys.dm_exec_sessions DMV. Copy and be ready to run the following code on that window:

```
DBCC FREEPROCCACHE
DBCC DROPCLEANBUFFERS
GO
SELECT * FROM Production.Product p1 CROSS JOIN
Production.Product p2
```

Copy the following code to a second window, replacing @session_id with the value you obtained in the first window:

```
DECLARE @session_id tinyint = 56
SELECT cpu_time, reads, total_elapsed_time, logical_reads, row_count
FROM sys.dm_exec_requests
WHERE session_id = @session_id
SELECT cpu_time, reads, total_elapsed_time, logical_reads, row_count
FROM sys.dm_exec_sessions
WHERE session_id = @session_id
```

Run the query on the first session, and at the same time run the code on the second session several times to see the resources used. The next output shows a sample execution while the query is still running and has not completed yet. Notice that the sys.dm_exec_requests DMV shows the partially used resources and that sys.dm_exec_sessions shows no used resources yet. Most likely, you will not see the same results for sys.dm_exec_requests.

cpu_time	reads	total_elapsed_time	logical_reads	row_count
468	62	4767	5868	1

cpu_time	reads	total_elapsed_time	logical_reads	row_count
0	0	5	0	1

After the query completes, the original request no longer exists and sys.dm_exec_ sessions now records the resources used by the first query:

cpu_time	reads	total_elapsed_time	logical_reads	row_count

cpu_time	reads	total_elapsed_time	logical_reads	row_count
671	62	6996	8192	254016

If you run the query on the first session again, sys.dm_exec_sessions will accumulate the resources used by both executions, so the values of the results will be slightly more than twice their previous values, as shown next:

cpu_time	reads	total_elapsed_time	logical_reads	row_count
cpu_time	reads	total_elapsed_time	logical_reads	row_count
1295	124	14062	16384	254016

Keep in mind that CPU time and duration may vary slightly during different executions, and most likely you will get different values as well. Logical reads is 8,192 for this execution, and we see the accumulated value 16,384 for two executions. In addition, the sys.dm_exec_requests DMV shows information about only currently executing queries, so you may not see this particular data if a query completes before you are able to see it. In summary, sys.dm_exec_requests and sys.dm_exec_sessions are useful to inspect the resources currently used by a request or the accumulation of resources used by requests on a session since creation.

sys.dm_exec_query_stats

If you ever worked with any version of SQL Server prior to SQL Server 2005, you may remember how difficult it was to determine the most expensive queries in your instance. Performing that kind of analysis would usually require running a server trace in your instance for a period of time and then analyzing the collected data, usually in the size of gigabytes, using third-party tools or your own created methods; this was a very time-consuming process. Not to mention the fact that running such a trace could also affect the performance of a system, which most likely is having a performance problem already.

As mentioned, DMVs were introduced with SQL Server 2005 and are a great help to diagnose problems, tune performance, and monitor the health of a server instance. In particular, sys.dm_exec_query_stats provides a rich amount of information not previously available in SQL Server regarding aggregated performance statistics for cached query plans. This information helps you avoid the need to run a trace in most cases. This view returns a row for each statement available in the plan cache, and SQL Server 2008 added enhancements such as the query hash and plan hash values, which will be explained soon.

Let's take a quick look at understanding how sys.dm_exec_query_stats works and the information it provides. Create the following stored procedure with three simple queries:

```
CREATE PROC test
AS
SELECT * FROM Sales.SalesOrderDetail WHERE SalesOrderID = 60677
SELECT * FROM Person.Address WHERE AddressID = 21
SELECT * FROM HumanResources.Employee WHERE BusinessEntityID = 229
```

Run the following code to clean the plan cache (so it is easier to inspect), remove all the clean buffers from the buffer pool, execute the created test stored procedure, and inspect the plan cache. Note that the code uses the sys.dm_exec_sql_text DMF, which requires a sql_handle or plan_handle value, which we are, of course, obtaining from the sys.dm_exec_query_stats DMV, and it returns the text of the SQL batch.

```
DBCC FREEPROCCACHE
DBCC DROPCLEANBUFFERS
GO
EXEC test
GO
SELECT * FROM sys.dm_exec_query_stats
CROSS APPLY sys.dm_exec_sql_text(sql_handle)
WHERE objectid = OBJECT_ID('dbo.test')
```

Examine the output. Because the number of columns is too large to show in this book, only some of the columns are shown next:

statement_ start_offset	statement_ end_offset	execution_ count	total_ worker_time	last_ worker_time	min_ worker_time	max_ worker_time	text
44	168	1	532	532	532	532	CREATE PROC ...
174	270	1	622	622	622	622	CREATE PROC ...
276	406	1	667	667	667	667	CREATE PROC ...

As you can see by looking at the query text, all three queries were compiled as part of the same batch, which we can also verify by validating they have the same plan_handle and sql_handle. The statement_start_offset and statement_end_offset values can be used to identify the particular queries in the batch, a process that will be explained later in this section. You can also see in this output the number of times the query was executed and several columns showing the CPU time used by each query, as total_worker_time, last_worker_time, min_worker_time, and max_worker_time. Should the query be executed more than once, the statistics would show the accumulated CPU time on total_worker_time. Additional performance statistics for physical reads, logical writes, logical reads, CLR time, and elapsed time are also displayed in the previous query but not shown in the book for page space. You can look at the SQL Server documentation online for the entire list of columns, including performance statistics and their documented descriptions.

Keep in mind that this view shows statistics for completed query executions only. You can look at sys.dm_exec_requests for information about queries currently executing. Finally, remember that certain types of execution plans may never be cached, and some cached plans may also be removed from the plan cache for several reasons, including internal or external memory pressure on the plan cache. Information for these plans would therefore not be available on sys.dm_exec_query_stats. Let's now take a look at the statement_start_offset and statement_end_offset values.

statement_start_offset and statement_end_offset

As you can see from the previous output of sys.dm_exec_query_stats, the sql_handle, the plan_handle, and the text column showing the code for the stored procedure are exactly the same in all three records. The same plan and query are used for the entire batch. So how do we identify each of the SQL statements—for example, supposing that only one of them is really expensive? We have to use the statement_start_offset and statement_end_offset columns. statement_start_offset is defined as the starting position of the query that the row describes within the text of its batch, whereas statement_end_offset is the ending position of the query that the row describes within the text of its batch. Both statement_start_offset and statement_end_offset are indicated in bytes, starting with 0, and a value of −1 indicates the end of the batch.

We can easily extend our previous query to inspect the plan cache to use statement_start_offset and statement_end_offset and get something like the following code:

```
DBCC FREEPROCCACHE
DBCC DROPCLEANBUFFERS
GO
EXEC test
GO
SELECT SUBSTRING(text, (statement_start_offset/2) + 1,
((CASE statement_end_offset
WHEN -1
THEN DATALENGTH(text)
ELSE
statement_end_offset
END
- statement_start_offset)/2) + 1) AS statement_text, *
FROM sys.dm_exec_query_stats
CROSS APPLY sys.dm_exec_sql_text(sql_handle)
WHERE objectid = OBJECT_ID('dbo.test')
```

This would produce output similar to the following (only a few columns are shown):

statement_text	statement_start_offset	statement_end_offset
SELECT * FROM Sales.SalesOrderDetail WHERE SalesOrderID = 60677	44	168
SELECT * FROM Person.Address WHERE AddressID = 21	174	270
SELECT * FROM HumanResources.Employee WHERE BusinessEntityID = 229	276	406

Basically, the query makes use of the SUBSTRING function as well as statement_start_offset and statement_end_offset values to obtain the text of the query within the batch. Division by 2 is required because the text data is stored as Unicode. To test the concept for a particular query, you can replace the values for statement_start_offset and statement_end_offset directly for the first statement (44 and 168, respectively) and provide the sql_handle or plan_handle, as shown next, to get the first statement returned:

```
SELECT SUBSTRING(text, 44 / 2 + 1, (168 - 44) / 2 + 1) FROM sys.dm_exec_sql_text(
0x03000500996DB224E0B27201B7A1000001000000000000000000000000000000000000000000000000000)
```

sql_handle and plan_handle

The sql_handle value is a hash value that refers to the batch or stored procedure the query is part of and can be used in the sys.dm_exec_sql_text DMF to retrieve the text of the query, as demonstrated previously. Consider the preceding example:

```
SELECT * from sys.dm_exec_sql_text(0x03000500996DB224E0B27201B
7A1000001000000000000000000000000000000000000000000000000000000)
```

We would get the following in return:

dbid	objectid	number	encrypted	text
5	615673241	1	0	CREATE PROC test AS SELECT * FROM...

The sql_handle hash is guaranteed to be unique for every batch in the system. The text of the batch is stored in the SQL Manager Cache (SQLMGR), which you can inspect by running the following query:

```
SELECT * FROM sys.dm_os_memory_objects WHERE type = 'MEMOBJ_SQLMGR'
```

Since a sql_handle has a 1:N relationship with a plan_handle (that is, there can be more than one generated executed plan for a particular query), the text of the batch will remain on the SQLMGR cache store until the last of the generated plans is evicted from the plan cache. The plan_handle value is a hash value that refers to the execution plan the query is part of and can be used in the sys.dm_exec_query_plan DMF to retrieve such an execution plan. It is guaranteed to be unique for every batch in the system and will remain the same even if one or more statements in the batch are recompiled. Here is an example:

```
SELECT * FROM sys.dm_exec_query_plan(0x05000500996DB224B0C9B
8F80100000001000000000000000000000000000000000000000000000000000000)
```

Running the code will return the following output, and clicking the query_plan link will display the requested graphical execution plan:

dbid	objectid	number	encrypted	query_plan
5	615673241	1	0	`<ShowPlanXML xmlns="http://schemas.microsoft.com/ sqlserver/2004/07/ showplan" ...`

Cached execution plans are stored in the OBJCP and SQLCP cache stores: object plans, including stored procedures, triggers, and functions, are stored in the OBJCP cache stores, whereas plans for ad hoc, auto-parameterized, and prepared queries are stored in the SQLCP cache store.

query_hash and plan_hash

Although the sys.dm_exec_query_stats DMV was a great resource, providing performance statistics for cached query plans when it was introduced in SQL Server 2005, one of its limitations was that it was not easy to aggregate the information for the same query when this query was not parameterized. The query_hash and plan_hash columns, introduced with SQL Server 2008, provide a solution to this problem. To understand the problem, let's look at an example of the behavior of sys.dm_exec_query_stats when a query is auto-parameterized:

```
DBCC FREEPROCCACHE
DBCC DROPCLEANBUFFERS
GO
SELECT * FROM Person.Address
WHERE AddressID = 12
GO
SELECT * FROM Person.Address
WHERE AddressID = 37
GO
SELECT * FROM sys.dm_exec_query_stats
```

Because in this case `AddressID` is part of a unique index, the predicate `AddressID = 12` would always return a maximum of one record, so it is safe for the query optimizer to auto-parameterize the query and use the same plan. Here is the output:

sql_handle	execution_count	query_hash	query_plan_hash
0x020000002D83010497EDC81695B0146B2F0000B7 B2D2 8D19000000000000000000000000000000000000000000	2	0x10E4AFA44470632D	0x1C9E602B6F826BBC

In this case, we have only one plan, reused for the second execution, as shown in the execution_count value. Therefore, we can also see that plan reuse is another benefit of parameterized queries. However, we can see a different behavior with the following query:

```
DBCC FREEPROCCACHE
DBCC DROPCLEANBUFFERS
GO
SELECT * FROM Person.Address
WHERE StateProvinceID = 79
GO
SELECT * FROM Person.Address
WHERE StateProvinceID = 59
GO
SELECT * FROM sys.dm_exec_query_stats
```

Because a filter with an equality comparison on `StateProvinceID` could return zero, one, or more values, it is not considered safe for SQL Server to auto-parameterize the query; in fact, both executions return different execution plans. Here is the output:

sql_handle	query_ hash	query_ plan_hash
0x020000000E311524E986FAF37BD4D922A18E2A758EFF1A2300000000000000000000 0000000000000000000000	0x1891A5DAEB303AE2	0x03D4D190651B0551
0x02000000EBFDF423379C4875CCC482ACD143308C504C72F100000000000000000000 0000000000000000000000	0x1891A5DAEB303AE2	0xAE5E89B0A490F3C9

As you can see, the sql_handle, the plan_handle (not shown), and the query_plan_hash have different values because the generated plans are actually different. However, the query_hash is the same because it is the same query, except with a different parameter. Supposing that this was the most expensive query in the system and there were multiple executions with different parameters, it would be very difficult to find out that all those execution plans actually did belong to the same query. This is where query_hash can help. You can use query_hash to aggregate performance statistics of similar queries that are not explicitly or implicitly parameterized. Both query_hash and plan_hash are available on the sys.dm_exec_query_stats and sys.dm_exec_requests DMVs.

The query_hash value is calculated from the tree of logical operators created after parsing but just before query optimization. This logical tree is used as the input to the query optimizer. Because of this, two or more queries do not need to have exactly the same text to produce the same query_hash value, as parameters, comments, and some other minor differences are not considered. And, as shown in the first example, two queries with the same query_hash value can have different execution plans (that is, different query_plan_hash values). On the other hand, the query_plan_hash is calculated from the tree of physical operators that make up an execution plan. Basically, if two plans are the same, although very minor differences are not considered, they will produce the same plan hash value as well.

Finally, a limitation of the hashing algorithms is that they can cause collisions, but the probability of this happening is extremely low. This basically means that two similar queries may produce different query_hash values or that two different queries may produce the same query_hash value, but again, the probability of this happening is extremely low and it should not be a concern.

Finding Expensive Queries

Let's now apply some of the concepts explained in this section and use the sys.dm_exec_query_stats DMV to find the most expensive queries in your system. A typical query to find the most expensive queries on the plan cache based on CPU is shown next. Notice that the query is grouping on the query_hash value to aggregate similar queries, regardless of whether or not they are parameterized.

```
SELECT TOP 20 query_stats.query_hash,
SUM(query_stats.total_worker_time) / SUM(query_stats.execution_count)
AS avg_cpu_time,
MIN(query_stats.statement_text) AS statement_text
FROM
(SELECT qs.*,
SUBSTRING(st.text, (qs.statement_start_offset/2) + 1,
((CASE statement_end_offset
WHEN -1 THEN DATALENGTH(ST.text)
ELSE qs.statement_end_offset END
- qs.statement_start_offset)/2) + 1) AS statement_text
FROM sys.dm_exec_query_stats qs
CROSS APPLY sys.dm_exec_sql_text(qs.sql_handle) AS st) AS query_stats
GROUP BY query_stats.query_hash
ORDER BY avg_cpu_time DESC
```

You may also notice that each returned row represents a query in a batch (for example, a batch with five queries would have five records on the sys.dm_exec_query_stats DMV, as explained earlier). We could trim the previous query into something like the following query to focus at the batch and plan level instead. Notice that there is no need to use the statement_start_offset and statement_end_offset columns to separate the particular queries and that this time we are grouping on the query_plan_hash value (as opposed to the query_hash value).

```
SELECT TOP 20 query_plan_hash,
SUM(total_worker_time) / SUM(execution_count) AS avg_cpu_time,
MIN(plan_handle) AS plan_handle, MIN(text) AS query_text
FROM sys.dm_exec_query_stats qs
CROSS APPLY sys.dm_exec_sql_text(qs.plan_handle) AS st
GROUP BY query_plan_hash
ORDER BY avg_cpu_time DESC
```

These examples are based on CPU time (worker time). Therefore, in the same way, you can update these queries to look for other resources listed on sys.dm_exec_query_stats, such as physical reads, logical writes, logical reads, CLR time, and elapsed time. Finally, we could also apply the same concept to find the most expensive queries currently executing, based on the sys.dm_exec_requests, as in the following query:

```
SELECT TOP 20 SUBSTRING(st.text, (er.statement_start_offset/2) + 1,
((CASE statement_end_offset
WHEN -1
THEN DATALENGTH(st.text)
ELSE
er.statement_end_offset
END
- er.statement_start_offset)/2) + 1) AS statement_text
, *
FROM sys.dm_exec_requests er
CROSS APPLY sys.dm_exec_sql_text(er.sql_handle) st
ORDER BY total_elapsed_time DESC
```

SET STATISTICS TIME / IO

We close this section with two statements that can give you additional information about your queries and that you can use as an additional tuning technique. These can be a great complement to using execution plans and DMVs to get additional performance information regarding your queries' optimization and execution process. One common misunderstanding I see is developers trying to compare plan cost to plan performance. You should not assume a direct correlation between a query-estimated cost and its actual runtime performance. Cost is an internal unit used by the query optimizer and should not be used to compare plan performance; SET STATISTICS TIME and SET STATISTICS IO can be used instead. This section explains both statements.

You can use SET STATISTICS TIME to see the number of milliseconds required to parse, compile, and execute each statement. For example, run this query:

```
SET STATISTICS TIME ON
```

And then run the following query:

```
SELECT DISTINCT(CustomerID) FROM Sales.SalesOrderHeader
```

To see the output, you will have to look at the Messages tab of the Edit window, which will show an output similar to the following:

```
SQL Server parse and compile time:
    CPU time = 16 ms, elapsed time = 226 ms.
SQL Server Execution Times:
    CPU time = 16 ms,  elapsed time = 148 ms.
```

"Parse and compile" refers to the time SQL Server takes to optimize the SQL statement, as explained earlier. SET STATISTICS TIME will continue to be enabled for any subsequently executed queries. You can disable it like so:

```
SET STATISTICS TIME OFF
```

As suggested previously, parse and compile information can also be seen on the XML execution plan, as in the following:

```
<QueryPlan DegreeOfParallelism="1" CachedPlanSize="16" CompileTime="226" CompileCPU="9"
CompileMemory="232">
```

Obviously, if you only need the execution time of each query, you can see this information in the status bar of the Management Studio Query Editor. SET STATISTICS IO displays the amount of disk activity generated by a query. To enable it, run the following statement:

```
SET STATISTICS IO ON
```

Run this next statement to clean all the buffers from the buffer pool to make sure that no pages for this table are loaded in memory:

```
DBCC DROPCLEANBUFFERS
```

Then run the following query:

```
SELECT * FROM Sales.SalesOrderDetail WHERE ProductID = 870
```

It will show an output similar to the following, which you can see in the Messages pane:

```
Table 'SalesOrderDetail'. Scan count 1, logical reads 1246, physical reads 3, read-ahead
reads 1277, lob logical reads 0, lob physical reads 0, lob read-ahead reads 0.
```

Here are the definitions of these items, which all use 8K pages:

▶ **Logical reads**   Number of pages read from the buffer pool.

▶ **Physical reads**   Number of pages read from disk.

▶ **Read-ahead reads**   Read-ahead is a performance optimization mechanism that anticipates the needed data pages and reads them from disk. It can read up to 64 contiguous pages from one data file.

▶ **Lob logical reads**   Number of large object (LOB) pages read from the buffer pool.

▶ **Lob physical reads**   Number of large object (LOB) pages read from disk.

▶ **Lob read-ahead reads**   Number of large object (LOB) pages read from disk using the read-ahead mechanism.

Now, if you run the same query again, you will no longer get physical and read-ahead reads, and you will get an output similar to this:

```
Table 'SalesOrderDetail'. Scan count 1, logical reads 1246, physical reads 0, read-ahead
reads 0, lob logical reads 0, lob physical reads 0, lob read-ahead reads 0.
```

"Scan count" is defined as the number of seeks or scans started after reaching the leaf level (that is, the bottom level of an index). The only case when scan count will return 0 is when you're seeking for only one value on a unique index, as in the following example:

```
SELECT * FROM Sales.SalesOrderHeader WHERE SalesOrderID = 51119
```

If you try the following query, in which `SalesOrderID` is defined in a nonunique index and can return more than one record, you can see that scan count now returns 1:

```
SELECT * FROM Sales.SalesOrderDetail WHERE SalesOrderID = 51119
```

Finally, in the following example, scan count is 4 because SQL Server has to perform four seeks:

```
SELECT * FROM Sales.SalesOrderHeader
WHERE SalesOrderID IN (51119, 43664, 63371, 75119)
```

Indexes

Indexing is one of the most important techniques used in query tuning and optimization. By using the right indexes, SQL Server can speed up your queries and dramatically improve the performance of your applications. There are several kinds of indexes in SQL Server, so the focus of this section will be on clustered and nonclustered indexes.

SQL Server can use indexes to perform seek and scan operations. Indexes can be used to speed up the execution of a query by quickly finding records without performing table scans, by delivering all the columns requested by the query without accessing the base table (that is, covering the query), or by providing sorted order, which will benefit queries with GROUP BY, DISTINCT, or ORDER BY clauses.

Part of the query optimizer's job is to determine whether an index can be used to resolve a predicate in a query. This is basically a comparison between an index key and a constant or variable. In addition, the query optimizer needs to determine whether the index covers the query—that is, whether the index contains all the columns required by the query (in which case it is referred to as a *covering index*). It needs to confirm this because a nonclustered index usually contains only a subset of the columns of the table.

SQL Server can also consider using more than one index and joining them to cover all the columns required by the query. This operation is called *index intersection*. If it's not possible to cover all of the columns required by the query, SQL Server may need to access the base table, which could be a clustered index or a heap, to obtain the remaining columns. This is called a *bookmark lookup operation* (which could be a Key Lookup or an RID Lookup operation). However, because a bookmark lookup requires random I/O, which is a very expensive operation, its usage can be effective only for a relatively small number of records.

Also keep in mind that although one or more indexes are available for selection, it does not mean that they will finally be selected in an execution plan, as this is always a cost-based decision. So after creating an index, make sure you verify that the index is, in fact, used in a plan, and, of course, verify that your query is performing better, which is probably the primary reason why you are defining an index. An index that is not being used by any query will take up valuable disk space and may negatively affect the performance of update operations without providing any benefit. It is also possible that an index that was useful when it was originally created is no longer used by any query. This could be the result of changes in the database, the data, or even the query itself.

Creating Indexes

Let's start this section with a summary of some basic terminology used in indexes:

▶ **Heap** A heap is a data structure where rows are stored without a specified order. In other words, it is a table without a clustered index.

▶ **Clustered index** In SQL Server, you can have the entire table logically sorted by a specific key in which the bottom, or leaf level, of the index contains the actual data rows of the table. Because of this, only one clustered index per table is possible. The data pages in the leaf level are linked in a doubly linked list (that is, each page has a pointer to the previous and next pages). Both clustered and nonclustered indexes are organized as B-trees.

▶ **Nonclustered index** A nonclustered index row contains the index key values and a pointer to the data row on the base table. Nonclustered indexes can be created on both heaps and clustered indexes. Each table can have up to 999 nonclustered indexes, but usually, you should keep this number to a minimum. A nonclustered index can optionally contain nonkey columns when using the INCLUDE clause, which are particularly useful when covering a query.

▶ **Unique index** As the name suggests, a unique index does not allow two rows of data to have identical key values. A table can have one or more unique indexes, although it should not be very common. By default, unique indexes are created as nonclustered indexes unless you specify otherwise.

▶ **Primary key** A primary key uniquely identifies each record in the table and creates a unique index, which, by default, will also be a clustered index. In addition to the uniqueness property required for the unique index, its key columns are required to be defined as NOT NULL. By definition, only one primary key can be defined on a table.

Although creating a primary key is straightforward, not everybody is aware of the fact that when a primary key is created, by default, it is created using a clustered index. This can be the case, for example, when using the Table Designer in SQL Server Management Studio (Table Designer is accessed when you right-click Tables and select New Table) or when using the CREATE TABLE and ALTER TABLE statements, as shown next. If you run the following code to create a primary key, where the CLUSTERED or NONCLUSTERED keywords are not specified, the primary key will be created using a clustered index:

```
CREATE TABLE table1 (
col1 int NOT NULL,
col2 nchar(10) NULL,
CONSTRAINT PK_table1 PRIMARY KEY(col1))
```

Or

```
CREATE TABLE table1 (
col1 int NOT NULL,
col2 nchar(10) NULL)
GO
ALTER TABLE table1 ADD CONSTRAINT
PK_table1 PRIMARY KEY (col1)
```

The code generated by the Table Designer will explicitly request a clustered index for the primary key, as in the following code (but you usually don't see such code):

```
ALTER TABLE table1 ADD CONSTRAINT
PK_table1 PRIMARY KEY CLUSTERED (col1)
```

Creating a clustered index along with a primary key can have some performance consequences, so it is important that you understand this is the default behavior. Obviously, it is also possible to have a primary key that is a nonclustered index, but this needs to be explicitly specified. Changing the previous code to create a nonclustered index will look like the following statement, where the CLUSTERED clause was changed to NONCLUSTERED:

```
ALTER TABLE table1 ADD CONSTRAINT
PK_table1 PRIMARY KEY NONCLUSTERED (col1)
```

After the preceding code is executed, PK_table1 will be created as a unique nonclustered index. Although the preceding code created an index as part of a constraint definition (in this case, a primary key), most likely, you will be using the

CREATE INDEX statement to define indexes. Next is a simplified version of the CREATE INDEX statement:

```
CREATE [UNIQUE ] [ CLUSTERED | NONCLUSTERED ] INDEX index_name
ON <object> ( column [ ASC | DESC ] [ ,...n ] )
[ INCLUDE ( column_name [ ,...n ] ) ]
[ WHERE <filter_predicate> ]
[ WITH ( <relational_index_option> [ ,...n ] ) ]
```

The UNIQUE clause creates a unique index in which no two rows are permitted to have the same index key value. CLUSTERED and NONCLUSTERED define clustered and nonclustered indexes, respectively. The INCLUDE clause enables you to specify nonkey columns to be added to the leaf level of the nonclustered index. The WHERE <filter_predicate> clause enables you to create a filter index that will also create filtered statistics. Filtered indexes and the INCLUDE clause will be explained in more detail later in this section. The WITH <relational_index_option> clause specifies the options to use when the index is created, such as FILLFACTOR, SORT_IN_TEMPDB, DROP_EXISTING, or ONLINE.

In addition, the ALTER INDEX statement can be used to modify an index and perform operations such as disabling, rebuilding, and reorganizing indexes. The DROP INDEX statement will remove the specified index from the database. Using DROP INDEX with a nonclustered index will remove the index data pages from the database. Dropping a clustered index will not delete the index data but will keep it stored as a heap instead.

As shown in Figure 5-7, a clustered index is organized as a B-tree, which consists of a root node (the top node of the B-tree), leaf nodes (the bottom-level nodes, which contain the data pages of the table), and intermediate levels (the nodes between the root and leaf nodes). To find a specific record on a clustered index B-tree, SQL Server uses the root and intermediate-level nodes to navigate to the leaf node, as the root and intermediate nodes contain index pages and a pointer either to an intermediate-level page or a leaf node page. To put this in perspective, and based on the example in Figure 5-7, with only one intermediate level, SQL Server is required to read three pages to find a specific row. A table with a larger number of records could have more than one intermediate level, requiring SQL Server to read four or more pages to find a row. This is the operation performed by an Index Seek operator, and it is very effective when only one row is required or when a partial scan can be used to satisfy the query.

This operation, however, can be very expensive when it needs to be performed for many records, each one requiring access to at least three pages. This is the problem we usually see when we have a nonclustered index that does not cover the query and needs to look at the clustered index for the remaining columns required by the query.

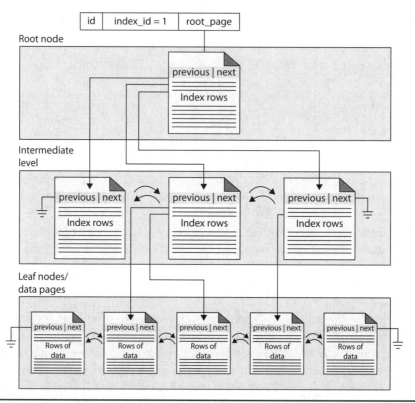

Figure 5-7 *Structure of a clustered index*

In this case, SQL Server has to navigate both the B-trees of the nonclustered and the clustered indexes. The query optimizer places a high cost on these operations, and this is why sometimes when a large number of records are required by the query, SQL Server decides to perform a clustered index scan instead.

Clustered Indexes vs. Heaps

One of the main decisions you have to make while creating a table is whether to use a clustered index or a heap. This is sometimes a topic for debate in the SQL Server community, and there is no right or wrong answer. Although the best solution may depend on your table definition and workload, it is usually recommended that you define each table with a clustered index, and this section will show you why. Let's start with a summary of the advantages and disadvantages of organizing tables as clustered indexes or heaps.

Here are some good reasons to leave a table as a heap:

▶ If the table is very small, a heap is best—although a clustered index could work fine for a small table, too.

▶ If the row identifier (RID) is smaller than a candidate clustered index key, use a heap. Individual rows in a heap are identified by an RID, which is a row locator that includes information such as the database file, page, and slot numbers to allow a specific record to be easily located. An RID uses 8 bytes and, in many cases, could be smaller than a clustered index key. Because every row in every nonclustered index contains the RID or the clustered index key to point to the corresponding record on the base table, a smaller size could greatly benefit the amount of resources used.

You definitely want to use a clustered index in the following cases:

▶ You frequently need to return data in a sorted order or query ranges of data. In this case, you would need to create the clustered index key on the column's desired order. You may need the entire table in a sorted order or only a range of the data. These operations are called *ordered scans* and *partial ordered scans*, respectively.

▶ You frequently need to return data grouped together. In this case, you would need to create the clustered index key on the columns used by the GROUP BY clause. To perform aggregate operations, SQL Server requires sorted data, and if it is not already sorted, a likely expensive sort operation may need to be added to the query plan.

Clustered Index Key

Deciding which column or columns will be part of the clustered index key is also a very important design consideration; they need to be chosen carefully. As a best practice, indexes should be unique, narrow, static, and ever increasing. But remember that as with other general recommendations, this may not apply to all cases, so you should also test thoroughly for your database and workload. Let me explain why these considerations may be important and how they may affect the performance of your database:

▶ **Unique** If a clustered index is not defined using the UNIQUE clause, SQL Server will add a 4-byte uniquifier to each record, increasing the size of the clustered index key. As a comparison, an RID used by nonclustered indexes on heaps is only 8 bytes long.

▶ **Narrow**   As mentioned earlier in this chapter, because every row in every nonclustered index contains, in addition to the columns defining the index, the clustered index key to point to the corresponding row on the base table, a small size key could greatly benefit the amount of resources used. A small key size will require less storage and memory, which will also benefit performance. Again, as a comparison, an RID used by nonclustered indexes on heaps is only 8 bytes long.

▶ **Static or nonvolatile**   Updating a clustered index key can have some performance consequences, such as page splits and fragmentation created by the row relocation within the clustered index. In addition, because every nonclustered index contains the clustered index key, the changing rows in the nonclustered index will have to be updated as well to reflect the new clustered key value.

▶ **Ever increasing**   A clustered index key would benefit of having ever-increasing values instead of having more random values, like in a last name column, for example. Having to insert new rows based on random entry points creates page splits and therefore fragmentation. On the other hand, you need to be aware that in some cases, having ever-increasing values can also cause contention, as multiple processes could be writing on the last page in a table, which could result in locking and latching bottlenecks.

Statistics

The SQL Server query optimizer is a cost-based optimizer; therefore, the quality of the execution plans it generates is directly related to the accuracy of its cost estimations. In the same way, the estimated cost of a plan is based on the algorithms or operators used as well as their cardinality estimations. For this reason, to estimate the cost of an execution plan correctly, the query optimizer needs to estimate, as precisely as possible, the number of records returned by a given query. During query optimization, SQL Server explores many candidate plans, estimates their relative costs, and selects the most efficient one. As such, incorrect cardinality and cost estimation may cause the query optimizer to choose inefficient plans, which can have a negative impact on the performance of your database.

SQL Server creates and maintains statistics to enable the query optimizer to calculate cardinality estimation. A *cardinality estimate* is the estimated number of rows that will be returned by a query or by a specific query operation such as a join or a filter. *Selectivity* is a concept similar to cardinality estimation, which can be described as the fraction of rows in a set that satisfy a predicate, and it is always a value between 0 and 1, inclusive. A highly selective predicate returns a small number of rows.

Creating and Updating Statistics

Statistics are created in several ways: automatically by the query optimizer (if the default option to create statistics automatically, AUTO_CREATE_STATISTICS, is on), when an index is created, and explicitly (for example, via the CREATE STATISTICS statement). Statistics can be created on one or more columns, and both the index and explicit creation methods support single- and multicolumn statistics. However, the statistics that are automatically generated by the query optimizer are always single-column statistics. The components of statistics objects are the histogram, the density information, and the string statistics. Both histograms and string statistics are created only for the first column of a statistics object, and the latter is created only if the column is of a string data type.

Density information is calculated for each set of columns, forming a prefix in the statistics object. Filtered statistics, on the other hand, are not created automatically by the query optimizer, but only when a filtered index is created or when a CREATE STATISTICS statement with a WHERE clause is issued. Both filtered indexes and statistics are a feature introduced in SQL Server 2008.

With the default configuration (AUTO_UPDATE_STATISTICS is on), the query optimizer automatically updates statistics when they are out of date. As noted, the query optimizer does not automatically create multicolumn or filtered statistics, but once they are created, by using any of the methods described earlier, they can be automatically updated. Alternatively, index rebuild operations and statements such as UPDATE STATISTICS can also be used to update statistics. Because both the auto-create and auto-update default choices will give you good quality statistics most of the time, it is strongly recommended that you keep these defaults. Naturally, you also have the choice of using some other statements if you need more control over the quality of the statistics.

So, by default, statistics may be automatically created (if nonexistent) and automatically updated (if out of date) as necessary during query optimization. By "out of date" we refer to the data being changed and therefore the statistics not being representative of the underlying data (more on the exact mechanism later). If an execution plan for a specific query exists in the plan cache and the statistics that were used to build the plan are now out of date, then the plan is discarded, the statistics are updated, and a new plan is created. In a similar way, updating statistics, either manually or automatically, invalidates any existing execution plan that used those statistics, and will cause a new optimization the next time the query is executed.

When it comes to determining the quality of your statistics, a fact to consider is the size of the sample of the target table used to calculate said statistics. The query optimizer determines a statistically significant sample by default when it creates or updates statistics, and the minimum sample size is 8MB (1024 pages) or the size of the table if it's smaller than 8MB. The sample size will increase for bigger tables, but it may still be only a small percentage of the table.

If needed, you can use the CREATE STATISTICS and UPDATE STATISTICS statements to explicitly request a bigger sample or scan the entire table to have better quality statistics. To do that, you need to specify a sample size or use the WITH FULLSCAN option to scan the entire table. A sample size can be specified as a number of rows or a percentage and, because the query optimizer has to scan all the rows on a data page, these values are approximate. Using WITH FULLSCAN or using a larger sample can be of benefit, especially with data that is not randomly distributed throughout the table. Scanning the entire table will naturally give you the most accurate statistics possible. Consider that if statistics are built after scanning 50 percent of a table, then SQL Server will assume that the 50 percent of data that it has not seen is statistically exactly the same as the 50 percent it has seen. In fact, given that statistics are always created alongside a new index, and given that this operation scans the entire table anyway, index statistics are initially created with the equivalent of the WITH FULLSCAN option. However, if the query optimizer needs to update these index statistics automatically, it has to go back to a default sample, because it may take too long to scan the entire table again.

By default, SQL Server needs to wait for the update statistics operation to complete before optimizing and executing the query; that is, statistics are updated synchronously. A database configuration option introduced with SQL Server 2005, AUTO_UPDATE_STATISTICS_ASYNC, can be used to change this default and let the statistics be updated asynchronously. As you might have guessed, with asynchronous statistics update, the query optimizer does not wait for the update statistics operation to complete, and instead just uses the current statistics for the optimization process. This can help in situations where applications experience timeouts caused by delays related to the automatic update of statistics. Although the current optimization will use the out-of-date statistics, they will be updated in the background and will be used by any later query optimization. However, asynchronous statistics updates usually benefit only OLTP workloads and may not be a good solution for more expensive queries, where getting a better plan is more important than an infrequent delay in statistics update.

SQL Server defines when statistics are out of date by using column modification counters, or colmodctrs, which count the total number of modifications for the leading statistics column since the last time statistics were updated. Basically, for tables bigger than 500 rows, a statistics object is considered out of date if the colmodctr value of the leading column has changed by more than 500 plus 20 percent of the number of rows in the table. The same formula is used by filtered statistics, but, because they are built only from a subset of the records of the table, the colmodctr value is first multiplied by the selectivity of the filter. The colmodctrs are exposed in the modification_counter column of the sys.dm_db_stats_properties DMF, which is available starting with SQL Server 2008 R2 Service Pack 2 and SQL Server 2012 Service Pack 1. (Previously, colmodctrs were available only using a dedicated administrator connection and looking at the rcmodified column of the sys.sysrscols base system table in SQL Server 2008 or the sysrowset columns for SQL Server 2005.)

> ### NOTE
>
> *SQL Server 2000 used rowmodctrs, or row modification counters, instead to keep track of the number of changes in a table or index. The main difference between colmodctrs and rowmodctrs is that rowmodctrs track any change to the row, whereas colmodctrs track changes only to the leading column of the statistics object. Currently, the sp_updatestats statement, which is another way to update statistics, is still based on rowmodctrs, whose values are available as the rowmodctr column of the sys.sysindexes compatibility view.*

Trace flag 2371 was introduced with SQL Server 2008 R2 Service Pack 1 as a way to update statistics automatically in a lower and dynamic percentage rate, instead of the mentioned 20 percent threshold. With this dynamic percentage rate, the higher the number of rows in a table, the lower this threshold will become to trigger an automatic update of statistics. Tables with fewer than 25,000 records will still use the 20 percent threshold, but as the number of records in the table increases, this threshold will be lower and lower. For more details about this trace flag, see the article "Changes to Automatic Update Statistics in SQL Server – Traceflag 2371," located at https://blogs.msdn.microsoft.com/saponsqlserver/2011/09/07/changes-to-automatic-update-statistics-in-sql-server-traceflag-2371/.

The density information on multicolumn statistics might improve the quality of execution plans in the case of correlated columns or statistical correlations between columns. As mentioned previously, density information is kept for all the columns in a statistics object, in the order that the columns appear in the statistics definition. By default, SQL Server assumes columns are independent; therefore, if a relationship or dependency exists between columns, multicolumn statistics can help with cardinality estimation problems in queries that are using these columns. Density information will also help on filters and GROUP BY operations. Filtered statistics can also be used for cardinality estimation problems with correlated columns

The New Cardinality Estimator

SQL Server 2014 introduced a new cardinality estimator, and starting with this version, the old cardinality estimator is still available. This section explains what a cardinality estimator is, why a new cardinality estimator was built, and how to enable the new and the old cardinality estimators.

The cardinality estimator is the component of the query processor whose job it is to estimate the number of rows returned by relational operations in a query. This information, along with some other data, is used by the query optimizer to select an efficient execution plan. Cardinality estimation is inherently inexact, because it is a mathematical model that relies on statistical information. It is also based on several assumptions that, although not documented, have been known over the years—some of them include the uniformity, independence, containment, and inclusion assumptions. A brief description of these assumptions follows:

▶ **Uniformity**   Used when the distribution for an attribute is unknown—for example, inside of range rows in a histogram step or when a histogram is not available

▶ **Independence**   Used when the attributes in a relation are independent, unless a correlation between them is known

▶ **Containment**   Used when two attributes might be the same; in this case, they are assumed to be the same

▶ **Inclusion**   Used when comparing an attribute with a constant; it is assumed there is always a match

The current cardinality estimator was written along with the entire query processor for SQL Server 7.0, which was released back in December 1998. Obviously this component has faced multiple changes during several years and multiple releases of SQL Server, including fixes, adjustments, and extensions to accommodate cardinality estimation for new T-SQL features. You may be thinking, why replace a component that has been successfully used for about the last 15 years?

In the 2012 paper "Testing Cardinality Estimation Models in SQL Server" by Campbell Fraser, *et al.*, the authors explain some of the reasons for the redesign of the cardinality estimator, including the following:

▶ It accommodates the cardinality estimator to new workload patterns.

▶ Changes made to the cardinality estimator over the years made the component difficult to "debug, predict, and understand."

▶ Trying to improve on the current model was difficult using the current architecture, so a new design was created, focused on the separation of tasks of deciding how to compute a particular estimate, and actually performing the computation.

I was also surprised to read in the paper that the authors admit that, according to their experience in practice, the previously listed assumptions are "frequently incorrect."

A major concern that comes to mind with such a huge change inside the query optimizer is plan regressions. The fear of plan regressions has been considered the biggest obstacle to query optimizer improvements. Regressions are problems introduced after a fix has been applied to the query optimizer and are sometimes referred to as the classic "two wrongs make a right." This can happen when two bad estimations—for example, one overestimating a value and the second one underestimating it—cancel each other out, luckily giving a good estimate. Correcting only one of these values may lead to a bad estimation, which may negatively impact the choice of plan selection, thus causing a regression.

To help avoid regressions related to the new cardinality estimator, SQL Server provides a way to enable or disable it, depending on the database compatibility level. This can be changed using the ALTER DATABASE statement, as indicated earlier. Setting a database to the compatibility level 120 or greater, depending on the version of SQL Server, will use the new cardinality estimator, whereas a compatibility level less than 120 will use the old cardinality estimator. In addition, once you are using a specific cardinality estimator, there are two trace flags you can use to change to the other. Use trace flag 2312 to enable the new cardinality estimator, and use trace flag 9481 to disable it. You can even use the trace flags for a specific query using the QUERYTRACEON hint. Both trace flags and their use with the QUERYTRACEON hint are documented and supported.

Finally, SQL Server includes several new extended events you can use to troubleshoot problems with cardinality estimation, or just to explore how it works. These events include query_optimizer_estimate_cardinality, inaccurate_cardinality_estimate, query_optimizer_force_both_cardinality_estimation_behaviors, and query_rpc_set_cardinality.

Cardinality Estimation Errors

Cardinality estimation errors can lead to the query optimizer making poor choices as to how best to execute a query and, therefore, to badly performing execution plans. Fortunately, you can easily check whether you have cardinality estimation errors by comparing the estimation against the actual number of rows, as shown in graphical or XML execution plans, or by using the SET STATISTICS PROFILE statement. In the next query, I show you how to use the SET STATISTICS PROFILE statement, where SQL Server is making a blind guess regarding the selectivity of certain columns:

```
SET STATISTICS PROFILE ON
GO
SELECT * FROM Sales.SalesOrderDetail
WHERE OrderQty * UnitPrice > 10000
GO
SET STATISTICS PROFILE OFF
GO
```

This is the resulting output, with the EstimateRows column manually moved just after the Rows column and edited to fit the page:

```
Rows    EstimateRows StmtText
------  ------------ -------------------------------------------------------
772     36395.1      SELECT * FROM [Sales].[SalesOrderDetail] WHERE [Or
772     36395.1      |--Filter(WHERE:([Expr1003]>($10000.0000)))
0       121317           |--Compute Scalar(DEFINE:([AdventureWorks20
0       121317               |--Compute Scalar(DEFINE:([AdventureWo
121317  121317                   |--Clustered Index Scan(OBJECT:([
```

Using this output, you can easily compare the actual number of rows, shown on the Rows column, against the estimated number of records, shown on the EstimateRows column, for each operator in the plan. Introduced with SQL Server 2012, the `inaccurate_cardinality_estimate` extended event can also be used to detect inaccurate cardinality estimates by identifying which query operators output significantly more rows than those estimated by the query optimizer.

Because each operator relies on previous operations for its input, cardinality estimation errors can propagate exponentially throughout the query plan. For example, a cardinality estimation error on a Filter operator can impact the cardinality estimation of all the other operators in the plan that consume the data produced by that operator. If your query is not performing well and you find cardinality estimation errors, check for problems such as missing or out-of-date statistics, very small samples being used, correlation between columns, use of scalar expressions, guessing selectivity issues, and so on.

Recommendations to help with these issues may include topics such as using the auto-create and auto-update statistics default configurations, updating statistics using WITH FULLSCAN, avoiding local variables in queries, avoiding nonconstant-foldable or complex expressions on predicates, using computed columns, and considering multicolumn or filtered statistics, among other things. In addition, parameter-sniffing and parameter-sensitive queries are covered in more detail in the next section. That's a fairly long list, but it should help convince you that you are already armed with pragmatically useful information.

Some SQL Server features, such as table variables, have no statistics, so you might want to consider instead using a temporary table or a standard table if you're having performance problems related to cardinality estimation errors. Multistatement table-valued user-defined functions have no statistics either. In this case, you can consider using a temporary table or a standard table as a temporary holding place for their results. In both these cases (table variables and multistatement table-valued user-defined functions), the query optimizer will guess at one row (which has been updated to 100 rows for multistatement table-valued user-defined functions in SQL Server 2014).

In addition, for complex queries that are not performing well because of cardinality estimation errors, you may want to consider breaking down the query into two or more steps while storing the intermediate results in temporary tables. This will enable SQL Server to create statistics on the intermediate results, which will help the query optimizer to produce a better execution plan. More details about breaking down complex queries is covered at the end of this chapter.

> **NOTE**
>
> *Trace flag 2453, available starting with SQL Server 2012 Service Pack 2, can be used to provide better cardinality estimation while using table variables. For more details, see https://support.microsoft.com/kb/2952444.*

Statistics Maintenance

As mentioned, the query optimizer will, by default, automatically update statistics when they are out of date. Statistics can also be updated with the UPDATE STATISTICS statement, which you can schedule to run as a maintenance job. Another statement commonly used, sp_updatestats, also runs UPDATE STATISTICS behind the scenes.

There are two important benefits of updating statistics in a maintenance job. The first is that your queries will use updated statistics without having to wait for the automatic update of statistics to be completed, thus avoiding delays in the optimization of your queries (although asynchronous statistics updates can also be used to partially help with this problem). The second benefit is that you can use a bigger sample than the query optimizer will use, or you can even scan the entire table. This can give you better quality statistics for big tables, especially for those where data is not randomly distributed in their data pages. Manually updating statistics can also be a benefit after operations such as batch data loads, which update large amounts of data, are performed.

On the other hand, note that the update of statistics will cause a recompiling of plans already in the plan cache that are using these statistics, so you may not want to update statistics too frequently, either.

An additional consideration for manually updating statistics in a maintenance job is how they relate to index rebuild maintenance jobs, which also update the index statistics. Keep the following items in mind when combining maintenance jobs for both indexes and statistics, remembering that there are both index and nonindex column statistics and that index operations obviously may impact only the first of these:

▶ Rebuilding an index (for example, by using the ALTER INDEX ... REBUILD statement) will also update index statistics by scanning all the rows in the table, which is the equivalent of using UPDATE STATISTICS WITH FULLSCAN. Rebuilding indexes does not update any column statistics.

► Reorganizing an index (for example, using the `ALTER INDEX … REORGANIZE` statement) does not update any statistics, not even index statistics.

► By default, the `UPDATE STATISTICS` statement updates both index and column statistics. Using the `INDEX` option will update index statistics only, and using the `COLUMNS` option will update nonindexed column statistics only.

Therefore, depending on your maintenance jobs and scripts, several scenarios can exist. The simplest maintenance plan is if you want to rebuild all the indexes and update all the statistics. As mentioned, if you rebuild all your indexes, then all the index statistics will also be automatically updated by scanning all the rows in the table. Then you just need to update your nonindexed column statistics by running `UPDATE STATISTICS WITH FULLSCAN, COLUMNS`. Because the index rebuild job updates only index statistics, and the second one updates only column statistics, it does not matter which one is executed first.

Of course, more complicated maintenance plans can exist—for example, when indexes are rebuilt or reorganized depending on their fragmentation level. You should keep in mind the items mentioned previously so that you can avoid problems such as updating the index statistics twice, which could occur when both index rebuild and update statistics operations are performed. You should also avoid discarding previously performed work—for example, when you rebuild the indexes of a table, which also updates statistics by scanning the entire table—and later running a job updating the statistics with a default or smaller sample. In this case, previously updated statistics are replaced with statistics that have potentially less quality.

NOTE

I strongly recommend Ola Hallengren's "SQL Server Maintenance Solution" for backups, integrity checks, and index and statistics maintenance. You can find this solution at https://ola.hallengren.com.

Parameter Sniffing

SQL Server can use the histogram of statistics objects to estimate the cardinality of a query and then use this information to try to produce an optimal execution plan. The query optimizer accomplishes this by first inspecting the values of the query parameters. This behavior, called *parameter sniffing*, is a very good thing: getting an execution plan tailored to the current parameters of a query naturally improves the performance of your applications. The plan cache can store these execution plans so that they can be reused the next time the same query needs to be executed. This saves optimization time and CPU resources because the query does not need to be optimized again.

However, although the query optimizer and the plan cache work well together most of the time, some performance problems can occasionally appear. Given that the query optimizer can produce different execution plans for syntactically identical queries, depending on their parameters, caching and reusing only one of these plans may create a performance issue for alternative instances of this query that would benefit from a better plan. This is a known problem with T-SQL code using explicit parameterization, such as stored procedures. In this section, I'll show you more details about this problem, along with a few recommendations on how to fix it.

To see an example, let's write a simple stored procedure using the Sales .SalesOrderDetail table on the AdventureWorks database.

```
CREATE PROCEDURE test (@pid int)
AS
SELECT * FROM Sales.SalesOrderDetail
WHERE ProductID = @pid
```

Run the following statement to execute the stored procedure requesting the actual execution plan:

```
EXEC test @pid = 897
```

The query optimizer estimates that only a few records will be returned by this query, and it produces the execution plan shown in Figure 5-8, which uses an Index Seek operator to quickly find the records on an existing nonclustered index, and a Key Lookup operator to search on the base table for the remaining columns requested by the query.

This combination of Index Seek and Key Lookup operators was a good choice, because, although it's a relatively expensive combination, the query was highly selective. However, what if a different parameter is used, producing a less selective predicate? For example, try the following query, including a SET STATISTICS IO ON statement to display the amount of disk activity generated by the query:

```
SET STATISTICS IO ON
GO
EXEC test @pid = 870
GO
```

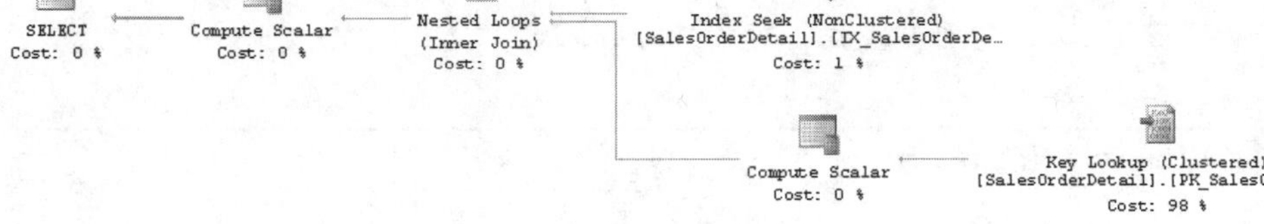

Figure 5-8 *Plan using Index Seek and Key Lookup operators*

The Messages tab will show the following output:

```
Table 'SalesOrderDetail'. Scan count 1, logical reads 18038, physical reads 57, read-
ahead reads 447, lob logical reads 0, lob physical reads 0, lob read-ahead reads 0.
```

As you can see, on this execution alone, SQL Server is performing 18,038 logical reads when the base table has only 1246 pages; therefore, it's using more than 14 times more I/O operations than just simply scanning the entire table. The reason for this difference is that performing Index Seeks plus Key Lookups on the base table, which uses random I/Os, is a very expensive operation. Note that you may get slightly different values in your own copy of the AdventureWorks database.

Now clear the plan cache to remove the execution plan currently held in memory and then run the stored procedure again, using the same parameter, as shown next:

```
DBCC FREEPROCCACHE
GO
EXEC test @pid = 870
GO
```

This time, you'll get a totally different execution plan. The I/O information now will show that only 1246 pages were read, and the execution plan will include a Clustered Index Scan, as shown in Figure 5-9. Because this time, there was not a plan for the stored procedure in the plan cache, SQL Server optimized it from scratch using the new parameter and created a new optimal execution plan.

Of course, this doesn't mean you're not supposed to trust your stored procedures any more or that maybe all your code is incorrect. This is just a problem that you need to be aware of and research, especially if you have queries where performance changes dramatically when different parameters are introduced. If you happen to have this problem, you have a few choices available, which we'll explore next.

Another related problem is that you don't have control over the lifetime of a plan in the cache, so every time a plan is removed from the cache, the newly created execution plan may depend on whichever parameter happens to be passed next. Some of the following choices enable you to have a certain degree of plan stability by asking the query optimizer to produce a plan based on a typical parameter or the average column density.

Figure 5-9   *Plan using a Clustered Index Scan*

Optimizing for a Typical Parameter

There might be cases when most of the executions of a query use the same execution plan and you want to avoid an ongoing optimization cost by reusing that plan. In these cases, you can use a hint introduced with SQL Server 2005 called OPTIMIZE FOR, which is useful when an optimal plan can be generated for the majority of values used in a specific parameter and in addition can provide more plan stability. As a result, only the few executions using an atypical parameter may not have an optimal plan.

Suppose that almost all the executions of our stored procedure would benefit from the previous plan using an Index Seek and a Key Lookup operator. To take advantage of that, you could write the stored procedure as shown next:

```
ALTER PROCEDURE test (@pid int)
AS
SELECT * FROM Sales.SalesOrderDetail
WHERE ProductID = @pid
OPTION (OPTIMIZE FOR (@pid = 897))
```

When you run the stored procedure for the first time, it will be optimized for the value 897, no matter what parameter value was actually specified for the execution. If you want to check, test the case by running the following:

```
EXEC test @pid = 870
```

You can find the following entry close to the end of the XML plan (or the Parameter List property of the root node in a graphical plan):

```
<ParameterList>
          <ColumnReference Column="@pid" ParameterCompiledValue="(897)"
                ParameterRuntimeValue="(870)" />
 </ParameterList>
```

This entry clearly shows which parameter value was used during optimization and which one was used during execution. In this case, the stored procedure is optimized only once, and the plan is stored in the plan cache and reused as many times as needed. The benefit of using this hint, in addition to avoiding optimization cost, is that you have total control over which plan is produced during the query optimization and stored in the plan cache. The OPTIMIZE FOR query hint can also enable you to use more than one parameter, separated by commas.

Optimizing on Every Execution

If using different parameters produces different execution plans and you want the best performance for every query, the solution might be to optimize for every execution. You will get the best possible plan on every execution but will end up paying for the optimization cost, so you'll need to decide if that's a worthwhile trade-off. To do this, use the RECOMPILE hint, as shown next:

```
ALTER PROCEDURE test (@pid int)
AS
SELECT * FROM Sales.SalesOrderDetail
WHERE ProductID = @pid
OPTION (RECOMPILE)
```

Using OPTION (RECOMPILE) can also allow the values of local variables to be sniffed, as shown in the next section.

Using Local Variables and the OPTIMIZE FOR UNKNOWN Hint

Another solution that has been traditionally implemented in the past is the use of local variables in queries instead of parameters. The query optimizer is not able to see the values of local variables at optimization time because these values are known only at execution time. However, by using local variables, you are disabling parameter sniffing, which basically means that the query optimizer will not be able to access the statistics histogram to find an optimal plan for the query. Instead, it will rely on just the density information of the statistics object.

This solution will simply ignore the parameter values and use the same execution plan for all the executions, but at least you're getting a consistent plan every time. A variation of the OPTIMIZE FOR hint is the OPTIMIZE FOR UNKNOWN hint. This hint was introduced with SQL Server 2008 and has the same effect as using local variables. A benefit of the OPTIMIZE FOR UNKNOWN hint compared with OPTIMIZE FOR is that it does not require you to specify a value for a parameter. Also, you don't have to worry if a specified value becomes atypical over time.

Running the following two versions of our stored procedure will have equivalent outcomes and will produce the same execution plan. The first version uses local variables, and the second one uses the OPTIMIZE FOR UNKNOWN hint.

```
ALTER PROCEDURE test (@pid int)
AS
DECLARE @p int = @pid
SELECT * FROM Sales.SalesOrderDetail
WHERE ProductID = @p

ALTER PROCEDURE test (@pid int)
AS
```

```
SELECT * FROM Sales.SalesOrderDetail
WHERE ProductID = @pid
OPTION (OPTIMIZE FOR UNKNOWN)
```

In this case, the query optimizer will create the plan using the Clustered Index Scan shown previously, no matter which parameter you use to execute the stored procedure. Note that the OPTIMIZE FOR UNKNOWN query hint will apply to all the parameters used in a query unless you use the following syntax to target only a specific parameter:

```
ALTER PROCEDURE test (@pid int)
AS
SELECT * FROM Sales.SalesOrderDetail
WHERE ProductID = @pid
OPTION (OPTIMIZE FOR (@pid UNKNOWN))
```

Finally, keep in mind that parameter sniffing is a desired optimization, and you would want to disable it only when you have any of the problems mentioned in this section and if it improves the general performance of your query.

It is interesting to note that as of SQL Server 2005, where statement-level compilation was introduced to allow the optimization of an individual statement, it was technically possible to sniff the value of local variables in the same way as with a parameter. However, this behavior was not implemented because there was already a lot of code using local variables to explicitly disable parameter sniffing. Local variables, however, can be sniffed while using the RECOMPILE query hint. For example, let's use the following code with both local variables and the OPTION (RECOMPILE) hint:

```
ALTER PROCEDURE test (@pid int)
AS
DECLARE @p int = @pid
SELECT * FROM Sales.SalesOrderDetail
WHERE ProductID = @p
OPTION (RECOMPILE)
```

And then run the following:

```
EXEC test @pid = 897
```

The query optimizer will be able to see the value of the local variable (in this case, 897) and get a plan optimized for that specific value (in this case, the plan with the Index Seek/Key Lookup operations, instead of the plan with the Clustered Index Scan, shown earlier when no value could be sniffed). Finally, the benefit of using the OPTIMIZE FOR UNKNOWN hint is that you need to optimize the query only once and can reuse the produced plan many times. Also, there is no need to specify a value like in the OPTIMIZE FOR hint.

Disabling Parameter Sniffing

As mentioned, when you use local variables in a query to avoid using a stored procedure parameter or when you use the OPTIMIZE FOR UNKNOWN query hint, you are basically disabling parameter sniffing. Microsoft has also published trace flag 4136 to disable parameter sniffing at the instance level. As described in the Microsoft Knowledge Base article 980653 at https://support.microsoft.com/en-us/help/980653/sql-server-2008-r2-cu2-sql-server-2008-sp1-cu7-and-sql-server-2005-sp3, this trace flag was first introduced as a cumulative update for older versions of SQL Server such as SQL Server 2005 SP3, SQL Server 2008 SP1, and SQL Server 2008 R2, and it is available on the latest versions as well, including SQL Server 2017. There are still three cases where this trace flag has no effect:

▶ Queries using the OPTIMIZE FOR query hint

▶ Queries using the OPTION (RECOMPILE) hint

▶ Queries in a stored procedure using the WITH RECOMPILE option

As with using forced parameterization at the database level, you should consider this an extreme option that can be used only on some limited cases and should be used with caution; make sure you test your application thoroughly to validate that, in fact, it improves performance. In addition, you could use this trace flag if the majority of your queries benefit from disabling parameter sniffing and still use any of the three exceptions listed for queries that may not. Microsoft has recommended that users of their Dynamics AX application consider using this trace flag, as documented at https://blogs.msdn.com/b/axperf/archive/2010/05/07/important-sql-server-change-parameter-sniffing-and-plan-caching.aspx.

I will continue talking about parameter sniffing in the next chapter covering related features from the last two SQL Server releases.

Query Processor Limitations

Query optimization is an inherently complex problem, not only for SQL Server, but also for any other relational database system. Despite the fact that query optimization research dates back to the early 1970s, challenges in some fundamental areas are still being addressed today. The first major impediment to a query optimizer finding an optimal plan is the fact that, for many queries, it is just not possible to explore the entire search space. An effect known as *combinatorial explosion* makes this exhaustive enumeration impossible, because the number of possible plans grows very rapidly, depending on the number of tables joined in the query. To make the search a manageable process, heuristics are used to limit the search space (that is, the number of possible plans to be considered), as mentioned earlier in this chapter. However, if a query optimizer is not able to explore the entire search space, there is no way to prove that you can get an absolutely optimal plan, or even that the best plan is among the candidates being considered, whether it is selected or not. As a result, it is clearly extremely important that the set of plans a query optimizer considers contains plans with low costs.

This leads us to another major technical challenge for the query optimizer: accurate cost and cardinality estimation. Because a cost-based optimizer selects the execution plan with the lowest estimated cost, the quality of the plan selection is only as good as the accuracy of the optimizer's cost and cardinality estimations. Even supposing that time is not a concern and that the query optimizer can analyze the entire search space without a problem, cardinality and cost estimation errors can still make a query optimizer select a nonoptimal plan. Cost estimation models are inherently inexact because they do not consider all the hardware conditions, and they must necessarily make certain assumptions about the environment. For example, the costing model assumes that every query starts with a cold cache (that is, that its data is read from disk and not from memory), and this assumption could lead to costing estimation errors in some cases.

In addition, cost estimation relies on cardinality estimation, which is also inexact and has some known limitations, especially when it comes to the estimation of the intermediate results in a plan. Errors in intermediate results in effect get magnified as more tables are joined and more estimation errors are included within the calculations. On top of all that, some operations are not covered by the mathematical model of the cardinality estimation component, which means the query optimizer has to resort to guess logic or heuristics to deal with these situations.

NOTE

As covered earlier in this chapter, SQL Server 2014 has introduced a new cardinality estimator to help improve the accuracy and supportability of the cardinality estimation process.

Query Optimization Research

Query optimization research dates back to the early 1970s. One of the earliest works describing a cost-based query optimizer was "Access Path Selection in a Relational Database Management System," published in 1979 by Pat Selinger, *et al.*, to describe the query optimizer for an experimental database management system developed in 1975 at what is now the IBM Almaden Research Center. This database management system, called "System R," advanced the field of query optimization by introducing the use of cost-based query optimization, the use of statistics, as an efficient method of determining join orders and the addition of CPU cost to the optimizer's cost estimation formulas.

Yet despite being an enormous influence in the field of query optimization research, it suffered a major drawback: its framework could not be easily extended to include additional transformations. This led to the development of more extensible optimization architectures, which facilitated the gradual addition of new functionality to query optimizers. The trailblazers in this field were the Exodus Optimizer Generator, defined by Goetz Graefe and David DeWitt, and, later, the Volcano Optimizer Generator, defined by Goetz Graefe and William McKenna. Graefe then went on to define the Cascades Framework, resolving errors that were present in his previous two endeavors.

What is most relevant for us about this research is that SQL Server implemented a new cost-based query optimizer, based on the Cascades Framework, in 1999, when its database engine was rearchitected for the release of SQL Server 7.0. The extensible architecture of the Cascades Framework has made it much easier for new functionality, such as new transformation rules or physical operators, to be implemented in the query optimizer.

Break Down Complex Queries

In some cases, the SQL Server query optimizer may not be able to produce a good plan for a query with a large number of joins. The same is true for complex queries with both joins and aggregations. However, because it is rarely necessary to request all the data in a single query, a good solution for those cases could be to break down a large and complex query into two or more simpler queries while storing the intermediate results in temporary tables. Breaking down complex queries this way offers several advantages:

► **Better plans** Query performance is improved because the query optimizer is able to create efficient plans for simpler queries.

► **Better statistics** Because one of the problems of some complex plans is the degradation of intermediate statistics, breaking down these queries and storing the aggregated or intermediate results in temporary tables enables SQL Server to create new statistics, greatly improving the cardinality estimation of the remaining queries. It is worth noticing that temporary tables should be used and not table variables, as the latter do not have statistics support.

► **No hints required** Because using hints is a common practice to fix problems with complex plans, breaking down the query enables the query optimizer to create an efficient plan without requiring hints. This has the additional benefit, in that the query optimizer can automatically react to future data or schema changes. On the other hand, a query using hints would require future maintenance, because the hint used may no longer be helpful or may even impact its performance in a negative way after such changes. Hints, which should be used only as a last resort when no other solution is available, are covered later in this chapter.

In the paper "When to Break Down Complex Queries," which you can find at https://blogs.msdn.microsoft.com/sqlcat/2013/09/09/when-to-break-down-complex-queries, the author describes several problematic query patterns for which the SQL Server query optimizer is not able to create good plans. Although the paper was published in October 2011 and indicates that it applies to versions from SQL Server 2005 to SQL Server code-named "Denali," I was still able to see the same behavior in the most recent versions of SQL Server.

Hints

SQL is a declarative language; it defines only what data to retrieve from the database. It doesn't describe the manner in which the data should be fetched. That, as we know, is the job of the query optimizer, which analyzes a number of candidate execution plans for a given query, estimates the cost of each of these plans, and selects an efficient plan by choosing the cheapest of the choices considered.

But there may be cases when the execution plan selected is not performing as you have expected and, as part of your query troubleshooting process, you may try to find a better plan yourself. Before doing this, keep in mind that just because your query does not perform as you expected, this does not mean a better plan is always possible. Your plan may be an efficient one, but the query may be an expensive one to perform, or your system may be experiencing performance bottlenecks that are impacting the query execution.

However, although the query optimizer does an excellent job most of the time, it does occasionally fail to produce an efficient plan. That being said, even in cases when you're not getting an efficient plan, you should try to distinguish between those times when the problems arise because you're not providing the query optimizer with all the information it needs to do a good job and those times when the problems are a result of a query optimizer limitation. Part of the focus of this chapter has been to help you to provide the query optimizer with the information it needs to produce an efficient execution plan, such as the right indexes and good quality statistics, and also how to troubleshoot the cases when you are not getting a good plan.

Having said that, there might be cases when the query optimizer just gets it wrong, and because of that we may be forced to resort to hints. Hints are essentially optimizer directives that enable us to take explicit control over the execution plan for a given query, with the goal of improving its performance. In reaching for a hint, however, we are going against the declarative property of the SQL language and, instead, giving direct instructions to the query optimizer. Overriding the query optimizer is risky business; hints need to be used with caution and only as a last resort when no other option is available to produce a viable plan.

When to Use Hints

Hints are a powerful means by which we can cause our decisions to overrule those of the query optimizer. However, you should do so with extreme caution, because hints restrict the choices available to the query optimizer. They also make your code less flexible and will require additional maintenance. A hint should be employed only once you're certain you have no alternative options. At a minimum, before you reach for a hint, you should explore these potential issues:

▶ **System problems**   Make sure your performance problem is not linked to other system-related issues, such as blocking or bottlenecks in server resources such as I/O, memory, and CPU.

▶ **Cardinality estimation errors**   The query optimizer often misses the correct plan because of cardinality estimation errors. Cardinality estimation errors can sometimes be fixed by solutions such as updating statistics, using a bigger sample for your statistics (or scanning the entire table); using computed columns, multicolumn statistics, or filtered statistics; and so on. There might be cases where the cardinality estimation errors are caused by the use of features in which statistics are not supported at all, such as table variables and multistatement table-valued user-defined functions. In these particular instances, you may consider using standard or temporary tables if you are not getting an efficient plan.

▶ **Additional troubleshooting**   You may need to perform additional troubleshooting before considering the use of hints. One of the obvious choices for improving the performance of your queries is providing the query optimizer with the right indexes. You might also consider some other, less obvious, troubleshooting procedures, such as breaking your query down into steps or smaller pieces and storing any intermediate results in temporary tables, as shown earlier in this chapter. You can use this method just as a troubleshooting procedure—for example, to find out which part of the original query is expensive so you can focus on it. Alternatively, you can keep it as the final version of your query if these changes alone give you better performance.

Query optimizers have improved radically after more than 30 years of research, but they still face some technical challenges. The SQL Server query optimizer will give you an efficient execution plan for most of your queries, but it will be increasingly challenged as the complexity of the query grows with more tables joined, plus the use of aggregations and other SQL features. If, after investigating the troubleshooting options and recommendations described previously, you still determine that the query optimizer is not finding a good execution plan for your query, you may need to consider using hints to direct the query optimizer toward what you believe is the optimal execution path.

Always remember that, by applying a hint, you effectively disable some of the available transformation rules to which the query optimizer usually has access and thus restrict the available search space. Only transformation rules that help to achieve the requested plan will be executed. For example, if you use hints to force a particular join order, the query optimizer will disable rules that reorder joins. Always try to use the least restrictive hint, because this will retain as much flexibility as possible in your query and make maintenance somewhat easier. In addition, hints cannot be used to generate an invalid plan or a plan that the query optimizer normally would not consider during query optimization.

Furthermore, a hint that initially does a great job might actively hinder performance at a later point in time when some conditions change—for example, as a result of schema updates, service packs, new versions of SQL Server, or even enough data changes. The hints may prevent the query optimizer from modifying the execution plan accordingly, and thus result in degraded performance. It is your responsibility to monitor and maintain your hinted queries to make sure they continue to perform well after such system changes or to remove those hints if they are no longer needed.

Also, remember that if you decide to use a hint to change a single section or physical operator of a plan, then after you apply the hint, the query optimizer will perform a completely new optimization. The query optimizer will obey your hint during the optimization process, but it still has the flexibility to change everything else in the plan, so the end result of your tweaking may be unintended changes to other sections of the plan. Finally, note that the fact that your query is not performing as you hoped does not always mean that the query optimizer is not giving you a good enough execution plan. If the operation you are performing is simply expensive and resource intensive, then it's possible that no amount of tuning or hinting will help you achieve the performance you would like.

Types of Hints

SQL Server provides a wide range of hints, which can be classified as follows:

- ▶ **Query hints** Tell the optimizer to apply the hint throughout the entire query. They are specified using the OPTION clause, which is included at the end of the query.

- ▶ **Join hints** Apply to a specific join in a query and can be specified by using ANSI-style join hints.

- ▶ **Table hints** Apply to a single table and are usually included using the WITH keyword in the FROM clause.

Another useful classification is dividing hints into physical operator and goal-oriented hints:

- ▶ **Physical operator hints**   Request the use of a specific physical operator, join order, or aggregation placement. Most of the available hints are physical hints.

- ▶ **Goal-oriented hints**   Do not specify how to build the plan, but instead specify a goal to achieve, leaving the query optimizer to find the best physical operators to achieve that goal. Goal-oriented hints are usually safer and require less knowledge about the internal workings of the query optimizer. Examples of goal-oriented hints include the OPTIMIZER FOR and FAST N hints.

NOTE

Locking hints do not affect plan selection, so they are not covered here.

Summary

This chapter provided a quick introduction to query tuning and optimization. This material should be helpful for every database professional, and it also provides the background you may need to understand the following chapters of the book, which focus on new features in SQL Server 2017, especially those related to query processing topics.

The chapter started with a foundation into the architecture of the query processor, explaining its components and describing the work it performs. There are multiple tools to troubleshoot query performance, and this chapter covered execution plans, several useful DMVs and DMFs, and the SET STATISTICS TIME and SET STATISTICS IO statements. Some other important tools and features, such as the query store, extended events, and SQL trace, were mentioned but were not in scope for the chapter. A basic introduction to indexes, statistics, and parameter sniffing was provided as well, closing with the coverage of query processor limitations and hints.

In the next chapter, I will cover adaptive query processing, automatic tuning, and some other query processing–related topics, all new with SQL Server 2017.

Chapter 6

New Query Processing Features

In This Chapter

- ▶ Adaptive Query Processing
- ▶ Automatic Tuning
- ▶ SQL Server 2016 Service Pack 1
- ▶ USE HINT Query Option
- ▶ CXPACKET and CXCONSUMER Waits
- ▶ Wait Statistics on Execution Plans
- ▶ Recent Announcements
- ▶ Summary

Chapter 5 provided an introduction to SQL Server query tuning and optimization. This material is required reading for all SQL Server professionals and was intended to serve as a foundation for the contents of this chapter. The information in Chapter 5 is applicable to all the previous versions of SQL Server.

In this chapter, I will cover what is new in query processing in SQL Server 2017. In addition, a lot of new features were released early with SQL Server 2016 Service Pack 1. I don't remember a previous SQL Server service pack bringing so many changes and new features, so I will cover some of them briefly here as well.

Undoubtedly, the most important change brought by SQL Server 2016 Service Pack 1 was that, for the first time in SQL Server history, it provided a consistent programmability surface area for developers across all SQL Server editions. As a result, previously Enterprise Edition–only features, such as columnstore indexes, In-Memory OLTP, always encrypted, compression, partitioning, database snapshots, row-level security, and dynamic data masking, among others, were made available on all SQL Server editions, such as Express, Web, Standard, and Enterprise.

Most of this chapter, however, will focus on the most important query processing innovations in SQL Server 2017: adaptive query processing and automatic tuning. Adaptive query processing offers a new generation of query processing features that enable the query optimizer to make runtime adjustments to statistics and execution plans and discover additional information that can lead to better query performance. Several features were released with SQL Server 2017, and more are promised to be released in the future. Automatic tuning is a very ambitious feature that offers automatic detection and fixes for plan regressions. Another feature, automatic index management, which is available only in Azure SQL Database, lets you create recommended indexes automatically or drop indexes that are no longer used.

In addition to these features, SQL Server 2017 includes other benefits, such as the ability to resume online index rebuild operations; new DMVs such as sys.dm_db_stats_histogram, sys.dm_os_host_info, and sys.dm_db_log_info; support for LOB columns on clustered columnstore indexes; and improvements on In-Memory OLTP, the query store, and the Database Engine Tuning Advisor (DTA) tool. Resumable online index rebuilds can be useful to resume online index rebuild operations after a failure or to pause them manually and then resume for maintenance reasons. The sys.dm_db_stats_histogram DMV returns the statistics histogram for the specified database object, similar to the DBCC SHOW_STATISTICS statement. The sys.dm_os_host_info DMV has been added to return operating system information for both Windows and Linux. Finally, the sys.dm_db_log_info can be used to return virtual log file (VLF) information similar to the DBCC LOGINFO statement.

This chapter will also cover a few other query processing features released in SQL Server in the last few months, including some that are included in SQL Server 2016 Service Pack 1.

Adaptive Query Processing

Adaptive query processing provides a new generation of query processing improvements for SQL Server that enables the query optimizer to make runtime adjustments to statistics and execution plans and discover additional information that can lead to better query performance. For the SQL Server 2017 initial release, adaptive query processing includes the following algorithms:

- Batch mode adaptive joins
- Batch mode adaptive memory grant feedback
- Interleaved execution for multistatement table value functions

Microsoft has also mentioned that more features will be added in the future, including adaptive memory grant feedback for row mode, which was announced recently.

As mentioned in Chapter 5, the estimated cost of a plan is based on the query cardinality estimation, as well on the algorithms or operators used by the plan. For this reason, to estimate the cost of an execution plan correctly, the query optimizer needs to estimate the number of records returned by a given query. During query optimization, SQL Server explores many candidate plans, estimates their relative costs, and selects the most efficient one. As such, incorrect cardinality and cost estimation may cause the query optimizer to choose inefficient plans, which can have a negative impact on the performance of your database.

In addition, cost estimation is inexact and has some known limitations, especially when it comes to the estimation of the intermediate results in a plan. Errors in intermediate results in effect get magnified as more tables are joined and more estimation errors are included within the calculations. On top of all that, some operations are not covered by the mathematical model of the cardinality estimation component, which means the query optimizer has to resort to guess logic or heuristics to deal with these situations. For example, some SQL Server features such as table variables and multistatement table-valued user-defined functions have no support for statistics, and the query optimizer will use a fixed estimate of 100 rows, or 1 row on versions previous to SQL Server 2014.

Traditionally, if a bad cardinality estimation contributed to a suboptimal execution plan, no additional changes were allowed after that and the plan was used to execute the query anyway. So if the estimates were incorrect, the created plan was still used despite the fact that it may be a suboptimal plan. Adaptive query processing offers some improvements to this traditional query optimization model. Let us cover next the first three adaptive query processing algorithms available with SQL Server 2017.

Batch Mode Adaptive Joins

As hinted at in Chapter 5, choosing an incorrect join type due to cardinality estimation errors could seriously impact the performance of queries. Batch mode adaptive joins help with this problem by allowing a plan to select the physical join algorithm dynamically at execution time based on the real number of rows flowing through the join.

The current release of batch mode adaptive joins works only for hash joins or nested loops joins and assumes the join type will initially be a hash join. The adaptive join reads the build input and, if a calculated threshold is met, will continue as a hash join; otherwise, it will use the same input to execute as a nested loops join. The nested loops join will then use the rows already read by the hash join build input, which also means that even if a nested loops join is finally selected, the memory requested is that of a hash join.

Batch mode adaptive joins, as the name may suggest, are currently limited to queries accessing tables with columnstore indexes, although as indicated later, a known workaround could be to create a dummy columnstore index to encourage the use of the adaptive joins on row store structures, too. In any of these cases, the execution plan using adaptive joins will be cached and used for additional executions in which the join algorithm selection will happen at runtime depending on the original calculated threshold.

There are a few limitations with adaptive joins in the current release. First, batch mode adaptive joins currently work only for SELECT statements that are not used on data modification operations. In addition, as suggested earlier, an adaptive join always requires memory for the build phase, which would not be required for a nested loops join. Finally, this build phase is a blocking (or stop-and-go) operation, which will not allow any other processing in the plan until it is completed.

There are a few conditions for batch mode adaptive joins to be considered in a plan:

► The query must benefit from either a hash join or a nested loops join. This means that if the third kind of physical join, merge join, is a better choice, the adaptive join will not be used.

► The query must use a columnstore index, or, at least, a columnstore index must be defined on any of the tables referenced by the query.

► The generated alternative solutions of the hash join and the nested loops join should have the same first input, called build input or outer reference, respectively.

Let's now try the batch mode adaptive joins by creating a columnstore index on the AdventureWorks database. For this and the following exercises, make sure your database is in compatibility level 140 by running the following statement:

```
ALTER DATABASE AdventureWorks2014 SET COMPATIBILITY_LEVEL = 140
```

Create the columstore index on the SalesOrderHeader table:

```
CREATE NONCLUSTERED COLUMNSTORE INDEX CIX_SalesOrderID
ON Sales.SalesOrderHeader(SubTotal)
```

Try the following query:

```
SELECT SUM(soh.SubTotal)
FROM Sales.SalesOrderHeader soh
JOIN Sales.SalesOrderDetail sod ON soh.SalesOrderID = sod.SalesOrderID
```

We get the plan shown in Figure 6-1, which uses the Live Query Statistics feature to help visualize the number of rows read on each executed branch.

Live Query Statistics is a new query troubleshooting feature introduced with SQL Server 2016, which can be used to view a live query plan while the query is still in execution, enabling you to see query plan information in real time without the need to wait for the query to complete. Since the data required for this feature is also available in the SQL Server 2014 database engine, it can also work in that version if you are using SQL Server 2016 Management Studio or later. There are several ways to enable this feature in SQL Server Management Studio, including selecting Include Live Query Statistics on the SQL Editor toolbar or using similar choices on the Tools menu or Activity Monitor.

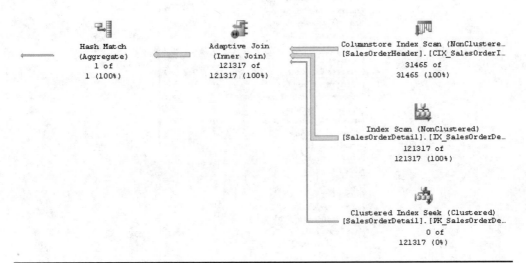

Figure 6-1 *Adaptive join query plan*

Among the items to notice in the plan is the new adaptive join operator. Different from the join operators we know so far, the adaptive join has the following three inputs:

▶ The first or top branch is the build input.

▶ The second or middle branch is the input used if the hash join is selected. Notice that live query statistics shows 121317 of 121317 rows, meaning the branch was executed.

▶ The third or bottom branch is the input used if the nested loops were selected. In this case the branch shows 0 of 121317 rows, meaning it was not executed.

Let us look at the properties of the adaptive join operator, which is shown in Figure 6-2.

Adaptive Join
Chooses dynamically between hash join and nested loops.

Physical Operation	Adaptive Join
Logical Operation	Inner Join
Actual Join Type	HashMatch
Actual Execution Mode	Batch
Estimated Join Type	HashMatch
Is Adaptive	True
Estimated Execution Mode	Batch
Adaptive Threshold Rows	1398.57
Actual Number of Rows	121317
Actual Number of Batches	135
Estimated Operator Cost	0 (0%)
Estimated I/O Cost	0
Estimated CPU Cost	0.0024263
Estimated Subtree Cost	0.483549
Estimated Number of Executions	1
Number of Executions	1
Estimated Number of Rows	121317
Estimated Row Size	15 B
Actual Rebinds	0
Actual Rewinds	0
Node ID	2

Output List
[AdventureWorks2014].[Sales].
[SalesOrderHeader].SubTotal
Hash Keys Probe
[AdventureWorks2014].[Sales].
[SalesOrderDetail].SalesOrderID
Outer References
[AdventureWorks2014].[Sales].
[SalesOrderHeader].SalesOrderID

Figure 6-2 *Adaptive join operator properties*

Several interesting new properties are available. One of them, Adaptive Threshold Rows, shows the number 1398.57. An estimation at or over this value will keep the hash join. An estimation lower will select the nested loops join. Adaptive join operator properties also show the Estimated Join Type and the Actual Join Type.

NOTE

Figure 6-2 shows the operator information from the actual execution plan. If you followed the live query statistics plan, you will see the estimated properties only.

Let us try a second example running the following query:

```
SELECT SUM(soh.SubTotal)
FROM Sales.SalesOrderHeader soh
JOIN Sales.SalesOrderDetail sod ON soh.SalesOrderID = sod.SalesOrderID
WHERE soh.OrderDate = '2011-05-31 00:00:00.000'
```

The live query statistics plan is shown in Figure 6-3.

As you can see, this time, the third branch was executed, showing 357 of 166 rows. Also notice that a new threshold was calculated. The threshold will depend on the query, and obviously this query is considered different from the previous one. The threshold is based on the estimated number of rows and the cost of using a hash join or a nested loops join for that number of rows. The adaptive threshold rows is now 107.307, (which you can see at the properties of the adaptive join operator as indicated earlier) and since only 43 rows qualified on the build input, the actual join type is nested loops, which can be verified on the actual execution plan.

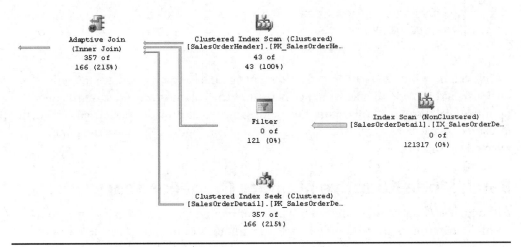

Figure 6-3   *Adaptive join query plan using nested loops*

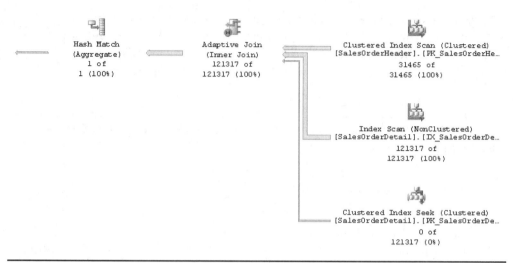

Figure 6-4   *Adaptive join query plan using row stores*

As mentioned, a current limitation of this feature is that it requires a columnstore index, a limitation that hopefully can be removed in a future release. A workaround to this limitation is to create a dummy columnstore index so the query optimizer can consider using an adaptive join. To test this, drop the current columnstore index:

```
DROP INDEX Sales.SalesOrderHeader.CIX_SalesOrderID
```

Now create a dummy columnstore index, in this case, using a filter predicate in which no rows qualify:

```
CREATE NONCLUSTERED COLUMNSTORE INDEX CIX_SalesOrderID
ON Sales.SalesOrderHeader(SubTotal)
WHERE SalesOrderID = 0
```

You can now run the last SELECT statement again. Using this workaround will obviously not provide the performance benefit of the columnstore index, so the query optimizer will use an adaptive join if using the row stores provides performance benefit measured, as usual, by cardinality and cost estimation. Figure 6-4 shows the plan selected for this query.

Batch Mode Adaptive Memory Grant Feedback

Although every query submitted to SQL Server requires some memory, sorting and hashing operations require significantly larger amounts of memory, which, in some cases, can contribute to performance problems. The buffer cache, which keeps data pages in memory, is different from a memory grant, which is a part of the server memory used to store temporary row data while a query is performing sort and hashing operations and is required only for the duration of the query. The memory grant is required to store the rows to be sorted or to build the hash tables used by hash join and hash aggregate operators. In rare cases, a memory grant may also be required for parallel query plans with multiple range scans.

The memory required by a query is estimated by the query optimizer when the execution plan is assembled, and it is based on the estimated number of rows and the average row size in addition to the type of operation required, such as a sort, a hash join, or a hash aggregate. Although this process usually correctly estimates the required memory, in some cases, some performance problem may occur:

▶   A plan underestimating the required memory could lead to additional data processing or to the query operator to use the disk (spilling).

▶   A system running multiple queries requiring sorting or hashing operations may not have enough memory available, requiring one or more queries to wait.

In the first case, usually due to bad cardinality estimations, the query optimizer may have underestimated the amount of memory required for the query and, as a result, the sort data or the build input of the hash operations may not fit into such memory. In the second case, SQL Server estimated the minimum memory needed to run the query, called required memory, but since there is not enough memory in the system, the query will have to wait until this memory is available. This problem is increased when, again due to a bad cardinality estimation, the amount of required memory is overestimated, leading to wasted memory and reduced concurrency.

As mentioned, bad cardinality estimations may happen for several different reasons, and there is no single solution that can work for all the possible statements. For example, some features such as table variables or multistatement table-value functions have a fixed and very small cardinality estimate. In other cases, you may be able to fix the problem, improving the quality of the statistics, for example, by increasing the sample size.

Batch mode adaptive memory grant feedback was designed to help with these situations by recalculating the memory required by a query and updating it in the cached query plan. The memory grant feedback may get information from spill events or from the amount of memory really used. Although this improved memory estimate may not help the first execution of the query, it can be used to improve the performance of the following executions. The batch mode adaptive memory grant process is in fact learning and getting feedback from real runtime information.

Finally, the batch mode memory grant feedback may not be useful and will be automatically disabled if the query has a very unstable and high variation on memory requirements, which could be possible, for example, with parameter-sensitive queries.

Let's try an example to see how the batch mode memory grant feedback works. We are using a table variable on purpose, which as you know will have a low fixed estimate of 100 rows to help us to create a low memory estimate. Run the following code and request the execution plan:

```
DECLARE @SalesOrderDetail TABLE
(
        [SalesOrderID] [int] NOT NULL,
        [SalesOrderDetailID] [int] NOT NULL,
        [CarrierTrackingNumber] [nvarchar](25) NULL,
        [OrderQty] [smallint] NOT NULL,
        [ProductID] [int] NOT NULL,
        [SpecialOfferID] [int] NOT NULL,
        [UnitPrice] [money] NOT NULL,
        [UnitPriceDiscount] [money] NOT NULL,
        [LineTotal]  money NOT NULL,
        [rowguid] [uniqueidentifier] ROWGUIDCOL  NOT NULL,
        [ModifiedDate] [datetime] NOT NULL)

INSERT @SalesOrderDetail
SELECT * FROM sales.SalesOrderDetail

SELECT * FROM @SalesOrderDetail o
INNER HASH JOIN sales.SalesOrderHeader h ON o.SalesOrderID = h.SalesOrderID
```

Figure 6-5 shows the created plan.

Notice the following warning on the hash join operator (you may need to look at the hash join operator properties or hover over the operator in the graphical plan): "Operator used tempdb to spill data during execution with spill level 2 and 1 spilled thread(s)." If you run the query a few more times, the hash join warning may not appear and query execution may be faster. In my system, the duration average went from 10 seconds to 3 seconds.

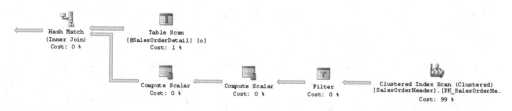

Figure 6-5   *Batch mode memory grant feedback plan*

This was the original memory grant information from the original XML plan:

```
<MemoryGrantInfo SerialRequiredMemory="1024" SerialDesiredMemory="1056"
RequiredMemory="1024" DesiredMemory="1056" RequestedMemory="1056"
GrantWaitTime="0" GrantedMemory="2080" MaxUsedMemory="1712"
MaxQueryMemory="715376" />
```

Next is the revised memory grant information later in the same execution plan. As you can see, `RequestedMemory` and `GrantedMemory` went from 1056 and 2080, respectively, to 34,224. Values are in kilobytes (KB).

```
<MemoryGrantInfo SerialRequiredMemory="1024" SerialDesiredMemory="34224"
RequiredMemory="1024" DesiredMemory="34224" RequestedMemory="34224"
GrantWaitTime="0" GrantedMemory="34224" MaxUsedMemory="29696"
MaxQueryMemory="715376" />
```

Optionally, you can use some extended events to get more information about how the process works. The spilling_report_to_memory_grant_feedback event will fire when batch mode iterators report spilling to the memory grant feedback process. In my case, the spilled_data_size field showed 6,744,890, which is the spilled data size in bytes.

The memory_grant_updated_by_feedback event occurs when the memory grant is updated by feedback. In my test, the event showed the following values for some of its fields:

▶ **history_update_count** 2 (number of memory grant updates in update history)

▶ **ideal_additional_memory_before_kb** 9920 (ideal additional memory grant before update in KB)

▶ **ideal_additional_memory_after_kb** 21,080 (ideal additional memory grant after update in KB)

Interleaved Execution for Multistatement Table-Value Functions

The previous two algorithms for adaptive query processing work in a different way. One uses a row threshold to decide the join type at runtime, and the second improves the memory grant size based on execution feedback. Interleaved execution for multistatement table-value functions works yet in a different way. I mentioned earlier that traditional query optimization creates a plan and, even if it is based on bad estimates, the created plan is executed anyway. For interleaved execution, the query processor engine will in fact pause query optimization, execute the multistatement table-value function, and use the new accurate cardinality to continue the optimization process. For the current release, interleaved execution works only with multistatement table-value functions, but more constructs will be added in the future.

Let's start with an example. Create a multistatement table-valued function:

```
CREATE FUNCTION dbo.ufn_SalesOrderDetail(@year int)
RETURNS @SalesOrderDetail TABLE
(
        [SalesOrderID] [int] NOT NULL,
        [SalesOrderDetailID] [int] NOT NULL,
        [CarrierTrackingNumber] [nvarchar](25) NULL,
        [OrderQty] [smallint] NOT NULL,
        [ProductID] [int] NOT NULL,
        [SpecialOfferID] [int] NOT NULL,
        [UnitPrice] [money] NOT NULL,
        [UnitPriceDiscount] [money] NOT NULL,
        [LineTotal] money NOT NULL,
        [rowguid] [uniqueidentifier] ROWGUIDCOL NOT NULL,
        [ModifiedDate] [datetime] NOT NULL)
AS
BEGIN
   INSERT @SalesOrderDetail
   SELECT * FROM sales.SalesOrderDetail
     WHERE YEAR(ModifiedDate) = @year
   RETURN
END
```

NOTE

This is not the best way to write such a function, but it is good enough to show the concept.

First let us look at the behavior before SQL Server 2017 by changing the database compatibility level to 130:

```
ALTER DATABASE AdventureWorks2014 SET COMPATIBILITY_LEVEL = 130
```

Now we are ready to run our query:

```
SELECT * FROM dbo.ufn_SalesOrderDetail(2014) o
JOIN Sales.SalesOrderHeader h ON o.SalesOrderID = h.SalesOrderID
```

The resulting execution plan is shown in Figure 6-6.

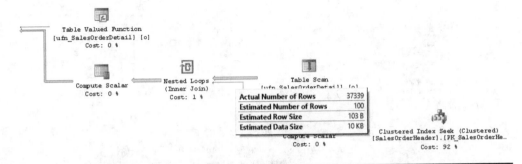

Figure 6-6   *Plan without interleaved execution*

Notice that, with a default estimated 100 rows from the multistatement table-valued function, the query optimizer decides to use a nested loops join, when in reality there are 37,339 rows. Obviously, in this case, a nested loops join was not the best choice for such a large number of rows, because it was required to execute the inner or bottom input 37,339 times. In addition, this incorrect estimation early in the plan could potentially create many problems, as decisions may be incorrect as data flows in the plan. Performance problems are likely in cases where these rows are used in downstream operations. A related example was shown earlier in the chapter, where a bad estimation on a table variable impacted a memory grant later in the plan.

Let's switch back the database compatibility level to 140 to test the SQL Server 2017 behavior:

```
ALTER DATABASE AdventureWorks2014 SET COMPATIBILITY_LEVEL = 140
```

Running the same query again returns the plan shown in Figure 6-7. You can see that it now reflects an accurate cardinality estimate.

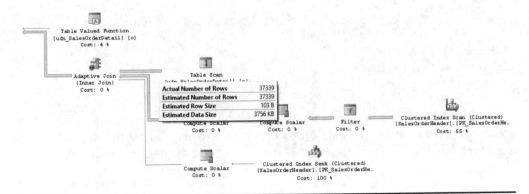

Figure 6-7   *Plan using interleaved execution*

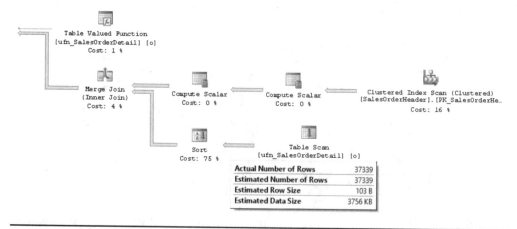

Actual Number of Rows	37339
Estimated Number of Rows	37339
Estimated Row Size	103 B
Estimated Data Size	3756 KB

Figure 6-8 *Plan using interleaved execution version 2*

Since we left the columnstore index created in the previous exercise, we also have an adaptive join. Let's take a look at an alternative plan that drops the columnstore index:

```
DROP INDEX Sales.SalesOrderHeader.CIX_SalesOrderID
```

Now we have the plan shown in Figure 6-8, which also has a correct estimate, but this time using a merge join.

The extended events interleaved_exec_status and interleaved_exec_status_ update can be used to track when interleaved execution is occurring and to track the cardinality estimates updated by it, respectively. In addition, an execution plan can show the properties `ContainsInterleavedExecutionCandidates` and `IsInterleavedExecuted` to detect whether there are interleaved execution candidates in the query and if the query was successfully executed, as shown in the following XML fragment example:

```
<QueryPlan … ContainsInterleavedExecutionCandidates="true">

<RunTimeInformation>
<RunTimeCountersPerThread … IsInterleavedExecuted="true" />
</RunTimeInformation>
```

Finally, in the current release, multistatement table-value functions must be read-only and cannot be part of a data modification operation to be candidates for interleaved execution. In addition, they cannot be used inside a CROSS APPLY operator.

Automatic Tuning

Automatic tuning is a new feature, which according to the SQL Server 2017 documentation, is intended to "provide insight into potential query performance problems, recommend solutions, and automatically fix identified problems." Although this may sound extremely broad and optimistic, and it has created a lot of hype in the SQL Server community, at the moment its only released feature is to help with plan regressions of queries, which were originally performing optimally. No announcements have yet indicated whether it will cover any additional features in a future release, or what those additional features could be. Although automatic tuning's current benefits are extremely limited, we hope they could be extended in the near future to cover additional query performance problems.

Automatic tuning also has a second feature, automatic index management, which is available only on Azure SQL Database. This feature is intended to automatically create recommended indexes or remove indexes that are no longer used by any query. I do not cover Azure SQL Database in this book, but you can get more details about this feature by looking at the online documentation at https://docs.microsoft.com/en-us/sql/relational-databases/automatic-tuning/automatic-tuning.

Automatic plan regression consists of automatically switching to the last known good plan of a query in case a regression is detected. The database engine will automatically force a recommendation only when the estimated CPU gain is better than 10 seconds, or when both the forced plan is better than the current one and the number of errors in the new plan is higher than the number of errors in the recommended plan. These thresholds currently cannot be changed.

In addition, the automatic plan regression process does not end at forcing that last known good plan, because the database engine continues to monitor the changes and can roll them back if the new plan is not performing better than the replaced plan.

Note that you could also implement this process manually, identifying the query and plan on the query store and running the sp_query_store_force_plan procedure. This process requires that you manually monitor the information on the query store to find the performance regression, locate the last known good plan, apply the required script to force the plan, and continue to monitor the performance of the changes. All of this functionality is available by using the query store, so it can be implemented starting with SQL Server 2016. A disadvantage of this manual process, as hinted, is that you also have to monitor the changes continually to see if they continue to bring performance benefits or otherwise decide to unforce the execution plan.

Finally, note that forcing a plan should be used only as a temporary fix while you look into a permanent solution. Forcing a plan is like a collection of hints, which, as discussed in Chapter 4, basically disables the work of the query optimizer. Finding a permanent solution may require applying standard query tuning techniques.

Let's try an example to see how the technology works by looking at automatic plan correction. (Automatic index management will not be covered here because it is implemented on Azure SQL Database only.)

Sometimes trying to create a real performance problem with AdventureWorks can be a challenge, because it is a very small database. Although one option could be to create tables with millions of rows, instead I can show the concept using the same scripts I showed in Chapter 5 while demonstrating parameter sniffing. So let's start by restoring a fresh copy of the AdventureWorks database.

In this case, let's assume that the desired plan is the one using an index seek and a key lookup, and if we suddenly have a table scan, we can consider it a regression. If you have not already done so, enable the query store on AdventureWorks by running the following statements:

```
ALTER DATABASE AdventureWorks2014 SET QUERY_STORE = ON
GO
ALTER DATABASE AdventureWorks2014 SET QUERY_STORE (OPERATION_MODE = READ_WRITE,
    MAX_STORAGE_SIZE_MB = 1024)
GO
```

If you already have the query store enabled, you can just run the following statement to purge its data and start clean:

```
ALTER DATABASE AdventureWorks2014 SET QUERY_STORE CLEAR ALL
```

Create the following stored procedure:

```
CREATE PROCEDURE test (@pid int)
AS
SELECT * FROM Sales.SalesOrderDetail
WHERE ProductID = @pid
```

Again, for this example, assume the following is the desired or optimal plan, using an index seek/key lookup combination:

```
EXEC test @pid = 898
```

Execute it a few more times so it can be captured by the query store:

```
EXEC test @pid = 898
GO 30
```

Performance and plan information about these procedure executions are now recorded in the query store. Now suppose that, for some reason, the plan is evicted from memory and a new nonoptimal plan is created instead. To simulate the plan being removed from memory, you can clear the plan cache for the AdventureWorks database by running the following statement:

```
ALTER DATABASE SCOPED CONFIGURATION CLEAR PROCEDURE_CACHE
```

Now run the following version of the stored procedure, which for the specified parameter will create a plan using a table scan:

```
EXEC test @pid = 870
```

At this point, we have a bad plan in memory that scans the entire table for any provided parameters. Since most of the provided parameters would return a small number of rows, they would instead benefit from the original plan with the index seek and key lookup operators.

Run the stored procedure again for the parameter returning nine rows:

```
EXEC test @pid = 898
GO 30
```

At this point, the database engine should be able to see the performance regression and make such information available using the sys.dm_db_tuning_recommendations DMV. Running the following statement will return one row (make sure you are connected to the database you want, in this case, AdventureWorks):

```
SELECT * FROM sys.dm_db_tuning_recommendations
```

The DMV sys.dm_db_tuning_recommendations returns detailed information about tuning recommendations based on the query store. Some of the columns at this point are interesting:

▶ **name**   Unique name of the tuning recommendation. In our case, returned PR_1.

▶ **type**   Type of automatic tuning recommendation. At this point, the only choice available in SQL Server could be FORCE_LAST_GOOD_PLAN.

▶ **reason**   Reason why this recommendation was provided. I got the value "Average query CPU time changed from 0.9ms to 22.26ms," which means that my index seek plan was using 0.9ms and the regressed plan using a table scan switched to 22.26ms. Once again, this is not a big difference because AdventureWorks is a very small database.

▶ **valid_since**   The first time the tuning recommendation was generated.

▶ **last_refresh**   The last time the tuning recommendation was generated. In our case, they are both the same because it is the first recommendation.

▶ **state**   State of the tuning recommendation as a JSON document. Currently only two fields are available: currentValue, which is the current state of the recommendation, and reason, which is the reason the tuning recommendation is in such a state. My values were

```
{"currentValue":"Active","reason":"AutomaticTuningOptionNotEnabled"}
```

In this case, the meaning of these values is that the recommendation is still active as the automatic tuning feature is not enabled. Later I will show you how to enable it.

Note that JSON (JavaScript Object Notation) is a popular open-standard textual data format used for exchanging data in web and mobile applications. SQL Server provides JSON support starting with SQL Server 2016.

▶ **details**   Details about the tuning recommendation, which is also a JSON document with multiple fields. In this case, you can take a look directly at the details column output or use SQL Server JSON capabilities to extract specific field information. My demo returned the following JSON document:

```
{"planForceDetails":{"queryId":1,"regressedPlanId":2,
"regressedPlanExecutionCount":15,"regressedPlanErrorCount":0,
"regressedPlanCpuTimeAverage":2.225853333333333e+004,
"regressedPlanCpuTimeStddev":8.224303041325482e+003,
"recommendedPlanId":1,"recommendedPlanExecutionCount":31,
"recommendedPlanErrorCount":0,"recommendedPlanCpuTimeAverage"
:8.970000000000000e+002,"recommendedPlanCpuTimeStddev"
:1.909332766414285e+002},"implementationDetails"
:{"method":"TSql","script":"exec sp_query_store_force_plan @query_id
= 1, @plan_id = 1"}}
```

For example, you can use the following script to get some of the details fields, including the script that can be used to force the plan:

```
SELECT name, reason, score,
    JSON_VALUE(details, '$.implementationDetails.script') as script,
    details.*
FROM sys.dm_db_tuning_recommendations
    CROSS APPLY OPENJSON(details, '$.planForceDetails')
    WITH (query_id int '$.queryId',
    regressed_plan_id int '$.regressedPlanId',
    last_good_plan_id int '$.recommendedPlanId') as details
WHERE JSON_VALUE(state, '$.currentValue') = 'Active'
```

NOTE

Running this query requires the use of the SQL Server 2017 compatibility level, so make sure your database is set to COMPATIBILITY_LEVEL 140.

The query returns some of the information discussed earlier, plus the fields `<script>`, which is the script to execute in case you decide to force a plan manually; `<queryId>`, which is the query_id of the regressed query; `<regressedPlanId>`, which is the plan_id of the regressed plan; and `<recommendedPlanId>`, which is the plan_id of the recommended plan. For this example, my created script was the following, which basically will force the plan with plan_id 1 for the query with query_id 1.

```
exec sp_query_store_force_plan @query_id = 1, @plan_id = 1
```

So far I have covered how to force a plan manually. This requires that I manually monitor the information on the query store to find the performance regression, find the last known good plan, apply the required script to force the plan, and continue to monitor the performance of the changes. All of this functionality is available by using the query store, however, so it can be implemented starting with SQL Server 2016. What is new in SQL Server 2017 is the ability to enable the database engine to implement these changes automatically. The sys.dm_db_tuning_recommendations DMV is also new in SQL Server 2017.

In addition, the new sys.database_automatic_tuning_options DMV can help you track the automatic tuning options for a specific database. Run the following statement to inspect the current configuration:

```
SELECT * FROM sys.database_automatic_tuning_options
```

You will get the following output:

Name	desired_state	desired_state_desc	actual_state	actual_state_desc	reason	reason_desc
FORCE_LAST_GOOD_PLAN	0	OFF	0	OFF	NULL	NULL

To enable the automatic plan regression feature, run the following statement using the new AUTOMATIC_TUNING option and the FORCE_LAST_GOOD_PLAN choice

```
ALTER DATABASE AdventureWorks2014
SET AUTOMATIC_TUNING (FORCE_LAST_GOOD_PLAN = ON)
```

This changes the sys.database_automatic_tuning_options DMV output as follows:

Name	desired_state	desired_state_desc	actual_state	actual_state_desc	reason	reason_desc
FORCE_LAST_GOOD_PLAN	1	ON	1	ON	NULL	NULL

Notice that this automatic tuning option requires the query store. Trying to enable it without the query store will generate the following error message:

```
Msg 15705, Level 16, State 1, Line 3
Automatic Tuning option FORCE_LAST_GOOD_PLAN cannot be enabled, because Query
Store is not turned on.
Msg 5069, Level 16, State 1, Line 3
ALTER DATABASE statement failed.
```

Finally, it is important to remember that SQL Server will automatically force a recommendation only where the estimated CPU gain is better than 10 seconds, or both the forced plan is better than the current one and the number of errors in the new plan is higher than the number of errors in the recommended plan. Earlier, I showed how to see the difference in CPU performance information using the reason column of the sys.dm_db_tuning_recommendations DMV. The number of errors is available using the following fields of the details column of the same DMV:

▶ **regressedPlanErrorCount**   Number of errors detected during the execution of the regressed plan

▶ **recommendedPlanErrorCount**   Number of errors detected during the execution of the recommended plan

SQL Server 2016 Service Pack 1

As mentioned, SQL Server 2016 Service Pack 1 brought a consistent programmability surface area for developers across SQL Server editions. Starting with this release, features such as columnstore indexes, In-Memory OLTP, always encrypted, compression, partitioning, database snapshots, row-level security, and dynamic data masking, among others, are now available on all SQL Server editions such as Express, Web, Standard and Enterprise.

SQL Server 2016 Service Pack 1 also brought a variety of new query processing–related features including the following:

▶ **CREATE OR ALTER statement**   New CREATE OR ALTER statement can apply to stored procedures, triggers, user-defined functions, and views.

▶ **USE HINT query option**   New query option provides the ability to enable the behavior of some trace flags at the query level without using QUERYTRACEON and requiring sysadmin credentials.

▶ **Ability to programmatically identify whether the Lock Pages in Memory privilege and Instant File initialization are in effect at SQL Server service startup**   This information is available on the sys.dm_os_sys_info and sys.dm_server_services DMVs, respectively.

► **Additional diagnostics information on execution plans** Information such as top waits, enabled trace flags, and additional performance information is available on execution plans.

► **New EstimatedRowsRead attribute** Attribute can be used to troubleshoot and diagnose query plans with pushdown predicates.

For more details about SQL Server 2016 Service Pack 1, refer to the online article at https://blogs.msdn.microsoft.com/sqlreleaseservices/sql-server-2016-service-pack-1-sp1-released/.

USE HINT Query Option

Available for the first time in SQL Server 2016 Service Pack 1, the new USE HINT query option remains a highly unknown feature. USE HINT can be used to get the behavior of some trace flags at the query level without using the QUERYTRACEON hint. As you may know, the QUERYTRACEON hint lets you enable a plan-affecting trace flags for a single-query compilation.

A problem with using some of this functionality in the past is that QUERYTRACEON was only partially documented and required sysadmin privileges. By partially documented, I mean that you could use a large number of trace flags with QUERYTRACEON, but only a small portion was supported and documented. Using USE HINT, you can alter the query optimizer behavior by using any of the supported query hints listed in Table 6-1 without requiring sysadmin permissions. Table 6-1 lists the new hint names, the trace flag that provides a similar behavior, and, if available, the database option that can provide the same behavior at the database level.

NOTE

A list of supported QUERYTRACEON trace flags is available at https://support.microsoft.com/en-us/help/2801413/enable-plan-affecting-sql-server-query-optimizer-behavior-that-can-be.

The following hint names are supported:

► **DISABLE_OPTIMIZED_NESTED_LOOP** Disables a batch sort operation for optimized nested loops joins.

► **FORCE_LEGACY_CARDINALITY_ESTIMATION** Enables the old cardinality estimator when a performance regression has been found.

► **ENABLE_QUERY_OPTIMIZER_HOTFIXES** Enables query optimizer hotfixes released on service packs and cumulative updates.

► **DISABLE_PARAMETER_SNIFFING** Disables parameter sniffing.

USE HINT	Trace Flag	Database Option
DISABLE_OPTIMIZED_NESTED_LOOP	2340	N/A
FORCE_LEGACY_CARDINALITY_ESTIMATION	9481	LEGACY_CARDINALITY_ESTIMATION
ENABLE_QUERY_OPTIMIZER_HOTFIXES	4199	QUERY_OPTIMIZER_HOTFIXES
DISABLE_PARAMETER_SNIFFING	4136	PARAMETER_SNIFFING
ASSUME_MIN_SELECTIVITY_FOR_FILTER_ESTIMATES	4137 (Old Cardinality Estimator) 9471 (New Cardinality Estimator)	N/A
DISABLE_OPTIMIZER_ROWGOAL	4138	N/A
ENABLE_HIST_AMENDMENT_FOR_ASC_KEYS	4139	N/A
ASSUME_JOIN_PREDICATE_DEPENDS_ON_FILTERS	9476 (New Cardinality Estimator)	N/A
FORCE_DEFAULT_CARDINALITY_ESTIMATION	2312	N/A

Table 6-1   *Hint Names*

▶ **ASSUME_MIN_SELECTIVITY_FOR_FILTER_ESTIMATES**   Creates execution plans using minimum selectivity when estimating AND predicates for filters to account for correlation.

▶ **ASSUME_JOIN_PREDICATE_DEPENDS_ON_FILTERS**   Creates execution plans using the simple containment assumption instead of the default base containment assumption for joins on the old cardinality estimator.

▶ **ENABLE_HIST_AMENDMENT_FOR_ASC_KEYS**   Enables automatically generated quick statistics for any leading index column for which a cardinality estimation is needed.

▶ **DISABLE_OPTIMIZER_ROWGOAL**   Creates execution plans that do not use row goal adjustments with queries that contain TOP, IN, EXISTS, or OPTION (FAST N) keywords.

▶ **FORCE_DEFAULT_CARDINALITY_ESTIMATION**   Enables the new cardinality estimator where the database is configured to use the old cardinality estimator.

Let's take a look at a couple of examples. First of all, run the following query *not* as a system administrator:

```
SELECT * FROM Sales.SalesOrderDetail WHERE ProductID = 898
OPTION (QUERYTRACEON 9481)
```

Trying to run the query without sysadmin permissions will produce the following error message:

```
Msg 2571, Level 14, State 3, Line 1
User 'test' does not have permission to run DBCC TRACEON.
```

However, the following statement results in exactly the same behavior without the need of sysadmin credentials:

```
SELECT * FROM Sales.SalesOrderDetail WHERE ProductID = 898
OPTION (USE HINT('FORCE_LEGACY_CARDINALITY_ESTIMATION'))
```

Following on our parameter sniffing example in Chapter 4 and earlier in this chapter, create the test stored procedure:

```
CREATE PROCEDURE test (@pid int)
AS
SELECT * FROM Sales.SalesOrderDetail
WHERE ProductID = @pid
```

Running the procedure with the following parameter will get an estimated nine rows and a plan using an index seek and a key lookup operator. This execution uses parameter sniffing to inspect the value of the passed parameter and estimates the number of returned rows using the histogram of the statistics object (as covered in Chapter 5):

```
EXEC test @pid = 898
```

As you saw in Chapter 5, in a limited number of cases, we may want to disable parameter sniffing. We can accomplish this in different ways, including using trace flag 4136, as shown next. Remember that using QUERYTRACEON hint requires working with sysadmin privileges again.

```
ALTER PROCEDURE test (@pid int)
AS
SELECT * FROM Sales.SalesOrderDetail
WHERE ProductID = @pid
OPTION (QUERYTRACEON 4136)
```

In this case, running the test stored procedure as before will get an estimation of 456.079 and a new plan using a table scan.

NOTE

Chapter 5 also covered using the OPTIMIZE FOR UNKNOWN hint to obtain exactly the same behavior.

The following example will produce exactly the same behavior using the DISABLE_ PARAMETER_SNIFFING hint name without requiring elevated privileges:

```
ALTER PROCEDURE test (@pid int)
AS
SELECT * FROM Sales.SalesOrderDetail
WHERE ProductID = @pid
OPTION (USE HINT('DISABLE_PARAMETER_SNIFFING'))
```

There is also a DMV, sys.dm_exec_valid_use_hints, which returns the supported USE HINT hint names:

```
SELECT * FROM sys.dm_exec_valid_use_hints
```

SQL Server 2017 returns the following hint names, which are also listed in Table 6-1:

- ▶ DISABLE_OPTIMIZED_NESTED_LOOP
- ▶ FORCE_LEGACY_CARDINALITY_ESTIMATION
- ▶ ENABLE_QUERY_OPTIMIZER_HOTFIXES
- ▶ DISABLE_PARAMETER_SNIFFING
- ▶ ASSUME_MIN_SELECTIVITY_FOR_FILTER_ESTIMATES
- ▶ ASSUME_JOIN_PREDICATE_DEPENDS_ON_FILTERS
- ▶ ENABLE_HIST_AMENDMENT_FOR_ASC_KEYS
- ▶ DISABLE_OPTIMIZER_ROWGOAL
- ▶ FORCE_DEFAULT_CARDINALITY_ESTIMATION

Finally, Table 6-1 also covered three database scoped configuration options that you can use to get the same behavior as the trace flag or name hint but at the database level. For example, to disable parameter sniffing at the database level, you could run the following statement:

```
ALTER DATABASE SCOPED CONFIGURATION SET PARAMETER_SNIFFING = OFF
```

Now you can run the original version of our test stored procedure and get the behavior of parameter sniffing disabled without any hint:

```
ALTER PROCEDURE test (@pid int)
AS
SELECT * FROM Sales.SalesOrderDetail
WHERE ProductID = @pid
```

Running the procedure will get the estimate of 456.079 and the plan using a table scan. Don't forget to enable parameter sniffing again if you tried the previous examples:

```
ALTER DATABASE SCOPED CONFIGURATION SET PARAMETER_SNIFFING = ON
```

NOTE

It is also possible to disable parameter sniffing at the server level, enabling the trace flag 4136 mentioned earlier for the entire SQL Server instance. Keep in mind, however, that doing this at the server level may be an extreme solution and should be tested carefully.

CXPACKET and CXCONSUMER Waits

SQL Server can use parallelism to help some expensive queries execute faster by using several logical processors simultaneously. However, even if a query gets better performance by using parallel plans, it may still use more resources than a similar serial plan. Parallel plans may show CXPACKET waits, also called parallel processing waits. Having these waits does not necessarily mean that there is a problem, and, unfortunately, some wrong advice online shows otherwise, which sometimes gives parallelism a bad reputation. As a consequence, a bad reaction to this wait type can be to disable parallelism. The reality is that we may need to do additional research to see if, in fact, parallelism is the problem. Traditionally, to troubleshoot CXPACKET waits, we should start by looking at the waits on the additional child parallel threads.

Starting with SQL Server 2017 Cumulative Update 3 (and SQL Server 2016 Service Pack 2), Microsoft is planning to split parallelism CXPACKET waits into two different waits: CXPACKET and CXCONSUMER, which will allow easier troubleshooting.

The concept of the change is basically the separation between producer waits and consumer waits. In parallel operations, producers push data to consumers, and these are the waits that require attention. Consumers may simply have to wait for data from the producers, so a delay on the producers will impact them as well. Starting with this SQL Server change, producer waits will be reported as CXPACKET waits and consumer waits as CXCONSUMER waits. CXPACKET waits will be the actionable waits, and you will not have to worry much about the CXCONSUMER waits. As with any other waits, they will be visible on the usual places such as the sys.dm_os_wait_stats or the sys.dm_exec_session_wait_stats DMVs.

NOTE

SQL Server 2017 Cumulative Update 3 was not yet available at the time of this writing, although according to the announcement, CXPACKET and CXCONSUMER waits are already implemented on Azure SQL Database.

Wait Statistics on Execution Plans

Another very interesting recent development is the ability to see wait statistics on an actual execution plan, a feature that was also released with SQL Server 2016 Service Pack 1. The information is limited to the top 10 waits, and most common sleep and idle waits are not included in the plan.

You can try one of the queries we used earlier in this chapter while requesting the actual execution plan:

```
SELECT SUM(soh.SubTotal)
FROM Sales.SalesOrderHeader soh
JOIN Sales.SalesOrderDetail sod ON soh.SalesOrderID = sod.SalesOrderID
```

You can see the information in the WaitStats section of the graphical plan. Next is an XML fragment of the same information I got on my test execution:

```
<WaitStats>
<Wait WaitType="SOS_SCHEDULER_YIELD" WaitTimeMs="1" WaitCount="35" />
<Wait WaitType="MEMORY_ALLOCATION_EXT" WaitTimeMs="25" WaitCount="2007" />
<Wait WaitType="PAGEIOLATCH_SH" WaitTimeMs="377" WaitCount="11" />
</WaitStats>
```

The information shows the wait type, the wait time in milliseconds, and the wait count or times the wait occurred for the duration of the query.

Finally, there was been some discussion on the SQL Server community and a Microsoft connect request was submitted indicating that not all the important waits are reported on the execution plan. The request is still open, and you can read the details online at connect.microsoft.com/SQLServer/feedback/details/3137948.

Recent Announcements

Another of the major changes in SQL Server 2017 is the new servicing model. Although service packs will still be used for SQL Server 2016 and previous supported versions, no more service packs will be released for SQL Server 2017 and later. The new servicing model will be based on cumulative updates (and General Distribution Releases, or GDRs, when required).

Cumulative updates will be released more often at first and then less frequently in the new servicing model. A cumulative update will be available every month for the first 12 months and every quarter for the remainder 4 years of the full 5-year mainstream lifecycle. You can read more details about the new servicing model online at https://blogs.msdn.microsoft.com/sqlreleaseservices/announcing-the-modern-servicing-model-for-sql-server/.

Finally, as of this writing, there have been a few new releases and announcements coming in SQL Server. First, SQL Operations Studio is available for preview. SQL Operations Studio is a new tool for database development and operations intended to work with SQL Server on Windows, Linux and Docker, Azure SQL Database, and Azure SQL Data Warehouse. SQL Operations Studio can run on Windows, Mac, or Linux operating systems. For more details and to download, visit https://blogs .technet.microsoft.com/dataplatforminsider/2017/11/15/announcing-sql-operations-studio-for-preview/.

Microsoft also recently announced some improvements to the database engine, which will be included in a future release:

▶ **Table variable deferred compilation**   This feature would help to get better cardinality estimation for table variables, instead of the default fixed estimate of 100.

▶ **Batch mode for row store**   Batch mode execution, as introduced with SQL Server 2012, has been available only for the columnstore indexes technology.

▶ **Scalar UDF inlining**   This feature will provide better performance for scalar user-defined functions.

▶ **Adaptive query processing row mode memory grant feedback**   As explained earlier, this would be the adaptive query processing memory grant feedback for rowstores.

Summary

This chapter covered what is new in query processing in SQL Server 2017, and it also included some SQL Server 2016 features released recently. The most important query processing innovations on SQL Server 2017 are adaptive query processing and automatic tuning.

Adaptive query processing is a very promising collection of features that for the current release include three algorithms: batch mode adaptive joins, batch mode adaptive memory grant feedback, and interleaved execution for multistatement table-valued functions. A future feature, adaptive query processing row mode memory grant feedback, has been announced as well.

Automatic tuning is also a new collection of features that seems to be in its infancy, with only one feature available in SQL Server—automatic plan correction—plus another one, automatic index management, available only on Azure SQL Database.

The chapter also covered a few SQL Server 2016 Service Pack 1 enhancements. This service pack change indicated the first time in the history of SQL Server in which a consistent programmability surface area was available for developers across SQL Server editions. Starting with this groundbreaking release, features such as columnstore indexes and In-Memory OLTP, among others, are now available for all editions of SQL Server.

Chapter 7

High Availability and Disaster Recovery

In This Chapter

- ► **SQL Server High-Availability and Disaster-Recovery Features**
- ► **Always On Availability Groups**
- ► **Availability Groups on Windows vs. Linux**
- ► **Implementing Availability Groups**
- ► **Summary**

This chapter provides an introduction to high-availability and disaster-recovery solutions for SQL Server on Linux and focuses on Always On availability groups. As high availability and disaster recovery are very broad topics, this chapter does not intend to be a comprehensive reference, but it will teach you everything you need to know to get started using this feature with SQL Server on Linux. For additional information, refer to the SQL Server documentation.

Availability groups, failover cluster instances (FCIs), and log shipping are the most important availability features provided by SQL Server 2017 on Linux. Such features are used in high-availability and disaster-recovery configurations. With availability groups, they can also be used for migrations and upgrades or even to scale out readable copies of one or more databases. A SQL Server feature that is also sometimes considered for availability scenarios, *replication*, is not currently available in SQL Server for Linux but is planned to be included in a future release. Another related feature, *database mirroring*, has been deprecated as of SQL Server 2012 and will not be included in the Linux release. A flavor of availability groups, *basic availability groups*, is available with SQL Server Standard edition and is intended to provide an alternative to replace (the now defunct) database mirroring feature on installations not running the Enterprise Edition.

"Always On" is a term that encompasses both Always On availability groups and Always On FCIs. A great benefit of availability groups is that they can provide high-availability and disaster-recovery solutions over geographic areas. For example, a local secondary replica can provide high-availability capabilities and also a remote secondary replica on a different data center to provide disaster recovery. In this scenario, the local replica traffic can be replicated synchronously, thereby providing zero data loss high availability, which is possible when network latency is low. And the remote replica can run asynchronously, providing minimal data loss disaster recovery where low network latency is not guaranteed.

SQL Server High-Availability and Disaster-Recovery Features

Although SQL Server provides features to help with high availability and disaster recovery, a robust and tested backup and restore strategy still has to be the basis of any availability solution. Although high availability and disaster recovery have common objectives, high availability usually refers to redundancy on the same data center, while disaster recovery is related to the choice to recover a system when a data center is no longer available. So high availability could be helpful, for example, when a single server is not available; disaster recovery is required when a data center suffers a catastrophic event, such as a flood or earthquake, to make applications and databases available in some other data center or location.

SQL Server features such as log shipping and replication have been available for almost as long as the product itself. Failover clustering was introduced with SQL Server 6.5. Database mirroring was introduced with SQL Server 2005 and was subsequently deprecated with SQL Server 2012, which introduced availability groups. Although availability groups is an Enterprise Edition feature, basic availability groups can be used in the Standard Edition as well, which helps with the replacement of database mirroring. SQL Server installations using database mirroring can be replaced with basic availability groups on SQL Server Standard Edition or regular availability groups on the Enterprise Edition. Replication is not yet available on the Linux release.

Log shipping is the process of automating the continuous backup of transaction log files on a primary database server and then restoring them to a secondary server. Log shipping uses SQL Server Agent jobs that periodically take transaction log backups of the primary database, copy them to one or more secondary server instances, and restore them to the secondary databases. For availability groups and database mirroring, the SQL Server engine reads transactions from the transaction log and copies them from the principal server instance to the mirror or secondary replica. Availability groups can work in two different ways: synchronous-commit mode and asynchronous-commit mode. In *synchronous-commit mode*, the primary replica waits for the secondary replica to confirm that transaction log records have been written to disk, which is also called *hardening the log*. In *asynchronous-commit mode*, the database engine does not wait for any secondary replica to write incoming transaction log records to disk. Therefore, synchronous-commit guarantees that no data loss is possible on a synchronous replica database, whereas asynchronous-commit can result in some data loss depending upon several factors, such as network latency and transactional throughput.

Another main consideration between these availability features is the scope. Failover clustering is the only one of these features that works at the instance level, while availability groups, log shipping, and database mirroring all work at the database level. Contrast this with replication, which can be configured even at a granular level, where tables or subsets of tables can be replicated; these objects are known as *publications*. So in these scenarios, except failover clustering, instance-level objects such as logins or SQL Server Agent jobs would have to be manually synchronized in a full failover scenario.

Although FCIs provide failover at the instance level, they require some sort of shared storage, which also means that only a single copy of the data provides a single point of failure, as opposed to availability groups and the other features, in which two or more copies of a database can be involved.

A basic availability group supports only two replicas—a primary and a secondary—and the availability group can have only one database. However, although you can have only one database in a basic availability group, you can have several basic availability groups on the same SQL Server instance. Enterprise Edition availability groups can have multiple databases in a single availability group and up to nine replicas per availability group (one primary and eight secondaries). Additional benefits such as readable secondaries (providing scale-out reads) or offloading backups on secondary replicas are available only in the Enterprise Edition.

Always On Availability Groups

As mentioned, Always On availability groups are also available on SQL Server on Linux. The main difference between availability groups in Windows and Linux is that in Linux, availability groups depend on Pacemaker instead of Windows Server Failover Cluster (WSFC). WSFC is built into the Windows operating system, and SQL Server and availability groups are cluster-aware. So in Windows, all the elements—SQL Server, the operating system, and WSFC—are held tightly together because they are all from one vendor: Microsoft. Linux, on the other hand, does not provide a vendor-agnostic native clustering solution but instead relies on other solutions such as Pacemaker. Pacemaker is an open-source solution and external to Linux, and each of the three supported Linux distributions provides its own version of Pacemaker.

The SQL Server High-Availability package, also known as the SQL Server resource agent for Pacemaker, is an optional package in SQL Server that must be installed for a high-availability solution in Linux. You can think of the SQL Server High-Availability package as the integration between Pacemaker and SQL Server high-availability solutions—in this case, availability groups and failover cluster instances (FCIs). A SQL Server instance in Linux is not cluster-aware.

NOTE

As introduced in Chapter 1, the SQL Server Agent is optional but recommended for installation and is a requirement for a log-shipping configuration. Interestingly, although in Windows they are installed together, the database engine and the SQL Server Agent run as different Windows services. On Linux, although they are installed with different packages, the SQL Server Agent runs as part of the database engine process.

Configuration-only replicas are a new concept in Linux and are available only on SQL Server 2017 CU1 and later. A configuration-only replica can be hosted on any edition of SQL Server, including SQL Server Express, and does not count toward the maximum number of replicas per SQL Server edition. In the same way, configuration-only replicas can also be used with SQL Server Standard Edition, which is limited to two replicas. It is also recommended to have at least SQL Server Management Studio 17.1 to work with availability groups in Linux. At the time of writing, the latest SQL Server Management Studio version is 17.5, and the latest SQL Server cumulative update is CU3.

NOTE

SQL Server 2017 CU3 provided a security update related to a processor design vulnerability that impacted nearly every computer and phone. These vulnerabilities are referred to as speculative execution side-channel attacks, aka the Meltdown and Spectre side-channel vulnerabilities.

Availability groups can be used to configure both high-availability and disaster-recovery solutions. For example, availability groups can be configured to have a primary and secondary replica on the same data center, plus another secondary replica on a different data center, as shown in Figure 7-1. Availability groups can also be used in other scenarios, such as migration, upgrades, and creation of readable copies for running queries or taking backups.

A cluster type in SQL Server 2017 can be WSFC, External, or None. An availability group type of None can be used on both Windows and Linux and does not require an underlying cluster, removing the cluster configuration complexity. This configuration, however, is not a high-availability solution but can be used for migrations or upgrades or to add another read-only replica. The None cluster type option can technically enable high-availability and disaster-recovery capabilities where no automatic failover is required, but this configuration is not recommended.

For automatic failover, availability groups on Linux require the following configurations and states:

▶ The cluster type must be configured to External; cluster type None is not supported.

▶ The primary and secondary replicas are configured as synchronous commit.

▶ The secondary replica must be in a synchronized state (as opposed to synchronizing).

▶ The secondary replica sequence_number must match the one from the original primary replica.

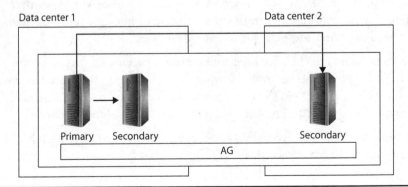

Figure 7-1 *Availability groups with replicas on two data centers*

Pacemaker uses constraints, which could be something similar to dependencies on a Windows failover cluster. Pacemaker provides three kinds of constraints:

▶ **Colocation**   Indicates whether or not two resources should be running on the same node

▶ **Location**   Enforces where a resource can or cannot run

▶ **Ordering**   Indicates the order in which the cluster resources should start

Pacemaker saves the configuration of the cluster in the corosync.conf file.

A Pacemaker cluster also uses the concept of *fencing*, which is the isolation of a failed node so that it does not cause disruption to a computer cluster; it is implemented by the Stonith (which stands for "Shoot the other node in the head") technique. At the time of this writing, Hyper-V does not include a solution for Stonith, which also impacts Microsoft Azure virtual machines. Microsoft is working on a solution to this.

Availability Groups on Windows vs. Linux

The following are some of the differences between availability groups on Windows and Linux:

▶ Linux does not provide a clustering component. Instead, each of the three Linux-supported distributions use Pacemaker, which is an open-source clustering solution.

▶ The Pacemaker configuration of the availability group is created after the availability group is configured. In the Windows world you are required to create a cluster first using WSFC and then configure availability groups.

▶ The Microsoft Distributed Transaction Coordinator (MSDTC) is not available on Linux. If your application requires MSDTC, you cannot use SQL Server on a Linux platform. The MSDTC service is a component of Windows that is responsible for coordinating transactions that span multiple resource managers, such as file systems, message queues, and databases.

▶ Automatic or manual failover is performed using Pacemaker. No support is available for T-SQL or SQL Server tools. However, a workaround can be used in cases where a failover using cluster tools may not work; it can be used to force a manual failover using the T-SQL `ALTER AVAILABILITY GROUP FAILOVER` statement.

▶ The SQL Server High-Availability package provides the integration between Pacemaker on Linux and SQL Server.

▶ Pacemaker cannot use a file share as a witness. As a solution to this limitation, you can use a configuration-only replica, which is available on SQL Server 2017 CU1 and later. In the same way, a configuration-only replica can also be used with SQL Server Standard Edition, which is limited to two replicas, plus the configuration-only replica could be on any edition.

Implementing Availability Groups

This section covers how to implement a high-availability solution using SQL Server availability groups on Red Hat Enterprise Linux and Ubuntu. References to implement on SUSE Linux Enterprise Server are provided. The implementation will use three replicas in synchronous-commit mode.

Let's start by creating three servers or virtual machines with Red Hat Enterprise Linux and SQL Server installed.

1. From Microsoft Azure, type **search "Red Hat SQL Server 2017"** to find the image named "Free SQL Server License: SQL Server 2017 Developer on Red Hat Enterprise Linux 7.4 (RHEL)." See Chapter 1 for more detailed instructions about how to create virtual machines and configure them as indicated there.

2. Name the virtual machines sqlonlinux1, sqlonlinux2, and sqlonlinux3. You are creating a primary replica and two secondary replicas.

3. Connect to each server, and make sure the servers can communicate with each other. When I create Azure, by default, I can ping each server, so in this case I don't have to do anything else. You may need to open firewall ports to connect. Make sure your configuration can resolve IP addresses to hostnames. You may also need to verify and update the information on /etc/hosts.

NOTE

/etc/hosts is a plain-text operating system file that maps computer hostnames to IP addresses.

```
$ ping sqlonlinux2
PING sqlonlinux2.ckea0p3oggauzez3101pol5gmd.dx.internal.cloudapp.net (10.1.3.23) 56(84) bytes of data.
64 bytes from 10.1.3.23 (10.1.3.23): icmp_seq=1 ttl=64 time=2.61 ms
64 bytes from 10.1.3.23 (10.1.3.23): icmp_seq=2 ttl=64 time=2.73 ms
64 bytes from 10.1.3.23 (10.1.3.23): icmp_seq=3 ttl=64 time=1.21 ms
64 bytes from 10.1.3.23 (10.1.3.23): icmp_seq=4 ttl=64 time=0.919 ms
^C
--- sqlonlinux2.ckea0p3oggauzez3101pol5gmd.dx.internal.cloudapp.net ping statistics ---
4 packets transmitted, 4 received, 0% packet loss, time 3004ms
rtt min/avg/max/mdev = 0.919/1.871/2.735/0.812 ms
```

Most of the steps indicated in this section are to be performed on every server. Pay attention to the few cases in which a step needs to be performed only on a specific server—for example, only on the primary replica or at the secondary replicas.

4. To finish the SQL Server configuration on each server, run the following command while specifying a strong system administrator (sa) password:

```
$ sudo /opt/mssql/bin/mssql-conf set-sa-password
Enter the SQL Server system administrator password:
Confirm the SQL Server system administrator password:
Configuring SQL Server...

The system administrator password has been changed.
Please run 'sudo systemctl start mssql-server' to start SQL Server.
```

5. Run the following `systemctl` command to start SQL Server as recommended by the preceding output:

```
$ sudo systemctl start mssql-server
```

SQL Server is now running, and you are ready to connect using the sa account. At this point, running `SELECT @@VERSION` on my instance returns Microsoft SQL Server 2017 (RTM) - 14.0.1000.169 (X64), which means this is the RTM (Release to Manufacturing) release and is missing a few cumulative updates (CUs).

Let's update to the latest cumulative update, which at the moment is CU3, by running the following `yum` command:

```
$ sudo yum update mssql-server
```

For more details about the `yum` command, see Chapter 3.

At the end of the software update process, my SQL Server version was updated to Microsoft SQL Server 2017 (RTM-CU3-GDR) (KB4052987) - 14.0.3015.40 (X64).

We will be using SQL Server Management Studio on Windows for most of the configuration in this section, although we could also use the sqlcmd utility on Linux. The latest version of SQL Server Management Studio is recommended, however, which at this writing is version 17.4. As indicated in Chapter 1, to connect to SQL Server from outside the virtual machine, you need to open the TCP port 1433. Here's a quick reminder of the steps required to open a port on the Microsoft Azure Portal:

1. Select your virtual machine.
2. Select Networking.
3. On the Inbound Port Rules section on the right, select Add Inbound.
4. At the Add Inbound Security Rule section, select the predefined MS SQL service and click OK. Note that the predefined service already defines TCP port 1433.

Refer to Chapter 1 for more details. Later in this section, you will need to open a port for availability groups as well; the default port is 5022.

In addition, and only for Red Hat Enterprise Linux, you need to run the following commands to open the same TCP port on the firewall. At this writing, this is not required for SUSE Enterprise Linux Server or Ubuntu Azure virtual machines.

```
$ sudo firewall-cmd --zone=public --add-port=1433/tcp –permanent
$ sudo firewall-cmd --reload
```

firewall-cmd is the command-line client of the firewalld daemon. In this particular case, the command adds the TCP port 1433. You can specify either a single port number or a port range. The defined protocol can be TCP, UDP, SCTP, or DCCP. Use the --permanent option to set the port permanently. These changes are not effective immediately but only after the service is reloaded or restarted or the system is rebooted. Use the --reload option to reload firewall rules and keep state information.

Next, enable the SQL Server instance to allow Always On availability groups. As introduced in Chapter 4, use the hadr.hadrenabled mssql-conf option to enable availability groups on SQL Server on Linux. After availability groups are enabled, restart the SQL Server instance as indicated:

```
$ sudo /opt/mssql/bin/mssql-conf set hadr.hadrenabled  1
SQL Server needs to be restarted in order to apply this setting. Please run
'systemctl restart mssql-server.service'.
$ sudo systemctl restart mssql-server
```

T-SQL Configuration

The remaining configuration in this section will be done in SQL Server using T-SQL statements. As mentioned, it could also be done at the server level using the sqlcmd utility or any other client tool that can submit T-SQL statements to the database engine. Here we will use SQL Server Management Studio. (In the next section I will cover the Availability Groups user interface, which requires SQL Server Management Studio.)

Start the AlwaysOn_health extended events session. AlwaysOn_health is a preconfigured extended events session that is useful and convenient to help you detect and troubleshoot potential issues with availability groups. Use ALTER EVENT SESSION to start the session, as shown next:

```
ALTER EVENT SESSION AlwaysOn_health ON SERVER WITH (STARTUP_STATE=ON)
```

NOTE

For more details about the AlwaysOn_health extended events session, see https://msdn.microsoft.com/en-us/library/dn135324(v=sql.110).aspx.

Next, create a login and username to be used by the availability group configuration. Specify a strong password for this and the other password required in this chapter:

```
CREATE LOGIN ag_login WITH PASSWORD = 'Pa$$w0rd!'
CREATE USER ag_user FOR LOGIN ag_login
```

For the SQL Server on Linux availability group configuration, we need a certificate to authenticate communication between the mirroring endpoints. For the SQL Server 2017 release, using certificates is the only authentication method supported, but Windows authentication will be enabled in a future release. This step basically requires that a master key and a certificate be created. The database master key is a symmetric key used to protect the private keys of certificates and asymmetric keys that are present in the database. The CREATE CERTIFICATE statement adds a certificate to a database in SQL Server. Finally, BACKUP CERTIFICATE is used to export both the certificate and the private key to files. In our case, the certificate will be saved in /var/opt/mssql/data/ag_certificate.cer'. In addition, the private key of the certificate will be exported to /var/opt/mssql/data/ag_certificate.pvk'.

Create and back up a certificate by running the following statements only on the primary replica sqlonlinux1:

```
CREATE MASTER KEY ENCRYPTION BY PASSWORD = 'Pa$$w0rd!';
CREATE CERTIFICATE ag_certificate WITH SUBJECT = 'ag';
BACKUP CERTIFICATE ag_certificate
   TO FILE = '/var/opt/mssql/data/ag_certificate.cer'
   WITH PRIVATE KEY (
          FILE = '/var/opt/mssql/data/ag_certificate.pvk',
          ENCRYPTION BY PASSWORD = 'Pa$$w0rd!'
       );
```

You can verify that both files were created on /var/opt/mssql/data/:

```
# ls -l /var/opt/mssql/data/ag*
-rw-rw----. 1 mssql mssql  667 Jan  8 04:13 /var/opt/mssql/data/ag_certificate.cer
-rw-rw----. 1 mssql mssql 1212 Jan  8 04:13 /var/opt/mssql/data/ag_certificate.pvk
```

Now let's copy such files to the same location on the other two servers and grant the same permissions they have on the principal replica. There are a few different ways to accomplish this. In Chapter 1, we used the PuTTY Secure Copy client or pscp utility to copy files between Windows and Linux. Because in this case, we will be copying files between Linux servers, we'll use scp, the secure copy command, which is a remote file copy program used to copy files between hosts on a network.

The scp command can use the following basic format to copy files:

```
scp file username@servername:/directory/subdirectory
```

Run the following command, replacing the host destination name, such as sqlonlinux2, or IP address and the user and directory destination. This command is executed at the primary replica and the files will be copied to my home directory on both of the secondary replicas:

```
sudo scp /var/opt/mssql/data/ag* bnevarez@23.99.95.94:/home/bnevarez
```

The files are copied as the user bnevarez, so I still need to copy them to the correct directory and give them the right permissions. Run the following commands to do that:

```
# cp /home/bnevarez/ag* /var/opt/mssql/data
# cd /var/opt/mssql/data
# chown mssql ag*
# chgrp mssql ag*
```

Run ls -l to validate permissions and ownership:

```
# ls -l
total 54216
-rw-r-----. 1 mssql mssql      667 Jan 14 04:50 ag_certificate.cer
-rw-r-----. 1 mssql mssql     1212 Jan 14 04:50 ag_certificate.pvk
```

Repeat the same operations to copy the files to the additional secondary replica.

So we just copied the files to the secondary replicas. Now the SQL Server instance needs to be aware of the certificates. Run the following statements on the other two servers, sqlonlinux2 and sqlonlinux3. This creates a master key and a certificate on the secondary servers from the backup created on the primary replica. Once again, use a strong password. Also, in this particular case, the password used on DECRYPTION BY PASSWORD has to be the same password used previously by the ENCRYPTION BY PASSWORD option when backing up the private key to a file.

```
CREATE MASTER KEY ENCRYPTION BY PASSWORD = 'Pa$$w0rd!';
CREATE CERTIFICATE ag_certificate
    AUTHORIZATION ag_user
    FROM FILE = '/var/opt/mssql/data/ag_certificate.cer'
    WITH PRIVATE KEY (
    FILE = '/var/opt/mssql/data/ag_certificate.pvk',
    DECRYPTION BY PASSWORD = 'Pa$$w0rd!'
            );
```

We are finally ready to create the database mirroring endpoints on all the servers. Database mirroring endpoints are still used in the availability groups terminology, although database mirroring is a separate feature that is also already deprecated. Database mirroring endpoints require a TCP port, so, once again, we need to open TCP ports on each virtual machine, which can be the default 5022 or any other available port of your choice.

Open the port from the Microsoft Azure Portal for each virtual machine, as indicated earlier when we opened TCP port 1433, and in the Inbound Port Rules section on the right, select Add Inbound. This time, there is no predefined service, so just select Custom and specify both Port ranges—in this case, 5022—and a default Name—in this case Port_5022. You may also need to change the Priority, for example, to 1020. Priority configures the order in which rules are being processed.

Run the `firewall-cmd` command, but this time for TCP port 5022. This is required only for Red Hat Enterprise Linux and is not needed for Ubuntu and SUSE Linux Enterprise Server.

```
$ sudo firewall-cmd --zone=public --add-port=5022/tcp --permanent
$ sudo firewall-cmd --reload
```

We are ready to run the CREATE ENDPOINT statement. The ROLE option of the statement defines the database mirroring role or roles that the endpoint supports and could be WITNESS, PARTNER, or ALL. As mentioned earlier, SQL Server Express now can be used to host a configuration-only replica, which supports only the WITNESS role.

Also, using a certificate is the only authentication method available on SQL Server 2017 on Linux. Windows authentication will be supported in a future release. The example statement also specifies that connections to this endpoint must use encryption using the AES algorithm, which is the default in SQL Server 2016 and later. No listener IP address will be defined for this exercise.

Finally, for each replica instance, create the new endpoint, start it, and grant connect permissions to it for the SQL Server login created earlier:

```
CREATE ENDPOINT [ag_endpoint]
    AS TCP (LISTENER_IP = (0.0.0.0), LISTENER_PORT = 5022)
    FOR DATA_MIRRORING (
        ROLE = ALL,
        AUTHENTICATION = CERTIFICATE ag_certificate,
        ENCRYPTION = REQUIRED ALGORITHM AES
        );
ALTER ENDPOINT [ag_endpoint] STATE = STARTED;
GRANT CONNECT ON ENDPOINT::[ag_endpoint] TO [ag_login];
```

Next we will create the availability group only on the primary replica, sqlonlinux1. The CREATE AVAILABILITY GROUP statement has a large variety of options. The following statement specifies several items. DB_FAILOVER with a value of ON specifies that any status other than ONLINE for a database in the availability group triggers an automatic failover. If the choice were OFF it means that only the health of the instance is used to trigger automatic failover.

CLUSTER_TYPE, which is new to SQL Server 2017, defines the cluster type, and the values can be WSFC, EXTERNAL, and NONE. WSFC is used to configure availability groups on Windows using a WSFC. EXTERNAL can be used on Linux when using an external cluster manager such as Pacemaker. NONE can be used when no cluster manager is used. This last choice can be useful for availability group configurations to be used as read-only replicas or migrations or upgrades. On a SQL Server instance on Linux, you will see only the EXTERNAL and NONE choices.

AVAILABILITY_MODE defines whether the primary replica should wait for the secondary replica to acknowledge the writing of log records to disk before the primary replica can commit a transaction on a database, as defined by the values ASYNCHRONOUS_COMMIT and SYNCHRONOUS_COMMIT. A third choice, new to SQL Server 2007 CU1, CONFIGURATION_ONLY, defines a configuration-only replica or a replica that is used only for availability group configuration metadata. CONFIGURATION_ONLY can be used on any edition of SQL Server and does not apply for CLUSTER_TYPE as WSFC. It is mainly used as a witness on Linux environments where a file share is not yet supported.

FAILOVER_MODE specifies the failover mode, which could be AUTOMATIC, MANUAL, or EXTERNAL. It is always EXTERNAL for Linux installations.

Finally, SEEDING_MODE defines how the secondary replica is initially seeded and can have the options AUTOMATIC or MANUAL. ENDPOINT_URL specifies the URL path for the database mirroring endpoint on the instance of SQL Server that hosts the availability replica. As you can see in the following example, ENDPOINT_URL requires a system name, a fully qualified domain name, or an IP address that unambiguously identifies the destination computer system and the port number that is associated with the mirroring endpoint of the partner server instance.

The following statement creates an availability group with three synchronous replicas. Replace the server, fully qualified domain name, and port with your own information. For simplicity, only the server name is used—in your case, add the fully qualified domain name as well.

```
USE master
GO
CREATE AVAILABILITY GROUP ag1
    WITH (DB_FAILOVER = ON, CLUSTER_TYPE = EXTERNAL)
    FOR REPLICA ON
```

```
      N'sqlonlinux1'
       WITH (
           ENDPOINT_URL = N'tcp://sqlonlinux1:5022',
           AVAILABILITY_MODE = SYNCHRONOUS_COMMIT,
           FAILOVER_MODE = EXTERNAL,
           SEEDING_MODE = AUTOMATIC
           ),
      N'sqlonlinux2'
       WITH (
           ENDPOINT_URL = N'tcp://sqlonlinux2:5022',
           AVAILABILITY_MODE = SYNCHRONOUS_COMMIT,
           FAILOVER_MODE = EXTERNAL,
           SEEDING_MODE = AUTOMATIC
           ),
      N'sqlonlinux3'
      WITH(
           ENDPOINT_URL = N'tcp://sqlonlinux3:5022',
           AVAILABILITY_MODE = SYNCHRONOUS_COMMIT,
           FAILOVER_MODE = EXTERNAL,
           SEEDING_MODE = AUTOMATIC
           );
```

Interesting to note is that if you run this twice, you get a Windows-related message, which I also saw on some other errors:

```
Msg 41171, Level 16, State 2, Line 31
Failed to create availability group 'ag1', because a Windows Server
Failover Cluster (WSFC) group with the specified name already exists.
The operation has been rolled back successfully.  To retry creating an
availability group, either remove or rename the existing WSFC group, or
retry the operation specifying a different availability group name.
```

Next, grant the CREATE ANY DATABASE permission to the availability group—for now, only for the primary replica sqlonlinux1:

```
ALTER AVAILABILITY GROUP ag1 GRANT CREATE ANY DATABASE;
```

Run the following statements on the other two replicas, sqlonlinux2 and sqlonlinux3. The JOIN option of ALTER AVAILABILITY GROUP is used by a local server instance to host a secondary replica in the specified availability group. Same as with sqlonlinux1, the CREATE ANY DATABASE permission is granted to the availability group.

```
ALTER AVAILABILITY GROUP ag1 JOIN WITH (CLUSTER_TYPE = EXTERNAL);
GO
ALTER AVAILABILITY GROUP ag1 GRANT CREATE ANY DATABASE;
```

At this moment, the availability group is completely configured. Now it is time to go back to the primary replica and add a database to the availability group. You can use an existing database or create a database now. The database needs to be in the full recovery mode and have an initial backup. Run the following statements to do just that:

```
CREATE DATABASE AdventureWorks
ALTER DATABASE AdventureWorks SET RECOVERY FULL
BACKUP DATABASE AdventureWorks
   TO DISK = N'/var/opt/mssql/data/AdventureWorks.bak'
```

Again, on the primary replica, sqlonlinux1, we can use the ADD DATABASE option of the ALTER AVAILABILITY GROUP statement to add one or more user databases to the availability group. Run the following statement:

```
ALTER AVAILABILITY GROUP ag1 ADD DATABASE AdventureWorks
```

Because the availability group was configured with SEEDING_MODE as AUTOMATIC, at this time the databases should be created on the secondary replicas. This would obviously depend on the size of the database. Validate that the database has been created by using Object Explorer on SQL Server Management Studio or by running the following statements:

```
SELECT * FROM sys.databases
GO
SELECT @@SERVERNAME, DB_NAME(database_id), synchronization_state_desc,
synchronization_health_desc
FROM sys.dm_hadr_database_replica_states
```

The synchronization_state_desc should be SYNCHRONIZED (perhaps you could briefly see it as NOT SYNCHRONIZING and then SYNCHRONIZING if you ran the ALTER AVAILABILITY GROUP statement). The synchronization_health_desc should be HEALTHY (also may show briefly as NOT_HEALTHY).

We have completed the configuration of the availability group in SQL Server. Now we need to configure Pacemaker on Linux. It is interesting to note that even when each supported Linux distribution has Pacemaker available, they are not exactly the same and there might be differences between distributions, as each one can be customized and have some different implementations and versions. Before going into the Pacemaker configuration, I'll also review briefly how to configure availability groups using the SQL Server Management Studio user interface.

SQL Server Management Studio Configuration

To get started configuring availability groups in SQL Server Management Studio, expand the Always On High Availability folder. Sometimes the warning about enabling the high-availability option appears, although it was already enabled. You can just ignore it.

As indicated earlier, unlike on Windows, you can configure availability groups on Linux before configuring Pacemaker.

You can configure availability groups either in SQL Server Management Studio using the New Availability Group choice or using the New Availability Group Wizard. Let's try the New Availability Group Wizard connected to the instance currently hosting the AdventureWorks database.

1. Start the New Availability Group Wizard. You will see the New Availability Group Introduction page, shown in Figure 7-2, which includes a summary of the information you need to provide in the wizard. Read the information on the page and click Next.

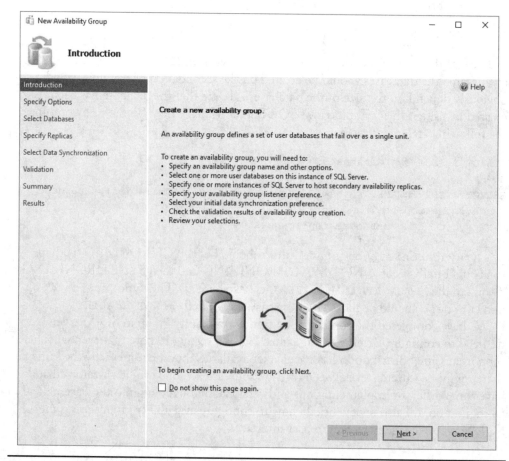

Figure 7-2   *Read the Introduction page.*

2. The Specify Availability Group Options page, shown in Figure 7-3, asks you to specify a name for the availability group. Type **ag1** for our example.

3. You have only two choices for Cluster type: EXTERNAL and NONE. WSFC is not available on a Linux instance. The Database Level Health Detection checkbox (or DB_FAILOVER option of the CREATE AVAILABILITY GROUP statement) is used to trigger the automatic failover of the availability group when a database is no longer in the online status. Leave the default of EXTERNAL and check the Database Level Health Detection box. Then click Next.

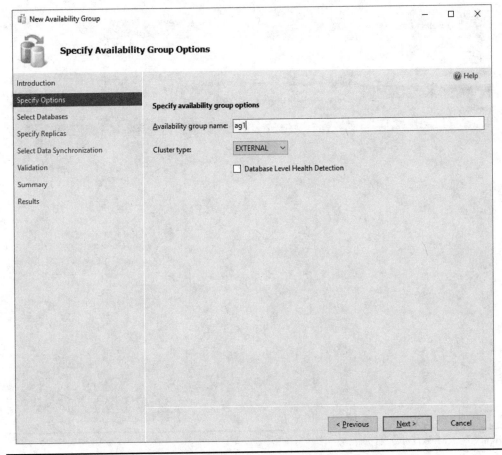

Figure 7-3 *Specify the group name and other options.*

4. On the Select Databases page, shown in Figure 7-4, you'll select one or more databases for the availability group. The size and status of the database are specified. A status of Meets Prerequisites, as shown, indicates that the database can be selected. If a database does not meet the prerequisites, the Status column will indicate the reason. (A common reason may be a database that is not in the full recovery mode.) You may also need to specify a password if the database contains a database master key. Check the AdventureWorks box and click Next.

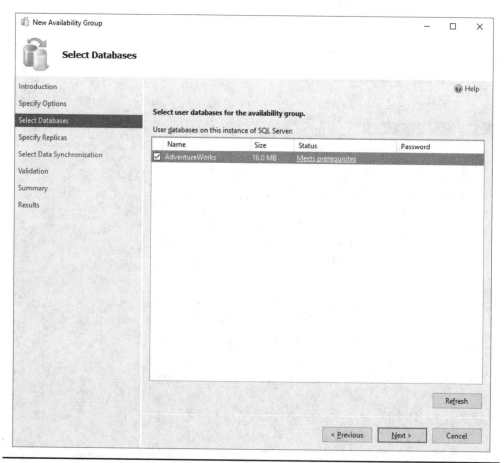

Figure 7-4 *Select Databases page*

5. The Specify Replicas page, shown in Figure 7-5, includes five tabs (Replicas, Endpoints, Backup Preferences, Listener, and Read-Only Routing) and a wealth of information; I will just cover the basics here.

    The Replicas tab is the main tab; here you can specify each instance of SQL Server that will host or currently hosts a secondary replica. Keep in mind that the SQL Server instance to which you are currently connected will host the primary replica. For our exercise, add sqlonlinux2 and sqlonlinux3 (click Add) and configure and change the Availability Mode to Synchronous Commit for all three replicas, as shown in Figure 7-5.

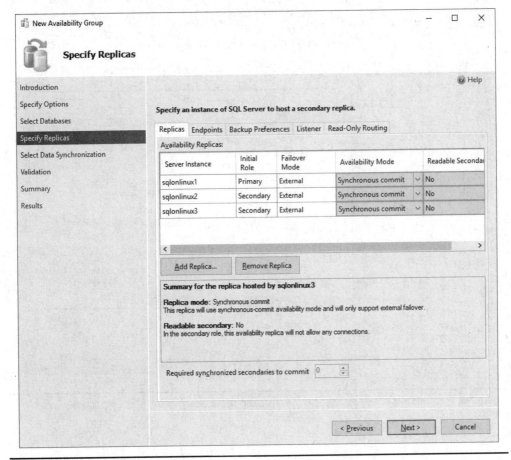

Figure 7-5   *Specify Replicas page*

The Endpoints tab, shown in Figure 7-6, is where you validate your existing database mirroring endpoints.

You may also want to check the Backup Preferences tab (Figure 7-7), where you can choose your backup preference for the availability group as a whole and your backup priorities for the individual availability replicas.

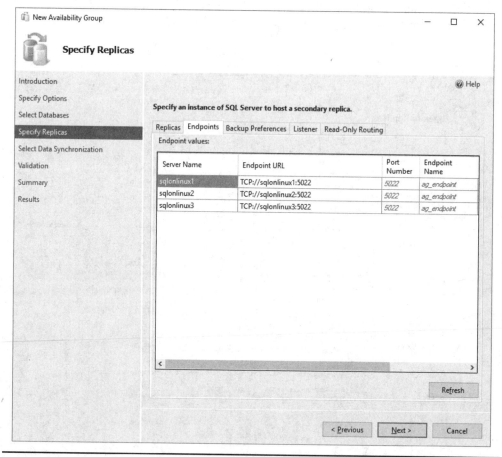

Figure 7-6   *Validate your existing database mirroring endpoints on the Specify Replicas page, Endpoints tab.*

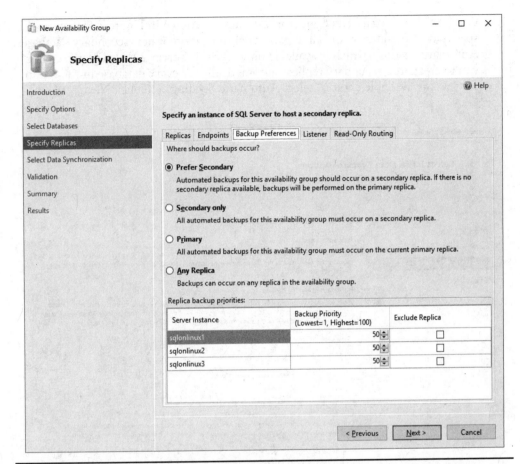

Figure 7-7   *Choose your backup preferences on the Backup Preferences tab.*

On the Listener tab, you can create an availability group listener. We are not going to define a listener for this exercise.

Use the Read-Only Routing tab to route qualifying read-only connection requests to an available readable secondary replica. A readable secondary replica is a replica that is configured to allow read-only workloads when running under the secondary role.

6.   Click Next.

7. On the Select Initial Data Synchronization page, shown in Figure 7-8, you can specify your preference for initial data synchronization of new secondary databases. Automatic seeding, which is available only on SQL Server 2016 and later, enables you to create the secondary replicas automatically for every database in the group. Review the available choices, select Automatic Seeding, and click Next.

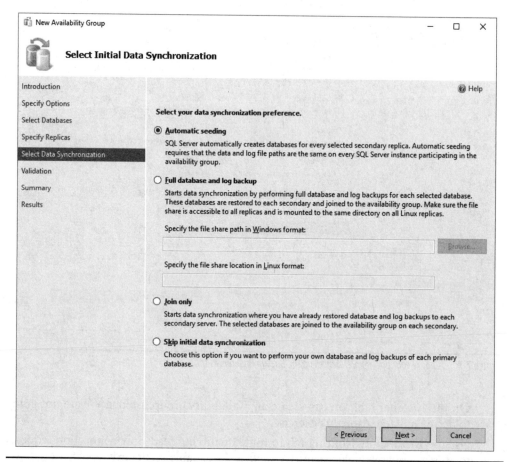

Figure 7-8   *Select Data Synchronization page*

8. On the Validation page, shown in Figure 7-9, you can validate that your environment supports all the configuration choices you made on previous pages of the wizard. The Result column can show Error, Skipped, Success, or Warning. Errors should be fixed before continuing with the availability group configuration. Warning messages should be reviewed as well to avoid potential issues with your future installation. Skipped means that the validation step was skipped because it is not required by your selections. Assuming you got no errors, click Next.

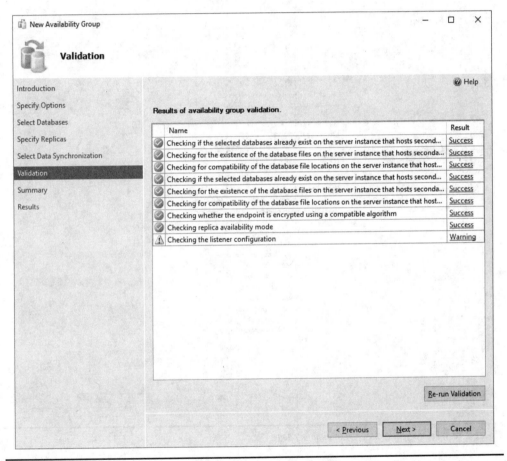

Figure 7-9   *Validate that your environment supports your configuration choices.*

9. The Summary page, shown in Figure 7-10, includes all the selections you made in the wizard and gives you the opportunity to review before submitting the changes to SQL Server. Click the Previous button to make any changes. Once you are satisfied with your choices, click Finish. Optionally, click the Script button to create a T-SQL script with all your selections. Then click Finish.

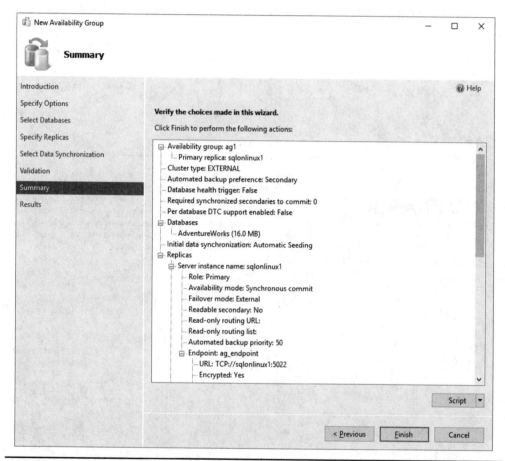

Figure 7-10   *Review your choices on the Summary page.*

10. On the Results page, shown in Figure 7-11, you can see the results of implementing the required changes. Results can show Error or Success. The page will list each of the activities performed, such as configuring endpoints and starting the AlwaysOn_health extended events session on each of the replicas, plus creating the availability group, waiting for the availability group to come online, and joining the secondary replicas to the availability group. Click Close to finish the New Availability Group Wizard.

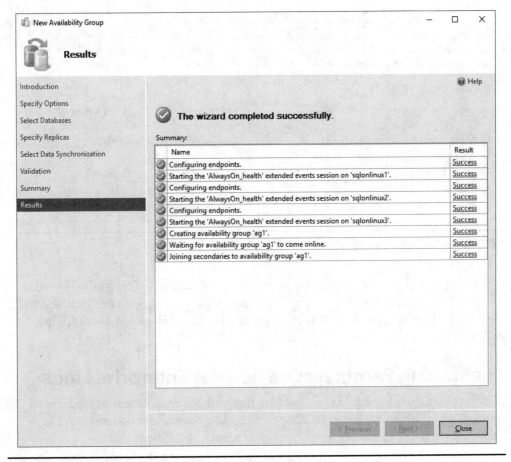

Figure 7-11   *View the results of implementing the required changes.*

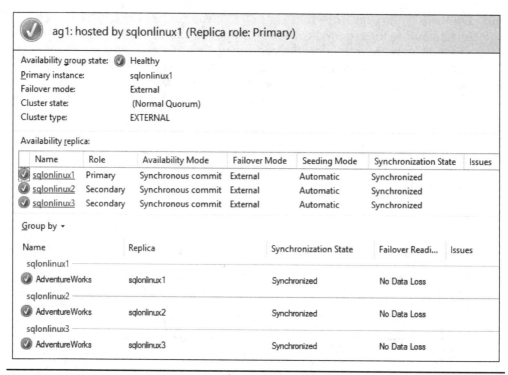

Figure 7-12 *Availability Group dashboard*

To see the status of the availability group, use the Availability Group Dashboard. To open it, go back to the Always On High Availability folder, open the Availability Group folder, right-click your availability group, and select Show Dashboard. The dashboard for this exercise is shown in Figure 7-12.

Configuring Pacemaker on Red Hat Enterprise Linux

Now let's configure Pacemaker on Red Hat Enterprise Linux. Pacemaker is an open-source, high-availability cluster solution that includes several components, such as Pacemaker clustering, fencing agents, resource agents, and Corosync.

NOTE

You can learn more about Pacemaker at www.opensourcerers.org/pacemaker-the-open-source-high-availability-cluster/.

The fencing agents in a Pacemaker cluster are designed to shut down a node that has become unstable or unresponsive so that it cannot damage the cluster or any cluster resources. Resource agents are packages that integrate applications and understand a specific application and its dependencies. Corosync is a heartbeat used for internal communications that provides intercluster communications between cluster nodes and may also provide a quorum if needed.

As of this writing, Red Hat Enterprise Linux does not provide support for fencing agents on any cloud environment, including Microsoft Azure. Microsoft has indicated that it is working on a solution to this. So, optionally, you can disable the fencing agents because they are not supported, or keep them enabled for evaluation purposes only.

NOTE

Access to the Red Hat Enterprise Linux High Availability Add-On requires a subscription to the Red Hat Developer Program, which provides no-cost subscriptions, and you can download the software for development use only. For more details, see https://developers.redhat.com/products/rhel/download.

Let's start the configuration. Most of the work on this section will be on the Linux side. Register the Red Hat High Availability Add-On on each server using the `subscription-manager` command. This command enables you to register systems to a subscription management service and attaches and manages subscriptions for software products. For this exercise, we will use the register, list, and attach modules. The register module is used to register this system to the customer portal or another subscription management service.

```
$ sudo subscription-manager register
Registering to: subscription.rhsm.redhat.com:443/subscription
Username: admin@benjaminnevarez.com
Password:
The system has been registered with ID: e716610b-3f8e-4803-99cc-0353efe97ea5
```

The list module, shown next, lists subscription and product information for this system:

```
sudo subscription-manager list --available
```

This is a partial output:

```
SKU:                  RH2262474
Contract:
Pool ID:              8a85f9825e880657015e892b8ec74358
Provides Management:  Yes
Available:            94
```

```
Suggested:              1
Service Level:          Self-Support
Service Type:           L1-L3
Subscription Type:      Standard
Ends:                   09/16/2018
System Type:            Virtual
```

Now, for each server, use the pool ID from the previous output to run the attach module, which is used to attach a specified subscription to the registered system:

```
$ sudo subscription-manager attach --pool=8a85f9825e880657015e892b8ec74358
Successfully attached a subscription for: Red Hat Enterprise Linux Developer Suite
```

Next, on all three servers, open the Pacemaker firewall ports, which basically opens the TCP ports 2224, 3121, and 21064, and the UDP port 5405. This involves using the firewall-cmd command-line client of the firewalld daemon. Instead of specifying a specific port or port range, it uses one of the firewall-cmd provided services. To get a list of the supported services, use firewall-cmd --get-services. For our example, we will use the high-availability service as shown next:

```
$ sudo firewall-cmd --permanent --add-service=high-availability
$ sudo firewall-cmd --reload
```

Now we can install Pacemaker and all the required components, such as fencing agents, resource agents, and Corosync, on all the nodes. As you may notice so far, Pacemaker terminology refer to the servers as "nodes," which differs from the primary and secondary replica terminology used in the previous section.

```
sudo yum install pacemaker pcs fence-agents-all resource-agents
```

In some of my testing while writing the book, one repository was not available, so I had to disable it and find and enable a replacement. I got the following partial error message:

```
4. Disable the repository permanently, so yum won't use it by default. Yum will then just ignore
the repository until you permanently enable it again or use --enablerepo for temporary usage:
yum-config-manager --disable rhel-7-server-rt-beta-rpms
or
subscription-manager repos --disable=rhel-7-server-rt-beta-rpms
```

For now I am running the following command to disable the repository. This may not be needed in your particular case, however.

```
$ subscription-manager repos --disable=rhel-7-server-rt-beta-rpms
Repository 'rhel-7-server-rt-beta-rpms' is disabled for this system.
```

I also had to enable the following repository:

```
yum-config-manager --enable rhel-ha-for-rhel-7-server-rpms
```

You can use the following statement to list the enabled repositories:

```
yum repolist
```

Now we are ready to try installing the four listed packages again. The output of the command will be huge, several pages long. Here is a quick summary that also asks for user input. Enter **y**.

```
Transaction Summary
Install 4 Package (+103 Dependent packages)
Total download size: 28 M
Installed size: 87 M
Is this ok [y/d/N]: y
```

Later, the command shows the installed packages, only a partial output here:

```
Installed:
  fence-agents-all.x86_64 0:4.0.11-66.el7_4.3
  pacemaker.x86_64 0:1.1.16-12.el7_4.5
  pcs.x86_64 0:0.9.158-6.el7_4.1
  resource-agents.x86_64 0:3.9.5-105.el7_4.3

Dependency Installed:
  OpenIPMI-modalias.x86_64 0:2.0.19-15.el7
  audit-libs-python.x86_64 0:2.7.6-3.el7
  autogen-libopts.x86_64 0:5.18-5.el7
...
  unbound-libs.x86_64 0:1.4.20-34.el7
Complete!
```

Finally, after such a large output, you could just verify the status of the installed packages by running the same command again. This is the entire output I got:

```
$ sudo yum install pacemaker pcs fence-agents-all resource-agents
Loaded plugins: langpacks, product-id, search-disabled-repos
Package pacemaker-1.1.16-12.el7_4.5.x86_64 already installed and latest version
Package pcs-0.9.158-6.el7_4.1.x86_64 already installed and latest version
Package fence-agents-all-4.0.11-66.el7_4.3.x86_64 already installed and latest version
Package resource-agents-3.9.5-105.el7_4.3.x86_64 already installed and latest version
Nothing to do
```

Next, change the password of the hacluster user, which was created when the Pacemaker package was installed. Use the same password for all nodes.

```
sudo passwd hacluster
```

Now we can enable and start the pcsd service and Pacemaker on all nodes. The pcsd daemon controls and configures the Pacemaker and Corosync clusters via pcs. Run the following commands:

```
$ sudo systemctl enable pcsd
Created symlink from /etc/systemd/system/multi-user.target.wants/pcsd.service to /usr/
lib/systemd/system/pcsd.service.
$ sudo systemctl start pcsd
$ sudo systemctl enable pacemaker
Created symlink from /etc/systemd/system/multi-user.target.wants/pacemaker.service to /
usr/lib/systemd/system/pacemaker.service.
```

Create the Pacemaker cluster, but this time only on sqlonlinux1. The cluster pcs command is used to configure cluster options and nodes. pcs is the pacemaker/corosync configuration system. Notice the auth, setup, and start options. The auth command is used to authenticate pcs to pcsd on nodes specified, or on all nodes configured in the local cluster if no nodes are specified. The list of nodes is specified in the command. User hacluster and password, as created earlier, are specified as well.

```
$ sudo pcs cluster auth sqlonlinux1 sqlonlinux2 sqlonlinux3 -u hacluster -p Pa$$w0rd!
sqlonlinux2: Authorized
sqlonlinux3: Authorized
sqlonlinux1: Authorized
```

Next, the setup option is used to configure Corosync and sync configuration out to listed nodes. The --name parameter will be the cluster name, in this case, sqlonlinuxc, and the list of all the nodes will follow.

```
$ sudo pcs cluster setup --name sqlonlinuxc sqlonlinux1 sqlonlinux2 sqlonlinux3
Destroying cluster on nodes: sqlonlinux1, sqlonlinux2, sqlonlinux3...
sqlonlinux1: Stopping Cluster (pacemaker)...
sqlonlinux3: Stopping Cluster (pacemaker)...
sqlonlinux2: Stopping Cluster (pacemaker)...
sqlonlinux3: Successfully destroyed cluster
sqlonlinux1: Successfully destroyed cluster
sqlonlinux2: Successfully destroyed cluster

Sending 'pacemaker_remote authkey' to 'sqlonlinux1', 'sqlonlinux2', 'sqlonlinux3'
sqlonlinux1: successful distribution of the file 'pacemaker_remote authkey'
sqlonlinux2: successful distribution of the file 'pacemaker_remote authkey'
sqlonlinux3: successful distribution of the file 'pacemaker_remote authkey'
Sending cluster config files to the nodes...
sqlonlinux1: Succeeded
sqlonlinux2: Succeeded
sqlonlinux3: Succeeded

Synchronizing pcsd certificates on nodes sqlonlinux1, sqlonlinux2, sqlonlinux3...
sqlonlinux2: Success
sqlonlinux3: Success
sqlonlinux1: Success
Restarting pcsd on the nodes in order to reload the certificates...
sqlonlinux2: Success
sqlonlinux3: Success
sqlonlinux1: Success
```

You may need to use the --force option if you previously tried a cluster configuration on the same nodes. The command would look like this:

```
$ sudo pcs cluster setup --force --name sqlonlinuxc sqlonlinux1 sqlonlinux2 sqlonlinux3
```

Finally, use the start option to start the cluster on the specified nodes:

```
$ sudo pcs cluster start -all
sqlonlinux2: Starting Cluster...
sqlonlinux3: Starting Cluster...
sqlonlinux1: Starting Cluster...
```

I needed to run this again after a virtual machine restart, so this could be configured to start automatically:

```
sudo pcs cluster start --all
```

You can use `pcs status` to view the current status of the cluster:

```
# pcs status
Error: cluster is not currently running on this node
```

This is the current configuration after you start the cluster on the specified nodes:

```
# pcs status
Cluster name: sqlonlinuxc
WARNING: no stonith devices and stonith-enabled is not false
Stack: unknown
Current DC: NONE
Last updated: Wed Jan 24 06:31:18 2018
Last change: Wed Jan 24 06:31:17 2018 by hacluster via crmd on sqlonlinux3

3 nodes configured
0 resources configured

Node sqlonlinux1: UNCLEAN (offline)
Node sqlonlinux2: UNCLEAN (offline)
Node sqlonlinux3: UNCLEAN (offline)

No resources

Daemon Status:
  corosync: active/disabled
  pacemaker: active/disabled
  pcsd: active/enabled
```

NOTE

_For more details about configuring the Red Hat High Availability Add-On with Pacemaker, see https://access .redhat.com/documentation/en-us/red_hat_enterprise_linux/6/html/configuring_the_red_hat_high_ availability_add-on_with_pacemaker/._

Next, we can install the SQL Server High Availability package. As we learned from Chapter 1, a SQL Server installation includes several packages, some of which can be optional. This needs to be installed on all nodes:

```
$ sudo yum install mssql-server-ha
Loaded plugins: langpacks, product-id, search-disabled-repos
Resolving Dependencies
--> Running transaction check
---> Package mssql-server-ha.x86_64 0:14.0.3008.27-1 will be installed
--> Finished Dependency Resolution
Dependencies Resolved
Installing:
Package mssql-server-ha
Arch x86_64
Version 14.0.3008.27-1
Repository packages-microsoft-com-mssql-server-2017
Size 2.7 M
Transaction Summary
Install  1 Package
Total download size: 2.7 M
Installed size: 12 M
Is this ok [y/d/N]: y
Downloading packages:
mssql-server-ha-14.0.3008.27-1.x86_64.rpm
2.7 MB  00:00:00
Running transaction check
Running transaction test
Transaction test succeeded
Running transaction
  Installing : mssql-server-ha-14.0.3008.27-1.x86_64
1/1
  Verifying  : mssql-server-ha-14.0.3008.27-1.x86_64
1/1
Installed:
  mssql-server-ha.x86_64 0:14.0.3008.27-1
Complete!
```

In the next step, we will disable Stonith, which is the Pacemaker fencing implementation. Stonith is configured by default when you install a Pacemaker cluster. Fencing may be defined as a method to bring a high-availability cluster to a known state. When the cluster resource manager cannot determine the state of a node or of a resource on a node, fencing brings the cluster to a known state again.

However, at this moment, Red Hat Enterprise Linux does not provide fencing agents for any cloud environments, including Azure. So I will disable it for this exercise.

NOTE

You should keep Stonith enabled on supported environments or for evaluation purposes. Microsoft is working on a solution for the environments not yet supported.

For now, we can disable Stonith by running the following command, where the `property` command is used to manage the Pacemaker properties. The following command sets the `stonith-enabled` property to `false` on the cluster:

```
sudo pcs property set stonith-enabled=false
```

NOTE

For more details about fencing and Stonith, see clusterlabs.org/pacemaker/doc/crm_fencing.html.

In the same way, set the `start-failure-is-fatal` property to `false`. This property is always used to treat start failures as fatal. We want to disable it to let the cluster decide whether to try starting on the same node again based on the resource current failure count and migration threshold. Run the following command:

```
sudo pcs property set start-failure-is-fatal=false
```

Note that you can list the Pacemaker cluster properties by using the following command, which lists the configured properties:

```
# pcs property list
Cluster Properties:
 cluster-infrastructure: corosync
 cluster-name: sqlonlinuxc
 dc-version: 1.1.16-12.el7_4.5-94ff4df
 have-watchdog: false
 master-ag_cluster: 0
 start-failure-is-fatal: false
 stonith-enabled: false
```

You can use the `--all` option to list all the properties, including unset properties with their default values. My installation returns 40 properties:

```
$ sudo pcs property list --all
```

This is the current cluster status:

```
# pcs status
Cluster name: sqlonlinuxc
Stack: corosync
Current DC: sqlonlinux2 (version 1.1.16-12.el7_4.5-94ff4df) - partition with quorum
Last updated: Wed Jan 24 06:35:11 2018
Last change: Wed Jan 24 06:35:07 2018 by root via cibadmin on sqlonlinux1

3 nodes configured
0 resources configured

Online: [ sqlonlinux1 sqlonlinux2 sqlonlinux3 ]

No resources

Daemon Status:
  corosync: active/disabled
  pacemaker: active/disabled
  pcsd: active/enabled
```

Next, create the following login on all three instances of SQL Server:

```
USE master
GO
CREATE LOGIN pacemakerLogin WITH PASSWORD = N'Pa$$w0rd!'
```

Grant the following permissions to the created login:

```
GRANT ALTER, CONTROL, VIEW DEFINITION ON AVAILABILITY GROUP::ag1 TO pacemakerLogin
GRANT VIEW SERVER STATE TO pacemakerLogin
```

Save the login information on every node. Create a text file with the following information, the SQL Server login name and password:

```
pacemakerLogin
Pa$$w0rd!
```

Save it to /var/opt/mssql/secrets/passwd. Change the permissions to be readable only by the root user:

```
sudo chown root:root /var/opt/mssql/secrets/passwd
sudo chmod 400 /var/opt/mssql/secrets/passwd
```

So at the end it would look like this:

```
$ sudo ls -l /var/opt/mssql/secrets/passwd
-r--------. 1 root root 32 Jan 20 07:25 /var/opt/mssql/secrets/passwd
$ sudo more /var/opt/mssql/secrets/passwd
pacemakerLogin
Pa$$w0rd!
```

Finally, create the availability group resource. Run the following command from sqlonlinux1:

```
sudo pcs resource create ag_cluster ocf:mssql:ag ag_name=ag1 master notify=true
```

Basically, this uses the pcs command to manage cluster resources. In this case, it creates a new resource called ag_cluster. The mssql is a resource provider installed with the SQL Server High Availability package. Since the master option is used, a master/slave resource is created.

This is the current status of the cluster:

```
# pcs status
Cluster name: sqlonlinuxc
Stack: corosync
Current DC: sqlonlinux2 (version 1.1.16-12.el7_4.5-94ff4df) - partition with quorum
Last updated: Wed Jan 24 06:37:52 2018
Last change: Wed Jan 24 06:37:50 2018 by root via cibadmin on sqlonlinux1

3 nodes configured
3 resources configured

Online: [ sqlonlinux1 sqlonlinux2 sqlonlinux3 ]

Full list of resources:

 Master/Slave Set: ag_cluster-master [ag_cluster]
     Stopped: [ sqlonlinux1 sqlonlinux2 sqlonlinux3 ]

Daemon Status:
  corosync: active/disabled
  pacemaker: active/disabled
  pcsd: active/enabled
```

By the way, the `providers` option lists the available Open Cluster Framework (OCF) resource agent providers:

```
$ sudo pcs resource providers
heartbeat
mssql
openstack
pacemaker
```

You may get the following error if you do not have the mssql-server-ha package installed:

```
# sudo pcs resource create ag_cluster ocf:mssql:ag ag_name=ag1 master notify=true
Error: Agent 'ocf:mssql:ag' is not installed or does not provide valid metadata:
Metadata query for ocf:mssql:ag failed: -5, use --force to override
```

Run the following command to create a virtual IP resource for the cluster. You will need to specify a valid static IP address:

```
$ sudo pcs resource create virtualip ocf:heartbeat:IPaddr2
ip=13.91.249.38
```

Notice that we are again creating a cluster resource, same as we did earlier to create an availability group resource. This time, though, it is a virtual IP resource.

We can use constraints to enforce whether or not two resources should be running on the same node, where a resource can or cannot run or the order in which the resources in a cluster should start. In this case, let's add a colocation constraint to ensure that the availability group primary replica and the virtual IP resources run on the same host. This requires a colocation constraint with a score of `INFINITY`. Run the following statement:

```
$ sudo pcs constraint colocation add virtualip ag_cluster-master INFINITY with-rsc-role=Master
```

The next constraint will make sure the availability group cluster resource is started first and then the virtual IP resource. This is required to avoid a case when the IP address is available but pointing to a node where the availability group resource is not yet available:

```
$ sudo pcs constraint order promote ag_cluster-master then start virtualip
```

Finally, you can use the `cluster destroy` command to destroy the cluster permanently on the current node, killing all cluster processes and removing all cluster configuration files. This could also be helpful to remove a test configuration and start all over again:

```
# sudo pcs cluster destroy
Shutting down pacemaker/corosync services...
Killing any remaining services...
Removing all cluster configuration files...
```

Similarly, you can drop the availability group from SQL Server by running the following:

```
DROP AVAILABILITY GROUP ag1
```

Configuring Pacemaker on Ubuntu

Configuring Pacemaker on Ubuntu is very similar to the Red Hat Enterprise Linux configuration, so in this section I will cover all the required commands. You may want to refer to the preceding sections on Red Hat Enterprise Linux for more details. Explanations will be summarized when they are similar to the instructions for Red Hat Enterprise Linux. Command output will not be included to save pages.

Let's start by creating the three servers or virtual machines with Ubuntu and SQL Server installed. If you are using Microsoft Azure, type **search "Ubuntu SQL Server 2017"** to find the image named "Free SQL Server License: SQL Server 2017 Developer on Ubuntu Server 16.04 LTS." Follow Chapter 1 for more detailed instructions about how to create the virtual machine and configure it as indicated. Name the virtual machines sqlonlinux1, sqlonlinux2, and sqlonlinux3. These will be a primary and two secondary replicas.

Open all the required firewall ports. As earlier, in addition to the TCP ports 1433 and 5022 required by the SQL Server instance and availability groups, respectively, we need to open the required Pacemaker firewall ports. In this case, we need to open the TCP ports 2224, 3121, and 21064 and the UDP port 5405. You can use the following command for the ports you need. ufw is a firewall configuration tool that is included with Ubuntu.

```
sudo ufw allow 1433/tcp
sudo ufw allow 5022/tcp
sudo ufw allow 2224/tcp
sudo ufw allow 3121/tcp
sudo ufw allow 21064/tcp
sudo ufw allow 5405/udp
sudo ufw reload
```

Run the following command to install Pacemaker and fencing agents, resource agents, and Corosync on all the nodes:

```
$ sudo apt-get install pacemaker pcs fence-agents resource-agents
Reading package lists... Done
Building dependency tree
Reading state information... Done
resource-agents is already the newest version (1:3.9.7-1).
fence-agents is already the newest version (4.0.22-2).
pacemaker is already the newest version (1.1.14-2ubuntu1.3).
pcs is already the newest version (0.9.149-1ubuntu1.1).
0 upgraded, 0 newly installed, 0 to remove and 81 not upgraded.
```

As you can see from my newly created Azure virtual machine, the operating system already has the required software, but it may be different in your case. Next, set the hacluster user password by running this command:

```
sudo passwd hacluster
```

Enable and start pcsd and Pacemaker on all nodes:

```
$ sudo systemctl enable pcsd
$ sudo systemctl start pcsd
$ sudo systemctl enable pacemaker
Synchronizing state of pacemaker.service with SysV init with /lib/systemd/systemd-sysv-install...
Executing /lib/systemd/systemd-sysv-install enable pacemaker
```

As mentioned, the Pacemaker cluster configuration is stored at /etc/corosync/corosync .conf. In the following example, you can see a list of nodes and logging configuration. This file is created during the pcs cluster setup. This same configuration file is also created for Red Hat Enterprise Linux.

```
totem {
    version: 2
    secauth: off
    cluster_name: sqlonlinuxc
    transport: udpu
}
nodelist {
    node {
        ring0_addr: sqlonlinux1
        nodeid: 1
    }
```

```
    node {
        ring0_addr: sqlonlinux2
        nodeid: 2
    }
    node {
        ring0_addr: sqlonlinux3
        nodeid: 3
    }
}
quorum {
    provider: corosync_votequorum
}
logging {
    to_logfile: yes
    logfile: /var/log/corosync/corosync.log
    to_syslog: yes
}
```

NOTE

At the time of writing, there is a bug in the installation related to the location of the log file that incorrectly points to /var/log/cluster/corosync.log. A workaround is simply to fix the location and change it to /var/log/corosync/corosync.log or just create the file on /var/log/cluster/corosync.log. The vendor is working on this fix.

Next, same as with Red Hat Enterprise Linux, run the following commands to create the three-node cluster:

```
$ sudo pcs cluster auth sqlonlinux1 sqlonlinux2 sqlonlinux3 -u hacluster -p Pa$$w0rd!
$ sudo pcs cluster setup --name sqlonlinuxc sqlonlinux1 sqlonlinux2 sqlonlinux3
$ sudo pcs cluster start --all
```

Install the SQL Server High Availability package:

```
$ sudo apt-get install mssql-server-ha
```

This time, I was not so lucky when I tried this on my Azure virtual machines, as I got an error. So I had to register the repository, as shown next:

```
sudo add-apt-repository "$(curl https://packages.microsoft.com/config/ubuntu/16.04/
mssql-server-2017.list)" && sudo apt-get update
```

Then I was able to run the `apt-get install` as indicated earlier.

Same as with Red Hat Enterprise Linux, disable Stonith by setting the `stonith-enabled` property to `false`:

```
$ sudo pcs property set stonith-enabled=false
```

Also set the `start-failure-is-fatal` property to `false`. This is always used to treat start failures as fatal, which lets the cluster decide whether to try to start on the same node again:

```
sudo pcs property set start-failure-is-fatal=false
```

Next, create the following login on all three instances of SQL Server:

```
USE [master]
GO
CREATE LOGIN [pacemakerLogin] with PASSWORD= N'Pa$$w0rd!'
```

Grant the following permissions to the created user:

```
GRANT ALTER, CONTROL, VIEW DEFINITION ON AVAILABILITY GROUP::ag1 TO pacemakerLogin
GRANT VIEW SERVER STATE TO pacemakerLogin
```

Save the login information on every node. Create a text file with the following information, the SQL Server login name and password:

```
pacemakerLogin
Pa$$w0rd!
```

And save it to /var/opt/mssql/secrets/passwd. Change the permissions to be readable only by the root user:

```
sudo chown root:root /var/opt/mssql/secrets/passwd
sudo chmod 400 /var/opt/mssql/secrets/passwd
```

Finally, create the availability group resource. Run the following command:

```
sudo pcs resource create ag_cluster ocf:mssql:ag ag_name=ag1 --master meta notify=true
```

Basically, this uses the `pcs` command to manage cluster resources. In this case, it creates a new resource called ag_cluster. mssql is a defined resource provider. Since the `master` option is used, a master/slave resource is created.

As with our Red Hat Enterprise Linux installation, run the following command to create a virtual IP resource for the cluster. You will need to specify a valid static IP address:

```
sudo pcs resource create virtualip ocf:heartbeat:IPaddr2 ip=13.91.249.38
```

Next, add a colocation constraint to ensure the availability group primary replica and the virtual IP resources run on the same host:

```
$ sudo pcs constraint colocation add virtualip ag_cluster-master INFINITY with-rsc-role=Master
```

Finally, run the following command to make sure the availability group cluster resource is started first and then the virtual IP resource:

```
$ sudo pcs constraint order promote ag_cluster-master then start virtualip
```

This completes the basic configuration of Pacemaker on Ubuntu. Remember that these commands are explained in more detail in the Red Hat Enterprise Linux section, so you may want to refer to it for additional details.

NOTE

Because of page/space constraints, installing SUSE Linux Enterprise Server (SLES) is beyond the scope of this book. For details, see the SQL Server documentation "Configure SLES Cluster for SQL Server Availability Group" at https://docs.microsoft.com/en-us/sql/linux/sql-server-linux-availability-group-cluster-sles, and additional links to the "SUSE Linux Enterprise High Availability Extension 12 SP3, Installation and Setup Quick Start" document at www.suse.com/documentation/sle-ha-12/singlehtml/install-quick/install-quick.html.

Operating an Availability Group Resource

This section introduces the Pacemaker cluster operation and shows you how to fail over an availability group manually using the pcs cluster tool. You can also bypass the external cluster manager in extreme cases when there is a problem with the cluster or the cluster management tools are not working as expected. In this case, a failover using T-SQL statements is a possible workaround.

Failing over an availability group resource requires two steps, which are the same for Red Hat Enterprise Linux and Ubuntu. The next command fails over an availability group resource named ag_cluster to a cluster node named sqlonlinux2:

```
$ sudo pcs resource move ag_cluster-master sqlonlinux2 --master
```

The move option moves the defined resource—in this case, the availability group resource ag_cluster—to the specified destination node—in this case, sqlonlinux2.

The second step requires that you remove the location constraint:

```
$ sudo pcs resource clear ag_cluster-master
$ sudo pcs constraint --full
```

Finally, if you have a problem and cannot use the tools for any reason, such as when the cluster is not responding properly, you can still temporarily do a manual failover using T-SQL statements from within SQL Server. To perform this manual failover, you first need to unmanage the availability group from Pacemaker, perform the manual failover using a T-SQL statement, and configure managing the availability group with Pacemaker again.

First, the unmanage option sets the listed resources to unmanaged mode. The cluster is not allowed to start or stop a resource when it is in unmanaged mode:

```
sudo pcs resource unmanage ag_cluster
```

Next, run the following statements on the secondary replica SQL Server instance, sqlonlinux2. This statement sets a key-value pair in the session context; in this case, set the session context variable external_cluster to 'yes'.

```
EXEC sp_set_session_context @key = N'external_cluster', @value = N'yes'
```

Run the following statement to initiate a manual failover of the availability group to the secondary replica to which you are connected. You could run this, for example, connected to the sqlonlinux2 instance to make this instance the new primary replica:

```
ALTER AVAILABILITY GROUP ag1 FAILOVER
```

A manual failover is performed without data loss and requires a synchronous-commit secondary replica that is currently synchronized with the primary replica. In this case, sqlonlinux2 will take over the primary role and recover its copy of each database, bringing them online as the new primary databases. The former primary replica, sqlonlinux1, concurrently transitions to the secondary role. A manual failover to sqlonlinux2 is shown in Figure 7-13.

Finally, let's get back to enabling Pacemaker. The following commands set the listed resources back to managed mode:

```
sudo pcs resource manage ag_cluster
```

Finally, the cleanup option makes the cluster forget the operation history of the resource and re-detect its current state:

```
sudo pcs resource cleanup ag_cluster
```

ag1: hosted by sqlonlinux2 (Replica role: Primary)

Availability group state: Healthy
Primary instance: sqlonlinux2
Failover mode: External
Cluster state: (Normal Quorum)
Cluster type: EXTERNAL

Availability replica:

Name	Role	Availability Mode	Failover Mode	Seeding Mode	Synchronization State	Issues
sqlonlinux1	Secondary	Synchronous commit	External	Automatic	Synchronized	
sqlonlinux2	Primary	Synchronous commit	External	Automatic	Synchronized	
sqlonlinux3	Secondary	Synchronous commit	External	Automatic	Synchronized	

Group by ▾

Name	Replica	Synchronization State	Failover Readi...	Issues
sqlonlinux1				
AdventureWorks	sqlonlinux1	Synchronized	No Data Loss	
sqlonlinux2				
AdventureWorks	sqlonlinux2	Synchronized	No Data Loss	
sqlonlinux3				
AdventureWorks	sqlonlinux3	Synchronized	No Data Loss	

Figure 7-13 *Manual failover to sqlonlinux2*

Summary

This chapter covered the basics of high availability and disaster recovery for SQL Server on Linux. Although several features were discussed, the majority of the chapter focused on Always On availability groups.

Availability groups on both Windows and Linux can be used in high-availability and disaster-recovery configurations and for migrations and upgrades, or even to scale out readable copies of one or more databases.

The main difference between availability groups in Windows and Linux is that in Windows, the Windows Server Failover Cluster, or WSFC, is built into the operating system and SQL Server and availability groups are cluster-aware. In Linux, availability groups depend on Pacemaker instead of WSFC. Because Linux does not provide a clustering solution out of the box, all three SQL Server–supported Linux distributions utilize their own version of Pacemaker. The SQL Server High Availability package, also known as the SQL Server resource agent for Pacemaker, is an optional package and must be installed for a high-availability solution in Linux.

For more details about availability groups in Windows, refer to the SQL Server documentation at https://docs.microsoft.com/en-us/sql/database-engine/availability-groups/windows/overview-of-always-on-availability-groups-sql-server.

For more information about availability groups in Linux, go to https://docs.microsoft .com/en-us/sql/linux/sql-server-linux-availability-group-overview.

Look for the Red Hat High Availability Add-On documentation at https://access .redhat.com/documentation/en-us/red_hat_enterprise_linux/7/html/high_availability_ add-on_reference/index.

The SUSE Linux Enterprise High Availability extension documentation is available at www.suse.com/documentation/sle_ha/book_sleha/data/book_sleha.html.

Chapter 8

Security

In This Chapter

This chapter provides an introduction to security in SQL Server, and its content applies to both Windows and Linux environments. It covers how SQL Server security works in terms of layers such as protecting the data itself, controlling access to the data, and monitoring data access. This chapter also covers some of the newest SQL Server security features introduced in the latest few versions of the product, including Transparent Data Encryption (TDE), Always Encrypted, Row-Level Security, and Dynamic Data Masking (DDM), in more detail.

All the security features available with Windows are available on Linux, with the exception of Active Directory, which will be included in a future update.

▶ **Transparent Data Encryption**   This security feature is designed to protect the database data and transaction log files against unauthorized access to physical media. It performs real-time I/O encryption at the page level, although the data is not encrypted after it is in memory or across other communication channels.

▶ **Always Encrypted**   This client-side encryption technology is designed to protect sensitive data; data remains encrypted in the database engine all the time.

▶ **Row-Level Security**   This security feature controls access to rows in a table based on the identity of the user executing a query. The benefit of this feature is that the access restriction logic is defined in SQL Server rather than at the application level.

▶ **Dynamic Data Masking**   This security feature is aimed at limiting sensitive data exposure by masking it to nonprivileged users.

Introduction to Security on SQL Server

SQL Server on Linux supports the same enterprise-level security capabilities available with SQL Server on Windows today, and all these features are built into the product. Microsoft defines SQL Server Security in terms of layers, as shown in Figure 8-1.

Let's review these layers in a bit more detail.

The first security layer is about protecting and encrypting the data itself, using, for example, encryption at rest to protect data in case files or disks are stolen. SQL Server provides features for encryption at rest, such as TDE, backup encryption, and cell-level encryption. Another type of encryption, encryption in transit, secures the communication for SQL Server and is based on the Transport Layer Security (TLS) protocol. A final type of encryption, client-side encryption, also called Always Encrypted, keeps data encrypted in the database engine all the time and is visible only on the client side. Both TDE and Always Encrypted are covered in detail in this chapter.

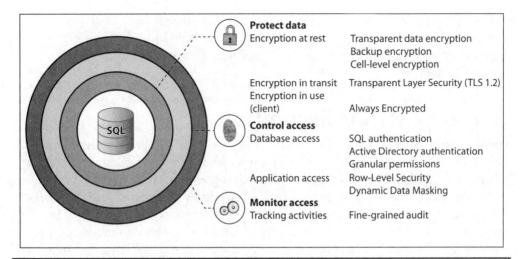

Protect data
Encryption at rest   Transparent data encryption
                      Backup encryption
                      Cell-level encryption

Encryption in transit Transparent Layer Security (TLS 1.2)
Encryption in use
(client)   Always Encrypted

Control access
Database access   SQL authentication
                      Active Directory authentication
                      Granular permissions

Application access   Row-Level Security
                      Dynamic Data Masking

Monitor access
Tracking activities   Fine-grained audit

Figure 8-1   *Layers of SQL Server security*

The second layer of security in SQL Server is about controlling access to the data through authentication and authorization processes. SQL Server has a very granular permissions system that enables you to control very specific access to almost every SQL Server object. SQL Server in Windows supports both SQL Server and Active Directory authentication. Active Directory authentication is currently not available on SQL Server on Linux, but it is planned to be implemented in the future. In addition, some features such as Row-Level Security and Dynamic Data Masking provide additional methods to control access to the data. Row-Level Security and Dynamic Data Masking are also covered in detail in this chapter.

The last and outer layer is about monitoring data access by logging user operations within an instance or database. SQL Server provides an audit feature that enables you to specify which users, actions, and objects should be tracked and will request the database engine to log all activity based on a defined policy. This process is commonly used to keep an audit trail to meet certain compliance standards.

Finally, starting on May 25, 2018, the General Data Protection Regulation (GDPR) will be introduced as a new European privacy law whose purpose is to protect personal data for individuals living within the European Union. Among other things, under the GDPR individuals have the right to access their personal data, correct errors in their personal data, and erase their personal data. Organizations, on the other hand, are required to protect personal data using appropriate security, notify authorities of personal data breaches, and provide clear notice of data collection. For more details about the GDPR you can read the white paper "Data Governance for GDPR Compliance: Principles, Processes, and Practices" at https://info.microsoft.com/DataGovernancefor GDPRCompliancePrinciplesProcessesandPractices-Registration.html.

The rest of this chapter provides an overview of Transparent Data Encryption, Always Encrypted, Row-Level Security, and Dynamic Data Masking features. For more information about these and other security features, refer to the SQL Server documentation.

Transparent Data Encryption

Transparent Data Encryption, also known as encryption at rest, protects the database data and transaction log files against unauthorized access to the physical media. When a database is configured for TDE, even accessing copies of the database files or database backups will not provide access to its data. TDE works by performing real-time I/O encryption at the page level, which means that pages are encrypted before they are written to disk and decrypted when the pages are read from disk into memory. Note that this data is not encrypted once in memory, and it is not encrypted across other communication channels.

Although this means that unauthorized parties will not be able to restore your database when enabling TDE, it also means that you will need the certificate and private key associated with the certificate used for the TDE configuration to do so, so you should immediately back them up. You will need them if you ever want to attach or restore the database on a different SQL Server instance. An example of how to do that is shown later in the section "Attach or Restore a TDE Database to Another SQL Server Instance."

The tempdb database will also be encrypted if there is at least one encrypted database in the SQL Server instance. This would help to encrypt temporary information used by the encrypted database but may also impact the performance of databases that are not encrypted. If a database is being used in database mirroring, log shipping, or availability group configurations, all the related databases—mirror, secondary, or replica, respectively—will be encrypted as well.

Let's work on an example to show how TDE works. First we need to create a master key and a certificate, similar to what we did in Chapter 7, where we used a certificate to authenticate communication between the mirroring endpoints for availability group configuration.

```
USE master;
GO
CREATE MASTER KEY ENCRYPTION BY PASSWORD = 'Pa$$w0rd!';
GO
CREATE CERTIFICATE MyCertificate WITH SUBJECT = 'My Certificate';
GO
```

The database master key is a symmetric key used to protect the private keys of certificates and asymmetric keys that are present in the database. The CREATE CERTIFICATE statement adds a certificate to a database in SQL Server. The CREATE DATABASE ENCRYPTION KEY statement can now be used to create a database encryption key and protect it by the certificate. Run the following statement:

```
USE AdventureWorks2012
GO
CREATE DATABASE ENCRYPTION KEY
WITH ALGORITHM = AES_128
ENCRYPTION BY SERVER CERTIFICATE MyCertificate;
GO
```

Notice the following warning about backing up the certificate and private key associated with the certificate:

```
Warning: The certificate used for encrypting the database encryption key
has not been backed up. You should immediately back up the certificate
and the private key associated with the certificate. If the certificate
ever becomes unavailable or if you must restore or attach the database
on another server, you must have backups of both the certificate and the
private key or you will not be able to open the database.
```

So let us follow that recommendation and back up the certificate and the private key associated with the certificate:

```
USE master
GO
BACKUP CERTIFICATE MyCertificate
TO FILE = 'MyCertificate '
WITH PRIVATE KEY
(
    FILE = 'SQLPrivateKeyFile',
    ENCRYPTION BY PASSWORD = 'Pa$$w0rd!'
)
GO
```

The BACKUP CERTIFICATE statement is used to export both the certificate and the private key associated with the certificate to files. In our case, the certificate will be saved in /var/opt/mssql/data/MyCertificate and the private key associated with the certificate will be exported to /var/opt/mssql/data/SQLPrivateKeyFile. If you are using the Windows platform, both files will be saved in the C:\Program Files\Microsoft SQL Server\MSSQL14.MSSQLSERVER\MSSQL\DATA folder.

Now we are ready to set the database to use encryption by using the ALTER DATABASE SET ENCRYPTION statement:

```
ALTER DATABASE AdventureWorks2012
SET ENCRYPTION ON
GO
```

So at this moment, the database is using TDE. Let's do a quick test, performing and restoring a backup:

```
BACKUP DATABASE AdventureWorks2012 TO DISK = 'AdventureWorks2012.bak'
```

The database backup will be saved in /var/opt/mssql/data/AdventureWorks2012 .bak. Now try to restore the backup file in the same SQL Server instance with a new database name:

```
RESTORE DATABASE [AdventureWorks2012New] FROM DISK = N'/var/opt/mssql/data/
AdventureWorks2012.bak' WITH  FILE = 1,  MOVE N'AdventureWorks2012' TO N'/var/
opt/mssql/data/AdventureWorks2012New.mdf',  MOVE N'AdventureWorks2012_log' TO
N'/var/opt/mssql/data/AdventureWorks2012New_log.ldf',  NOUNLOAD,  STATS = 5
```

Running the following query will show that the database was restored and is encrypted. Three databases will be listed: AdventureWorks2012, AdventureWorks2012New, and, as explained earlier, tempdb.

```
SELECT name, is_encrypted, * FROM sys.databases WHERE is_encrypted = 1
```

Trying to restore this database into another SQL Server instance will not work and instead will return the "Cannot find server certificate with thumbprint" error message. The following section explains how to restore a database using TDE on another SQL Server instance.

Attach or Restore a TDE Database to Another SQL Server Instance

Following on the previous example, I'll show you now how to restore a TDE database into another SQL Server instance. Keep in mind that at this time you can have only a single SQL Server instance on a Linux installation, but you could have multiple instances in a Windows environment. So on a Linux installation, this will also involve copying files to another server and probably updating its permissions as well.

We'll start by copying the database backup file, moving it to the /var/opt/mssql/data directory, and making sure the mssql user can access it. Run the following command, replacing the host destination name or IP address and the user and directory destination. This command is executed at the original server, and the files will be copied to my home directory at the destination server:

```
sudo scp /var/opt/mssql/data/AdventureWorks2012.bak
bnevarez@23.99.83.158:/home/bnevarez
```

Now run the following commands on the destination server:

```
sudo cp AdventureWorks2012.bak /var/opt/mssql/data
# cd /var/opt/mssql/data
# chown mssql AdventureWorks2012.bak
# chgrp mssql AdventureWorks2012.bak
```

Obviously, you could follow exactly the same exercise in Windows using the appropriate directories, such as C:\Program Files\Microsoft SQL Server\MSSQL14 .MSSQLSERVER\MSSQL\DATA or some other location. Going back to SQL Server Management Studio, try to restore on the second server using the original database name, AdventureWorks2012:

```
RESTORE DATABASE [AdventureWorks2012] FROM  DISK = N'/var/opt/mssql/data/
AdventureWorks2012.Bak' WITH  FILE = 1,  MOVE N'AdventureWorks2012' TO N'/var/
opt/mssql/data/AdventureWorks2012.mdf',  MOVE N'AdventureWorks2012_log' TO N'/
var/opt/mssql/data/AdventureWorks2012_log.ldf',  NOUNLOAD,  STATS = 5
```

You get a message similar to this:

```
Msg 33111, Level 16, State 3, Line 1
Cannot find server certificate with thumbprint
'0xD1046B72062A47A4B76797D8000E609CC96A3242'.
Msg 3013, Level 16, State 1, Line 1
RESTORE DATABASE is terminating abnormally.
```

As indicated in the previous section, to restore an encrypted database, we need the certificate and the private key associated with the certificate used for the encryption process. Copy the MyServerCert and SQLPrivateKeyFile files to the DATA directory on the new SQL Server instance if you are using a Windows installation.

For a Linux installation, follow the next steps, which are very similar to the preceding ones, where we copied the database backup file:

```
sudo scp /var/opt/mssql/data/MyCertificate bnevarez@104.42.5.46:/home/bnevarez
sudo scp /var/opt/mssql/data/SQLPrivateKeyFile bnevarez@104.42.5.46:/home/bnevarez
```

Same as before, the files are copied as the user bnevarez, so I still need to copy them to the correct directory and give them the right permissions. Copy the files to /var/opt/mssql/data and change the file ownership appropriately:

```
cp MyCertificate /var/opt/mssql/data
cp SQLPrivateKeyFile /var/opt/mssql/data
cd /var/opt/mssql/data
chown mssql MyCertificate
chown mssql SQLPrivateKeyFile
chgrp mssql MyCertificate
chgrp mssql SQLPrivateKeyFile
```

We've copied the files to the second server. Now the SQL Server instance needs to be aware of the certificates. Run the following statements to create a master key and a certificate on the second SQL Server instance, using the backup created on the original server. Once again, use a strong password. Also, in this particular case, the password used on DECRYPTION BY PASSWORD has to be the same password used previously by the ENCRYPTION BY PASSWORD option when backing up the private key to a file. An incorrect password will return the following error message:

```
Msg 15465, Level 16, State 6, Line 1
The private key password is invalid.
```

Run the following statements:

```
USE master;
GO
CREATE MASTER KEY ENCRYPTION BY PASSWORD = 'Pa$$w0rd!'
GO
CREATE CERTIFICATE TestSQLServerCert
FROM FILE = 'MyCertificate'
WITH PRIVATE KEY
(
    FILE = 'SQLPrivateKeyFile',
    DECRYPTION BY PASSWORD = 'Pa$$w0rd!'
)
```

At this point, you should finally be able to restore the TDE database:

```
RESTORE DATABASE [AdventureWorks2012] FROM DISK = N'/var/opt/mssql/data/
AdventureWorks2012.Bak' WITH FILE = 1, MOVE N'AdventureWorks2012' TO N'/var/
opt/mssql/data/AdventureWorks2012.mdf', MOVE N'AdventureWorks2012_log' TO N'/
var/opt/mssql/data/AdventureWorks2012_log.ldf', NOUNLOAD, STATS = 5
```

Finally, this procedure can work the same way if you need to attach a database. You would need to repeat all the steps in the same way, copy the database files to the appropriate location, and attach the database as usual.

Always Encrypted

Always Encrypted is a client-side encryption technology designed to protect sensitive data. The data remains encrypted in the database engine all the time, even during query processing operations. In addition, Always Encrypted is the only SQL Server security feature that can provide a separation between the entities that own the data and can access it and those that only need to manage the data but should not access it. This means that in an Always Encrypted configuration, only the required applications and users can access and see the data. Always Encrypted was introduced as an Enterprise Edition–only feature with SQL Server 2016, but after Service Pack 1 it is now available on any SQL Server edition.

A typical scenario for using Always Encrypted would be when the data is hosted by a cloud provider such as Microsoft Azure and the client application is on premises. In this case, cloud administrators would not have access to see the data they administer. A second scenario may be in the cases, either on premises or in the cloud, where data administrators are not required to access the data. The database stores only encrypted values, so database administrators or any privileged user won't be able to see the data.

Always Encrypted data could be a challenge to the query processor. Query performance may be impacted when some operations are performed on encrypted columns, since the query optimizer may not have information about the real data distribution and values of these columns. The way the columns are encrypted has query processing and performance implications when the columns are used for index lookups, equality joins, and grouping operations. Because of these implications, Always Encrypted implements deterministic and randomized encryption. *Randomized* encryption uses a method that encrypts data in a less predictable manner and can be used when you don't need to use these columns for query-processing operations—for example, with credit card information. *Deterministic* encryption always generates the same encrypted value for any given plain-text value and is better suited for use in the query processing operations mentioned earlier such as index lookups, equality joins, and grouping operations.

To help with these query processing limitations, a future enhancement of Always Encrypted has been recently announced which will include rich computations on encrypted columns, including pattern matching, range comparisons, and sorting. The feature is called Always Encrypted with secure enclaves where an enclave is a protected region of memory that acts as a trusted execution environment. In addition, this feature will provide in-place encryption, helping with schema changes that involve cryptographic operations on sensitive data. For more details about Always Encrypted with secure enclaves you can read the following article https://blogs.msdn.microsoft .com/sqlsecurity/2017/10/05/enabling-confidential-computing-with-always-encrypted-using-enclaves-early-access-preview/.

Some of the tasks required to implement the Always Encrypted feature are not supported by T-SQL as, by definition, the database engine cannot be involved in data encryption and decryption operations. These tasks need to be done at the client side. You can also use PowerShell or SQL Server Management Studio. I'll show you how to use the Always Encrypted Wizard on SQL Server Management Studio next; this can also optionally generate a PowerShell script required to implement the wizard selections. In summary, the database engine is not involved with provisioning column master keys, column encryption keys, and encrypted column encryption keys with their corresponding column master keys.

Finally, the client application needs to be aware of which columns are using Always Encrypted and should be coded accordingly.

NOTE

For an example of creating a client application that works with the encrypted data, see the article at https://docs.microsoft.com/en-us/azure/sql-database/sql-database-always-encrypted.

Next let's look at how Always Encrypted works. We'll create a small table in which we will encrypt two columns. Run the following statement:

```
CREATE TABLE Employee (
ID int IDENTITY(1, 1),
FirstName varchar(50),
LastName varchar(50),
SSN char(11),
BirthDate date)
```

Insert a couple of values:

```
INSERT INTO Employee VALUES ('Freddie', 'Mercury', '123-45-6789', '01/04/1960')
INSERT INTO Employee VALUES ('Brian', 'May', '987-65-4321', '01/04/1960')
```

Now run the Always Encrypted Wizard. From SQL Server Management Studio Object Explorer, expand Databases, expand the database containing the table, expand Tables, and right-click the Employee table and select Encrypt Columns. The Always Encrypted Wizard Introduction page is shown in Figure 8-2. Then click Next.

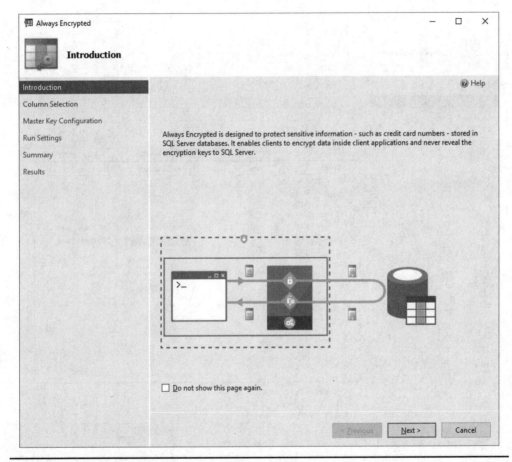

Figure 8-2   *Always Encrypted Wizard Introduction page*

On the Column Selection page, shown in Figure 8-3, you can select the columns to encrypt on the table. Select the SSN and BirthDate column checkboxes. For the Encryption Type column, select Deterministic for the SSN column and Randomized for the BirthDate column, as shown in Figure 8-3. Click Next.

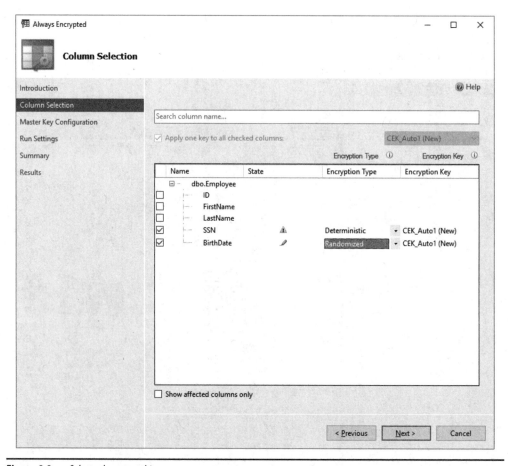

Figure 8-3   *Select columns on this page.*

On the Master Key Configuration page, shown in Figure 8-4, you set up your column master key and select the key store provider where the column master key will be stored. As of this writing, the choices for key store provider are a Windows Certificate Store and the Azure Key Vault. For this example, keep the default choices and select the Windows Certificate Store. Then click Next.

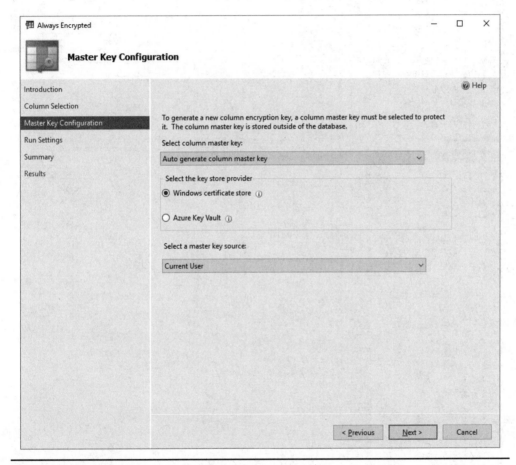

Figure 8-4   *Set up your column master key and select the key store provider.*

The Run Settings, shown in Figure 8-5, gives you the choice of generating a PowerShell script to run later or letting the wizard execute the current selections. In addition, it shows a warning: "While encryption/decryption is in progress, write operations should not be performed on a table. If write operations are performed, there is a potential for data loss. It is recommended to schedule this encryption/decryption operation during your planned maintenance window."

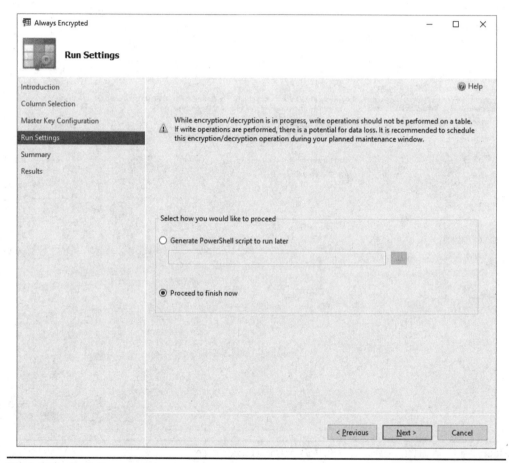

Figure 8-5   *Run Settings page*

This is the PowerShell script generated for my selections if the script choice were selected instead:

```
# Generated by SQL Server Management Studio at 2:21 AM on 3/4/2018

Import-Module SqlServer
# Set up connection and database SMO objects

$sqlConnectionString = "Data Source=104.42.5.46;Initial Catalog=demo;User ID=sa;
MultipleActiveResultSets=False;Connect Timeout=30;Encrypt=False;TrustServerCerti
ficate=False;Packet Size=4096;Application Name=`"Microsoft SQL Server Management
Studio`""
$smoDatabase = Get-SqlDatabase -ConnectionString $sqlConnectionString

# If your encryption changes involve keys in Azure Key Vault, uncomment one of
the lines below in order to authenticate:
#    * Prompt for a username and password:
#Add-SqlAzureAuthenticationContext -Interactive

#    * Enter a Client ID, Secret, and Tenant ID:
#Add-SqlAzureAuthenticationContext -ClientID '<Client ID>' -Secret '<Secret>'
-Tenant '<Tenant ID>'

# Change encryption schema

$encryptionChanges = @()

# Add changes for table [dbo].[Employee]
$encryptionChanges += New-SqlColumnEncryptionSettings -ColumnName dbo.Employee
.SSN -EncryptionType Deterministic -EncryptionKey "CEK_Auto1"
$encryptionChanges += New-SqlColumnEncryptionSettings -ColumnName dbo.Employee
.BirthDate -EncryptionType Randomized -EncryptionKey "CEK_Auto1"

Set-SqlColumnEncryption -ColumnEncryptionSettings $encryptionChanges
-InputObject $smoDatabase
```

Keep the default Proceed To Finish Now choice and click Next.

On the Summary page, shown in Figure 8-6, you can verify your selected settings before implementation. Click Finish to execute the wizard selection choices. Finally, the Results page, shown in Figure 8-7, will show the status of the operations performed by the wizard.

After the Always Encrypted wizard completes, you can query your data again, and this time the columns will be encrypted. Run the following statement to show encrypted values for both the SSN and BirthDate columns:

```
SELECT * FROM Employee
```

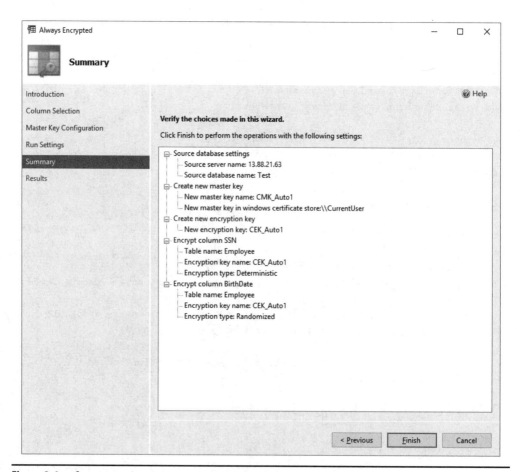

Figure 8-6   *Summary page*

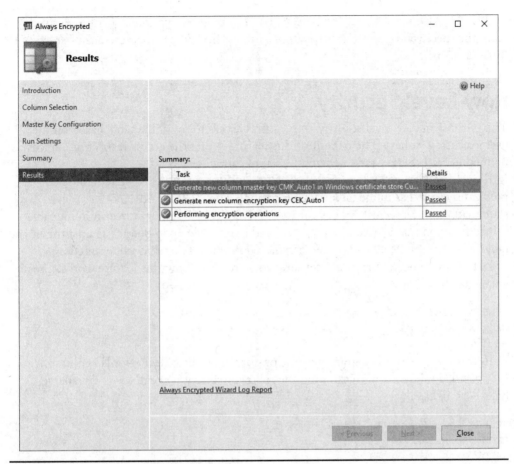

Figure 8-7   *Results page shows the status of operations*

In addition, notice that the schema has changed. The table definition is now the following, which includes some of the definitions used in the Always Encrypted Wizard such as encryption type. It also includes the encryption algorithm, which in this case is called AEAD_AES_256_CBC_HMAC_SHA_256.

```
CREATE TABLE [dbo].[Employee](
    [ID] [int] IDENTITY(1,1) NOT NULL,
    [FirstName] [varchar](50) NULL,
    [LastName] [varchar](50) NULL,
    [SSN] [char](11) COLLATE Latin1_General_BIN2 ENCRYPTED WITH (COLUMN_ENCRYPTION_KEY = [CEK_Auto1], ENCRYPTION_
TYPE = Deterministic, ALGORITHM = 'AEAD_AES_256_CBC_HMAC_SHA_256') NULL,
    [BirthDate] [date] ENCRYPTED WITH (COLUMN_ENCRYPTION_KEY = [CEK_Auto1], ENCRYPTION_TYPE = Randomized, ALGORITHM
= 'AEAD_AES_256_CBC_HMAC_SHA_256') NULL
) ON [PRIMARY]
GO
```

AEAD_AES_256_CBC_HMAC_SHA_256 is an encryption algorithm derived from the specification draft at http://tools.ietf.org/html/draft-mcgrew-aead-aes-cbc-hmac-sha2-05.

Row-Level Security

The purpose of row-level security is to control access to rows in a table based on the user executing a query. The benefit of this feature is that the access restriction logic is defined in SQL Server rather than at the application level.

Row-Level Security relies on the CREATE SECURITY POLICY statement and predicates created as inline table-value functions. The CREATE SECURITY POLICY statement creates a security policy for Row-Level Security and requires an inline table valued function that is used as a predicate and is enforced upon queries against the target table. The SCHEMABINDING option is required in this inline table-value function.

Let's copy some data from AdventureWorks to show how this feature works. Create a new database:

```
SELECT * INTO dbo.SalesOrderHeader
FROM AdventureWorks2014.Sales.SalesOrderHeader
```

In this case, we want to grant permissions based on the SalesPersonID column to the specified salesperson. By running the following query, you can see the available SalesPersonID values:

```
SELECT SalesPersonID, COUNT(*)
FROM dbo.SalesOrderHeader
GROUP BY SalesPersonID
```

For simplicity, let us focus only on SalesPersonIDs 274 and 275. Let's create a few users: two salespersons and a sales manager:

```
CREATE USER SalesManager WITHOUT LOGIN
CREATE USER SalesPerson274 WITHOUT LOGIN
CREATE USER SalesPerson275 WITHOUT LOGIN
```

Grant SELECT permissions on the SalesOrderHeader table to each user:

```
GRANT SELECT ON SalesOrderHeader TO SalesManager
GRANT SELECT ON SalesOrderHeader TO SalesPerson274
GRANT SELECT ON SalesOrderHeader TO SalesPerson275
```

At this time, users can access the entire table, as requested by the GRANT SELECT statement. Let us fix that by creating our filter predicate function:

```
CREATE FUNCTION fn_securitypredicate(@SalesPersonID AS sysname)
    RETURNS TABLE
WITH SCHEMABINDING
AS
    RETURN SELECT 1 AS fn_securitypredicate_result
WHERE @SalesPersonID = RIGHT(USER_NAME(), 3) OR USER_NAME() = 'Manager';
```

Create the security policy using the previously defined inline table-value function:

```
CREATE SECURITY POLICY SalesFilter
ADD FILTER PREDICATE dbo.fn_securitypredicate(SalesPersonId)
ON dbo.SalesOrderHeader
WITH (STATE = ON)
```

Since we have specified STATE ON, the security policy is now enabled. To test the change in permissions, try the following statements:

```
EXECUTE AS USER = 'SalesPerson274'
SELECT * FROM SalesOrderHeader
REVERT


EXECUTE AS USER = 'SalesPerson275'
SELECT * FROM SalesOrderHeader
REVERT


EXECUTE AS USER = 'SalesManager'
SELECT * FROM SalesOrderHeader
REVERT
```

So you can see how only the rows for the specific salesperson are listed, even when the user is submitting a SELECT for the entire table. SalesPerson274 can only see rows with SalesPersonID 274. SalesManager has no restrictions and can see all the data.

To clean up, you only need to drop the SalesFilter security policy and the fn_securitypredicate function:

```
DROP SECURITY POLICY SalesFilter
DROP FUNCTION fn_securitypredicate
```

Dynamic Data Masking

Dynamic Data Masking is another security feature introduced with SQL Server 2016; it is aimed at limiting sensitive data exposure by masking it to nonprivileged users. Dynamic Data Masking is implemented by using a masking rule that is defined on a column in a table by using either the CREATE TABLE or the ALTER TABLE statement. Four types of masks are currently available:

▶ **Default mask**   Works with most data types. For example, it replaces a string data type with 'xxxx', a numeric data type with a zero value, a date and time data type with '01.01.1900 00:00:00.0000000', and a binary data type with the ASCII value 0.

▶ **E-mail mask**   Replaces e-mail address values with the form 'aXXX@XXXX.com'.

▶ **Random mask**   Replaces a numeric data type with a random value based on a specified range.

▶ **Custom string mask**   Replaces a string data type with a string that exposes the first and last letters and adds a custom padding string in the middle.

Let's create a table to test some of these choices:

```
CREATE TABLE test (
field1 varchar(40) MASKED WITH (FUNCTION = 'default()'),
field2 int MASKED WITH (FUNCTION = 'default()'),
field3 datetime MASKED WITH (FUNCTION = 'default()'),
field4 binary(20) MASKED WITH (FUNCTION = 'default()'),
field5 varchar(40) MASKED WITH (FUNCTION = 'email()'),
field6 int MASKED WITH (FUNCTION = 'random(1, 12)'),
field7 varchar(20) MASKED WITH (FUNCTION = 'partial(1, "XXXXXXX", 0)'))
```

Insert a single row:

```
INSERT INTO test VALUES ('San Diego', 666, GETDATE(), CAST(123 AS
binary(20)), 'admin@benjaminnevarez.com', 123, 'Los Angeles')
```

Run the following statement to see the current data:

```
SELECT * FROM test
```

Now if you are running the query with a login with high-level privileges, you will still see the real data. Try it with a user without high-level privileges by running the following statements, which create a temporary user, and use EXECUTE AS to run the query as the specified user:

```
CREATE USER test_user WITHOUT LOGIN
GRANT SELECT ON test TO test_user
EXECUTE AS USER = 'test_user'
SELECT * FROM test
REVERT
```

You will see the values shown in the Masked column:

Column	Original	Masked
field1	San Diego	XXXX
field2	666	0
field3	14:03.8	00:00.0
field4	0x000000000000000000000000000000000000007B	0x30
field5	admin@benjaminnevarez.com	aXXX@XXXX.com
field6	123	2
field7	Los Angeles	LXXXXXXX

As mentioned, you can also use ALTER TABLE ALTER COLUMN for existing tables and columns. Try the following test:

```
ALTER TABLE test
ALTER COLUMN field7 ADD MASKED WITH (FUNCTION = 'partial(2, "XXXXXXX", 0)')
```

In this case, the value for field7 will now show as LoXXXXXXX.

Finally, although Dynamic Data Masking can help in a large variety of security cases, keep in mind that some techniques may bypass the Dynamic Data Masking definitions. For example, a malicious user may try brute-force techniques to guess values, and by doing that may be able to see the real data. As an example, see the following queries:

```
EXECUTE AS USER = 'test_user'
SELECT * FROM test
WHERE field2 > 600
REVERT

EXECUTE AS USER = 'test_user'
SELECT * FROM test
WHERE field2 < 600
REVERT
```

```
EXECUTE AS USER = 'test_user'
SELECT * FROM test
WHERE field2 = 666
REVERT
```

On the first query, the malicious user knows that field2 is greater than 600 and less than 700, as the query returns one row in each case. Continuing such techniques, the user can try other values such as `field = 666` until the required data is returned, and by doing that discovering its value.

Summary

This chapter served as an introduction to security on SQL Server on Linux. SQL Server on Linux supports the same enterprise-level security capabilities that are available on SQL Server on Windows today, and all these features are built into the product.

The chapter defined SQL Server Security in terms of layers. The first layer, or level, of security is about protecting the data itself, typically by using methods such as encryption. The second layer is about controlling access to the data, which is basically defining who is allowed to access which parts of the data. The third layer is about monitoring access by tracking activities that are happening against the data.

The chapter also covered Transparent Data Encryption, Always Encrypted, Row-Level Security, and Dynamic Data Masking in more detail. Transparent Data Encryption is a security feature designed to protect the database data and transaction log files and backup files against unauthorized access to physical media. Always Encrypted is a client-side encryption technology designed to protect sensitive data. Row-Level security is a security feature that controls access to rows in a table based on the user executing a query. Finally, Dynamic Data Masking is another security feature introduced with SQL Server 2016 that is aimed at limiting sensitive data exposure by masking it to nonprivileged users.

Index